STEPS OF COURAGE

STEPS OF COURAGE

My Parents' Journey from Nazi Germany to America

BETTINA HOERLIN

authorHOUSE®

AuthorHouse™
1663 Liberty Drive
Bloomington, IN 47403
www.authorhouse.com
Phone: 1-800-839-8640

First published by AuthorHouse   11/01/2011

ISBN: 978-1-4634-2618-7 (sc)
ISBN: 978-1-4634-2619-4 (hc)
ISBN: 978-1-4634-2617-0 (ebk)

Library of Congress Control Number: 2011910629

Printed in the United States of America

This book is printed on acid-free paper.

𝐵 Hoe

TABLE OF CONTENTS

To my children
Noah, Jason, Kristine and Steven
who knew Oma and Opa
and
to my grandchildren
who now will know them too

INTRODUCTION: LETTERS FROM THE PAST

The only concrete history that can be retrieved remains that carried by personal stories.

Saul Friedlander, <u>Nazi Germany and the Jews</u>

The small leather suitcase engraved with my father's initials, **H.W.H.**, had resided in the basement for several years. It was among the subterranean hodgepodge of items, some forgotten, some ignored but none quite ready to be discarded. The accumulated holdings had been expanded after the deaths of my parents, when I inherited sundry possessions, including the suitcase. Whether due to my lack of curiosity or—more probably, the pace and demands of everyday life, it remained unopened. But one day, perhaps a rainy one, it beckoned me. Inside, neatly stacked and carefully tied with faded blue ribbons in half-year packets, were over 400 letters my mother wrote my father from 1934 to 1938 in pre-war Germany. He had saved them all, and I wondered whether he even remembered keeping them. No one else in the family had a clue they were there; he had predeceased my mother, but she never mentioned any such letters. I assume she too had forgotten their existence.

It was another two years before I read the letters, the delay due in part because they were written in German *schrift*, an archaic lettering still used in Germany in the late 1930's. Until then it was the standard for people, like my mother, educated in the German school system. Initially the elaborately ornamental handwriting stymied me, but gradually I mastered it—simultaneously brushing up on my German. By that time, I had more than a passing interest in various unknowns of my heritage and decided to dig further through boxes stored in the basement. And I found another treasure: over 100 letters my father had written my mother during that same period, 1934 to 1938. Added to my mother's 400 letters, I was able to reconstruct a great love story that unfolded in Nazi Germany, one of the most horrendous periods in world history.

Once I started reading the letters, I was mesmerized. Letters were the major mode of communication then, offering unique insights of the times and its witnesses. Most of all, they gave me fresh perspectives of my mother and father, who hardly spoke of their respective pasts. Here was an unedited version of a romance between two people who I had always seen through the eyes of a child: I knew my parents were remarkable (but not _how_ remarkable); I knew they had overcome many odds (but not _how_ many); and I knew they loved one another (but not _how_ much). In regard to one's parents, there is always that element of "other"—the quality that distinguishes them from you, a gap of generation and perspective. With the letters I was thrust into the midst of their courtship—its passion and excitement—and soon, its disregard of the dictates of Nazi laws.

"Hearing" my father and mother's voices, feeling their mutual love, and sensing their bravery during a period of tremendous upheaval were the key propellants that launched this book. In addition to the treasure trove of letters, I conducted extensive research, incorporating previously untapped archival records that allowed me to embed their personal story into a historical context. The story plays out against some of the most profound markers of the 20th century: the rise of the Third Reich, the American immigrant experience and ongoing threats of the Nuclear Age.

My parents had met because of a mountain, one of the world's highest, although neither was on its icy slopes when ten climbers perished. The 1934 German expedition to the Himalayas was seeking to do what had never been accomplished, the conquest of an eight thousand meter peak. Certain of victory, Hitler used the expedition as an opportunity to tout Aryan superiority and international supremacy. Instead, it made a mark of another kind: the largest mountaineering disaster that had ever occurred. My father had declined to join the elite team of climbers, staying in Germany to complete his doctoral studies. If he had agreed to go, he could have been among the casualties and would have never met my mother, who was the expedition's press liaison. To help her sort out its gruesome details, the German Alpine Club sent him, an expert mountaineer, to her side.

Hermann Wilhelm Hoerlin held several world records during a time called the "golden age of mountaineering," an era that combined scientific and exploratory pursuits with dramatic ascents. One morning, having spent several days immersed in studying a 1930 international expedition, I grumbled to my patient husband, "I have to bring my father to the top of the mountain today," as we ate breakfast. "Don't forget to get him down," he quipped. That day my father both ascended and descended a Himalayan mountain that entered the record books as the highest peak then scaled, a feat achieved some 80 years prior to my breakfast conversation. When he broke the record, my father became a poster boy for Aryan ideals, a perfect prototype with his fair hair and tall, handsome looks. Moreover, climbers were revered and celebrated. In Germany, mountaineering was akin to America's ongoing fascination with space exploration and baseball championships. My father was a Teutonic hero.

Attempting to capture my mother's character was another challenge. "She's taking over again," I complained to a good friend. My mother, Kate Tietz, had a propensity to dominate a room; I was not happy that she was threatening to take over my book. Beautiful and charismatic, she had an uncanny ability to attract people; flirtatious and lively, she held them in her sway. Among her friends was the cultural and corporate elite of Germany, representatives of an epoch of enormous intellectual and creative energy, albeit of economic hardships. Sadly and horribly, that came to an end with the rise of Hitler. My mother's life changed forever when her first husband. Willi Schmid, was murdered by the Nazis on June 30, 1934, which became known as the infamous "Night of the Long Knives." At least 90 people, allegedly enemies of the state, were rounded up by execution squads and summarily killed. The rule of law in Germany was over, replaced by a reign of terror. The Third Reich's acknowledgment of Schmid's death as a "mistake" was hardly a consolation to Kate and her three children.

My parents were an unlikely couple to fall in love. They lived in different worlds, my father in one of science and mountaineering, my mother one of music and literature. Hoerlin and Kate both lived in a country dear to them, one rapidly crumbling under the heavy boot of Fascism, and each of them fought Nazism in his and her own way. He confronted the nazification of physics and mountaineering, consistently speaking out against these hyper-political intrusions. She met innumerable times with Hitler's cabinet members and other high-ranking Nazi officials in Berlin, demanding retribution for the wrongful death of her husband from those very functionaries responsible for his murder and who later engineered the Holocaust.

While waging their respective battles, Kate and Hoerlin were united in their determination to marry and leave their homeland. They faced considerable obstacles, foremost among them a secret, deeply held then and perpetuated throughout my parents' lives. In 1938 they finally managed to flee to America, a comparative haven of safety but with its own set of challenges. Emigrants, even an accomplished physicist such as my father, were not necessarily welcome in a country struggling with its own economic security and its eventual entry into World War II. My parents' hyphenated status as German-Americans was painful, a source of suspicion and prejudice toward them during the war. As an "enemy alien," my father's assets were seized and his job threatened. It was only through an association with Eleanor Roosevelt that life returned to normal.

When peace was declared, they faced the tragedies wrought in their former homeland while forging a new life. As in Germany, they cultivated a fascinating group of friends: writers, artists, musicians and scientists. In 1953, they pulled up stakes again and moved to a chillingly futuristic destination, Los Alamos, New Mexico. The town, known as "the Atomic City," had birthed the nuclear bomb and now was deeply embedded in the Cold War arms race. In those tense times during the ever-present menace of nuclear war, my father's work concentrated on detection techniques of high altitude testing, a precursor to the first international arms control agreement. His 1962 Congressional testimony on this topic was convincing and pivotal.

The arc of my parents' love story spans an era from when a diabolic dictator set out to annihilate Jews to when weapons of mass destruction threatened to annihilate humankind. In relaying this story, I have portrayed the choices made and the persons who made them in an environment that too often alternated between fear and chaos. How those factors shaped individuals is hard to imagine. Once I told a confidant that I had found someone boring because she had "no corners." The characters in this book have corners, and corners behind corners, some less attractive than others. When at long last I discovered the secret my parents had harbored for so many years, it was one among many corners in their complex personalities. On my father's 80th birthday, surrounded by children and grandchildren, he told us the most critical quality to have in life was COURAGE. Both he and my mother had an abundance of it. As their daughter, I am eternally grateful to them.

PART I

GERMANY

Chapter 1

THE 54 STEPS

A 1937 photograph of the grand stairway, 200 feet wide, leading from
Schwaebisch Hall's town square up to its Roman-Gothic church.

There are 54 steps leading up to St. Michael's church in Schwaebisch Hall. Since 1507, children in this quintessential medieval German town have raced up and down them, their ears deaf to the obligatory parental cautions of "Vorsicht!" (careful!). The contests of getting to the top first have endured over time. It was probably not until 1908 when my father, age five, had sturdy enough legs to fully participate in this ritual. But I have no doubt that from that time onward he led his peers with skill and speed on both the assault and descent. It might be considered as the first of his many conquests.

The steps <u>ask</u> to be counted and climbed. They beckon to any first time visitor, as they did to me when I was thirteen. My father had brought me to Germany to meet, for the first time, my grandmother. At age 78, she guided me slowly up the welcoming staircase and reached the top with misty eyes but a triumphant smile. Almost twenty years later, after I had become the mother of two children of a widower, I watched them, ages seven and ten, jump excitedly up and down the steps. Then, to settle the kind of impassioned argument that occurs only between siblings, they walked up slowly hand in hand and counted out loud the exact number of steps. One of them, I no longer remember whom, was right: it was fifty-four. As I accompanied them they did not know, and I only suspected, that a new baby brother, my first born, was partaking in his special version of conquest, ascending the steps safely tucked in his mother's womb. Over 30 years later the feat of summitry for all my four of my children [1] was complete when the youngest climbed the steps with his fiancée. That evening they spoke with an elderly resident of Schwaebisch Hall and asked if, by chance, he had heard of my son's grandfather. The gentleman replied, "Ja, Hermann Hoerlin, ja." He paused … and continued: "Er war (he was) Sportsmann." My father's reputation as a one-time world record holder for first ascents on three continents, Europe, Asia and South America, lived on.

In no small part inspired by my son's glowing reports of the town's beauty, my husband of twenty years and I put it on our 2005 travel agenda. Schwaebisch Hall sits on the banks of a gently meandering river crisscrossed by several wood shingled bridges. Entering the town feels like a stroll through history with harmoniously varied architecture styles, narrow cobble-stoned streets, thick protective walls and impressive watch towers. But the highlight of the town is the famous steps. When we reverentially ascended them to the top, we could glimpse the distant hills of the Swabian Alb, a perfect hiking area and, if one was so inclined, a challenging rock climbing destination with 500 foot cliffs. My father was so inclined and he, like other budding alpinists, used it was a training ground for more demanding ventures.

A medieval street in Schwaebisch Hall with one of many towers.

Not far from the church lays the town's Baroque town hall, which houses the record of my father's birth on July 5, 1903. As I held the yellowed document with his parents' signatures, I noted that it had taken Adolf and Maria over a month to register their son's name: Hermann Julius Wilhelm Hoerlin.

Perhaps the delay and his multiple names portended the various names given my father in subsequent years. Although usually known by friends and later on by colleagues as Hermann (the extra "n" was dropped as a concession to

his subsequent immigration to America), fellow mountaineers referred to him as Pallas. His valiant feats stirred comparisons to the eponymous god of Greek mythology, the father of Victory, Rivalry, Strength and Power. And the name Pallas was derived from pallo, "to brandish (a spear)." If one substituted an ice axe for a spear, his friends would regard the picture as complete. My mother, not part of this brotherhood and accordingly not entitled to use "Pallas", never liked the name Hermann (or Herman). She created her own imprimatur, simply calling him Hoerlin. To me, he was Father for years, but that morphed—some place along the way—to Papa.

WILH. KLEMM   Schw. Hall
Kgl. Hof-Photograph   Röverantagen.

Hermann Julius Wilhelm Hoerlin, three years old.

Little "Hermannle", as his mother called him, or "Maxile", as his sister Liesel inexplicably chose to name him, grew up with the comfortable trimmings of bourgeois life. The family lived above the store owned for generations by the Hoerlins, the "Wilhelm Hoerlin Glas, Porzellan Haus-und Kuechengeraete," specializing in wedding giftware. His father, Adolf, was a successful businessman whose distinguished looks were softened by a perpetual twinkle in his eyes. His pious mother exuded more reserved and solemn airs, reading the Bible and reciting her prayers on a daily basis.

His sister, five years younger than he, was wispy in her loveliness, a pale and gentle soul. Altogether they were a good-looking family, proper citizens involved in town affairs, attendees of the Lutheran church. Mother/daughter were more resolutely devout than father/son, neither of whom were regular church-goers. Life was generally well ordered although my father had an early mischievous streak. Occasionally during World War I, he and his friends got away with clandestinely ringing the town's church bells, the public communiqué of a German battle victory resulting in early dismissal from school. As the war dragged on, there were fewer and fewer times the bell rang, warranted or not.

Maria and Adolf Hoerlin, 1899

Townspeople took for granted that Hermann would follow in his father's footsteps, but Adolf Hoerlin had other ideas. With a genealogical past dominated by farmers and craftsmen, Adolf wanted his only son to have a university education and venture out into the world. He harbored regrets that he himself had never traveled and experienced other cultures. Adolf had led a rather predictable life: running the family business, marrying a girl from a nearby town[2], being a good parent and an upright citizen. It was a life of merit but not of excitement. He wanted more for his son. This longing was shared openly, so the ground was well prepared for Hermann to go and explore relatively unknown territories. As my father wrote, [3] "Who does not wish to travel untrodden paths?" Neither my father, and certainly not his own father, could have anticipated how far afield these paths would be.

In 1922 his journey from home began when he enrolled nearby in Stuttgart's Institute of Technology, distinguishing himself there more by his enthusiasm for climbing and skiing than for academics. He joined a number of sports clubs [4] and, given the number of his climbs listed in their yearly reports, it is difficult to imagine when he had time to study at all, much less major in physics. The tenor of the clubs encouraged extreme sports adventures, as well as partying and carousing. Camaraderie was sealed by exploits on snow and rock, winter and summer climbing and/or skiing tours of the Alps, and nights spent over campfires or in alpine huts. Although women sometimes joined these excursions and were even officially club members, Hoerlin sensed the overall tone as ". . . anti-feminine" [5] with a concentration on male prowess and achievements. Considered as bastions of young German manhood, the clubs—much to my father's dismay—later became fertile ground for promoting Aryan ideals when Nazism came into power. Political rhetoric urged the nascent idols to seek glory for the Fatherland on mountain tops. Climbing for love of country became the goal, one that subsequently spawned tragic consequences.

But in the 20's, the mountaineering community was relatively innocent, small, low-key and friendly. Climbing was just beginning to emerge as a 'sport,' becoming more popular and international. Young Alpinists from all over continental Europe and Great Britain sought ever increasingly degrees of difficulty by finding new routes or scaling virgin peaks. My father was among them, exalting in the reward of summitry and appreciative of being at one with nature. By 1926, he had made numerous ascents in the Austrian, Swiss and Italian Alps, climbing approximately 20 peaks. In 1927 alone, he summitted 30 more. [6] His was an auspicious resume, getting the attention of other climbers who knew it required great athleticism, stamina and—not least of all—judgment.

On one of his excursions, Hoerlin met a wild Austrian named Erwin Schneider, who would become his most trusted and frequent climbing companion. The two shared natural affinities for mountaineering and similar ambitions, always seeking new challenges. While summer ascents in the Alps were becoming more commonplace, winter ascents—which combined expertise on skis as well as rock and ice climbing skills—were rare. Hoerlin and Schneider, undaunted by Europe's highest mountain, set their sites on Mont Blanc and its surrounding peaks. Resembling a snow and ice castle, the huge massif looks majestically over France, Italy and Switzerland. First summited in 1786, Mont Blanc begins in deep valleys and builds gradually from wide open meadows to giant glaciers, rock and ice buttresses, and longer ridges leading to its imposing white dome. Steep needle-like peaks (Aiguilles) pierce the mountain's contours and are regarded as more technically difficult to climb than the mountain itself. The climbing partners decided that winter ascents of these narrow spires held the promise of great adventure and perhaps, with luck, wider recognition of their talents. This was on another level from other climbs, offering a welcome chance to test their limits. As my father articulated in a mountaineering journal, "Alpinists find a solitude in winter climbs that we seek in vain during the summer. The precipitous interchange of ice and fields of the wintry Mont Blanc landscape is unique." And he continued to describe the special attraction of winter ascents: ". . . {they} offer the additional challenges of short and cold days, avalanches, snow and wind—in summary . . . the difficulties are greater and multifaceted." [7]

Hoerlin and Schneider were a curious pair. Schneider, a head shorter than my father, had thick black hair—long by the standards of the day—that regularly fell over his rugged-looking face. Ebullient and outrageous, the shaggy Austrian from Tyrol cracked a steady stream of jokes. My father shared with him a certain rebelliousness, but it was much more subtle and controlled. Pallas was quiet and contemplative, always neat, with a natural air of elegance. But on ice, snow and rock, their dissimilarities faded and they fashioned a formidable team.

To plan their climbs, the two partners poured over a large two-by-three map, that had become a classic in its time, the 1924 Carte Albert Barbey of La Chaine du Mont Blanc. The map folds neatly into pocket size, still sturdy and impressive in detail even today. [8] When I touch its smooth surfaces, it feels as though I am coming into contact with my father's skin. Climbing was indeed under his skin and played a key role in forming who he was as he himself noted: "These excursions, during which one learns so much about oneself, deeply shape our minds." [9] Qualities of modesty, calm, integrity and thoughtfulness were all central to his persona, whether on or off a mountain.

During consecutive winters, Hoerlin and Schneider made ascents of various Aiguilles from the French and Italian approaches, from Chamonix and Courmayeur respectively In the winter of 1928, the pair along with two other climbers,[10] made their way up to the Aiguille Verte, considered the most difficult and stunning peak on the Mont Blanc range. Using lanterns to light their way, the team took off at 4 a.m. on skis to cross a hazardous glacier in single file.

A precarious winter ascent of the Aiguille de Bionnassay

The skis had to be taken off and on, depending on what was required to navigate through the glacier's maze of treacherous crevasses, ice towers and abysses. Reaching the almost vertical couloirs of the Aiguille, the team traded skis for spiked iron crampons that they attached to their boot bottoms. With perfect weather, the climb up avalanche-prone gullies was exhilarating. "It was like a fairy tale," my father exalted, ". . . winter, the sun shining, the sky deep blue and we were 4000 meters high." [11] At the narrow top, the youthful conquerors indulged in a victory dance accompanied by hoots and hollers, an act of sheer jubilation that also helped thaw frozen toes. This ritual, actually dancing on a pin(nacle), was repeated two days later when the team added another notch, a first winter ascent of Les Droites, to their triumphs.

In 1929, Pallas and his Austrian counterpart met again in Italy, bound for the Aiguilles Blanche and Noire de Peuterey, among the most risky climbs in the Alps and never ascended in winter. They were determined to succeed in honor of their companion—a team member from the previous year—who meanwhile had been killed in a freakish climbing accident. [12] In spite of fickle weather, Hoerlin and Schneider accomplished their mission. In fact their winter ascent of the Aiguille Blanche set an astonishing record: it was faster than the fastest of all summer ascents. This was followed by a first winter ascent of the Aiguille Noire, where a sudden storm broke out as they descending, forcing them to bivouac for the night without sleeping bags or warm clothing. They recovered from their ordeal the next day, basking in the sun, covered with Italian olive oil to improve their tans, albeit not their aroma. The victors could not help but bask in the glow of their conquests as well.

Their feats were not over: the indefatigable twosome made the first winter traverse across three mountains (Mont Blanc, Mont Maudit and Montblanc du Tacal), a grueling route that began in France and ended in Italy on a starry and moonlit night. On their way to Courmayeur, they wearily stumbled onto a modest farmhouse, whose sympathetic owner offered them beds. It was a fitting end to a glorious day. As my father later recalled, "What we hardly had hoped for in our wildest dreams became a reality."[13] Pallas and Schneider had set a number of mountaineering records, establishing themselves as an extraordinarily speedy pair with, as noted by a leading British mountaineer, "as brilliant a record of great climbs as any young mountaineers in Europe."[14] Years later, Hoerlin was credited further: ". . . between 1926 and 1930, in a time when the roots for today's measures of climbing difficulty were shaped, Hermann Hoerlin had already completed the most challenging summer and winter excursions in the west Alps." [15]

1928 winter ascent of the Aiguille Verte, one of Mont Blanc's most difficult pinnacles.

Although Pallas was at his happiest on top of a mountain, other matters called. After graduating from the Stuttgart Institute of Technology, he returned for a year to Schwaebisch Hall to help run the family store due to his father's illness. After a year, his father's health stabilized and the twenty-three year old decided to continue his studies, with a focus on photographic physics, at the Berlin Institute of Technology. People were abuzz with exciting developments in photography and the burgeoning film industry. My father found himself on the cutting edge of new discoveries in improved film quality and techniques for documentary photography and cinematography. Movies were coming into vogue and Berlin was at the forefront of European filmmaking. Germany's first talking film, "The Blue Angel," became an overnight sensation with its *femme fatale*, Marlene Dietrich, and its depiction of the times: the decadence of cabaret life, general raunchiness, shocking nudity, and open sexuality.

The young man from Swabia must have been wide-eyed with his exposure to this new world, a stark contrast to the conservative and traditional style of Stuttgart, and of course to Schwaebisch Hall. Berlin had shed its stern Prussian image and burst forth as a "... a capital of modernism." [16] Artists, musicians, and writers flocked to this vibrant city to participate in its boom and make their mark. Modern technology was evident everywhere, whether in the bright lights lining streets, the network of express trains, the advanced water and sewage systems, or the large flashy department stores with their swift escalators. The scientific atmosphere was also exhilarating with revelations like quantum mechanics and relativity theory; physics was changing the way the world was viewed, appealing to the best and brightest minds. Berlin's embrace of innovation was infectious and Hoerlin was enjoying it. Yet, he missed the splendor and thrills of mountain climbing.

When an invitation came to become a member of the 1930 International Expedition to Kanchenjunga, Hoerlin did not hesitate. Since excelling on the Mont Blanc Aiguilles, he had dreamed of climbing in the Himalayas, which boosted the world's highest mountains with fourteen peaks over 8000 meters (compared to Mt. Blanc's 4810 meters). No one had summitted any of them. The expedition's lofty aim was to ascend what was then thought to be the 2nd highest mountain in the world (it was actually the 3rd highest). Schneider had been invited to join the team as well, both he and Pallas enthusiastically recommended by a renowned mountaineer, Frank Smythe, with whom they crossed paths in 1928 when the Englishman blazed three new routes up Mont Blanc. The meeting had been fortuitous; Smythe regarded ". . . . Herr Hoerlin (as) one of Germany's most enterprising young mountaineers," [17] an opinion shared by the expedition's seasoned leader, Swiss Professor Gunter Dyhrenfurth.

With the invitation came an opportunity for Hoerlin to combine his budding vocation (physics) with his blooming avocation (mountaineering). In addition to being a key member of the climbing team, Hoerlin was going to conduct photographic research such as assessing films, exposures, lens, filters and the pros and cons of various types of cameras. [18] He also would be involved in shooting a movie, "The Himalayas, the Throne of the Gods," documenting the assault and introducing audiences to the unfamiliar civilizations and terrain of Nepal and Sikkim. For the first time ever, the technology of a motion film would be brought to the Himalayas, a literal high point in the industry's relatively young history.

For a 27 year old, it all was enormously exciting. In February he left Berlin, stopping to say goodbye to his family in Schwaebisch Hall before embarking for India from Venice. His father's habitually modest smile had broadened to a wide beam, confident in the knowledge that his son was pushing beyond customary boundaries, both intellectual and physical. It was just as he had dreamed, only more so. Hoerlin's sister was also thrilled, climbing with her adventuresome brother the 54 steps of St. Michael's church for luck and laughing about how many multiples of them it would take to reach the top of Kanchenjunga. His stoical mother hid her worries and in a loving gesture typical of mothers, baked a cake—Hermannle's favorite—a hazelnut torte (Haselnusstorte). By the time Hoerlin had traversed from the north to the south of Europe on trains to Venice, he had eaten all of the cake. Underneath a calm and collected demeanor laid an avid appetite, one that was not only culinary. Soon he would embark on a new adventure, sailing to lands and cultures scarcely known and striding on mountains never before trodden.

Chapter 2

THE THRONE OF THE GODS

The voyage from Venice to Bombay took 16 days, the steamship slowly chugging its way through the Suez Canal, the fabled 100 mile link between Europe and Asia. With desert on either side of the canal's tight cut, my father felt as though he could touch the oppressive heat. He, along with other team members, had to force themselves to exercise, finding reprieve afterwards in a makeshift pool on the upper deck. Evenings were cooler and the climbers donned ties and jackets for formal dinners, sometimes followed by dancing, a time to mingle with other passengers. Only one female was on the expedition, Hettie Dyhrenfurth, the wife of its leader, and she and a handful of other women aboard would dance into the night. Participation in the expedition already signaled the independent-minded Hettie's disregard for conventions, but dancing with Indians as easily as with Europeans caused consternation among at least one of the climbers. Frank Symthe, whose fellow Brits had already expressed their disapproval of a female presence in the group, roundly chastised Hettie for this perceived infraction saying "It is impossible for a lady to dance with colored people." With a smile on her face, Hettie politely disagreed.

When the expedition members finally disembarked on the terra firma of India, they stepped into a world exotic to them: a constant stream of humanity, chaotic street life and syncretic diversity. For the one Austrian, two Swiss, three English and five German climbers, India was a sharp contrast to their own countries, where order and homogeneity reigned. Furthermore, arriving mid-March 1930, they stepped into a nascent revolution. Gandhi was leading a non-violent march with thousands of followers protesting

British domination. [1] In cities throughout the Raj, there was turmoil, mass demonstrations and fierce confrontations that landed hundreds in jail. When Hoerlin saw the miserable conditions in which most Indians lived, he empathized with their desire for independence. "The disparities are great and I can understand why there is so much discontent," he observed, "however, the viewpoint of Germans living in India with whom I have spoken is that Indian independence would be a disaster at this time and could provoke terrible fighting between Muslims and Hindus." Unfortunately, these fears were all too real. Seventeen years later when the struggle was finally won, violent sectarian clashes broke out.

Following a few days of sightseeing in Bombay (now Mumbai), expedition members headed south to Delhi, where they had been invited to be the guests of the Viceroy of India, the Earl of Halifax, [2] the foremost representative of Great Britain's monarchy in the Raj. Their visit was on the heels of a letter to the Viceroy from Gandhi explicating why he regarded ". . . British rule as a curse." The Viceroy was doing his utmost to negotiate concessions between India's desire for freedom and Great Britain's wish to hang onto its empire, satisfying neither side in the process. "He was almost too much of a gentleman," my father commented years later, "and perhaps almost naïve in his approach." Lord Halifax's subsequent appointments as Britain's Foreign Minister and then Ambassador to the United States during World War II sorely tested that perceived naiveté.

After a whirlwind exposure to Indian politics and culture, the expedition members were relieved to embark on the last leg of their journey toward the cooler and calmer foothills of the Himalayas. A hot and dusty train ride of over 50 hours finally took them to Darjeeling, from where Kanchenjunga was dramatically visible, one of the few mountains of that stature that can be seen from the comforts of a relatively urbanized setting. Called the "Queen" of mountains, Kanchenjunga is a giant massif of five peaks, gleaming glaciers and colossal ice terraces. The mountain, only 860 feet lower than Everest, humbled the group who shared an almost mythical reverence for the thought of attaining such heights. By 1930 approximately ten serious attempts, involving either a few individuals or larger teams, had been made to conquer the three highest mountains in the world, all in the Himalayas: Everest, K2 or Chogori, and Kanchenjunga. Scaling their summits had so far eluded the climbers' grasp, although heights of over 8000 meters had been attained.

The British mountaineer, George Mallory, on his 3rd attempt of Everest, was last sighted climbing 250 meters below the summit of 8840 meters (29,002 feet).[3] Seventy-five years later, his frozen body, remarkably well preserved, was found at 8,160 meters.[4] His obsession with climbing Everest, which he famously explained as "because it is there," had ended badly.

None of the IHE members had been to the Himalayas before. Although premier mountaineers, their experience had been in the Alps. As Smythe cautioned: "There is only one way of learning Himalayan mountaineering, and that is to climb among the Himalayas. Useful asset though it is, a brilliant Alpine mountaineering record is no Open Sesame to a brilliant Himalayan record, the conditions are so different."[5] What climbers could accomplish in a few days in the Alps needed to be sustained for weeks and even months in the Himalayas, thereby earning its description as "extreme" mountaineering. In addition to prolonged physical exertion at impossibly high altitudes, climbers coped with torrential monsoons and enormous avalanches. Hoerlin shared the mindset of his companions: enduring superhuman hardships was worth the prospect of conquest, motivated by a mysterious mix of raw physicality, heroic resolve, exploratory thrills and spiritual redemption.

The 1930 International Himalayan Expedition from left to right, back row: Hermann Hoerlin, Erwin Schneider, Uli Wieland, Gunter Dyhrenfurth, Marcel Kurz, Wood Johnson; front row: Frank Smythe, Hettie Dyhrenfurth, Charles Duvanel, Helmut Richter.

IHE was distinguished by its cross-national membership, although it perhaps was a stretch to call it an "International" by today's standards. Dyhrenfurth was trying to make the symbolic point of setting aside nationalism and promoting cooperation and friendship between countries. The message appealed to my father, as well as others who had signed on, including his good friends Erwin Schneider and Uli Wieland. With the exception of Pallas and Schneider, none of the expedition members had a history of climbing together. Nevertheless, according to accounts written by Smythe, Dyhrenfurth and my father, the team was extraordinarily cohesive.

To fund the IHE, Dyhrenfurth had scrambled for support, tapping a strange range of sponsors: the London Times, Berlin's Verlag Sherl publishing house, the German Himalaya Club, the British Alpine Club and a total of 81 German, Swiss and British-Indian businesses. The latter contributed a potpourri of items ranging from alcohol to rice crispies. Extensive photographic equipment to shoot a movie was also donated; it took forty porters to carry the film supplies alone. Four firms donated chocolate and three firms tobacco; the Imperial Tobacco Company contributed 100,000 cigarettes, perks for the climbers and even more so for the porters. [6] Today's global tobacco epidemic, a major killer in developed and emerging countries, could be traced to seemingly innocent gestures like these. [7]

To beat the monsoon season responsible for Kanchenjunga's reputation for having the greatest annual snowfall of any mountain in Asia, there was no time to waste in selecting a legion of 400 porters, many of whom were reluctant to tread on Kanchenjunga's holy ground, sacred to them. They hesitated about disturbing the throne of the gods and angering the deities. Such beliefs had not factored into expedition planning. In this regard as well as others, Hettie's presence was a definite bonus. If a Western woman could brave the wrath of the gods, so could the porters. Called Memsahb, an abbreviation for Memsahib (a respectful colonial term for a married European woman), Hettie had impressed them by volunteering to be vaccinated against smallpox. In a gesture worthy of Catherine the Great [8], Memsahb served as a role model for enduring the small pinch that offered protection against deadly outbreaks common to the region. The recruits followed suit, judging correctly that compared to the burdens of carrying packs from 60 to 80 pounds through treacherous terrain, this was a fleeting discomfort.

Kanchenjunga sits between three territories, reflected in the mix of porters: Sikkim in the South and East, Nepal in the West and Tibet in the North. [9] Attaining the necessary permissions to approach it from any of these sides was highly political and cumbersome. A few days before the IHE was slated to leave on route through Sikkim, an amazing letter arrived. Dated March 29th, 1930, it came from the private secretary of the Maharajah of Nepal and gave unprecedented permission to go through the kingdom adding, "His Highness appreciates your remarks about the international character of the expedition which has for its object the cementation of international friendship and good-will among the countries concerned, coupled with the augmentation of human aesthetical and scientific knowledge, and desires me to inform you that he gladly accedes to your request. His Highness hopes that the expedition will be a great success in every way . . . ." [10] The letter also promised that all relevant local authorities would be alerted about the IHE and asked to cooperate with them. The expedition members could scarcely believe their good luck. They would be able to explore areas that Westerners had been in only once, in 1899. Plans were revamped quickly and on April 7, 1930, the IHE left to the cheers of a small crowd.

In addition to conquering "Kantsch," as it was known among German climbers, the expedition members intended to pursue scientific research in geology, topography, meteorology and physiology. Ponies carried the equipment necessary for those tasks, in addition to mountaineering gear and provisions in 180 sizeable crates, weighing approximately six and a half tons. Some gear were almost comical with today's hi tech advances. Climbing boots with sixty nails on their soles weighed six and a half pounds a pair and crampons four pounds a pair, meaning that a mountaineer was burdened with a load of ten and ½ pounds on his feet alone. Thick woolen expedition sweaters, complete with insignia, weighed two pounds ten ounces. Tents were constructed with heavy canvas and wooden pegs to anchor them; hefty ice axes were also made of wood. Climbers could each luxuriate in their own private tent and munch on canned items such as caviar and pate de foie gras, contributions made by firms based on their good intentions more than a climber's individual cravings. But as altitudes increased, appetites for such delicacies decreased.

In general there was a dearth of information on "best practices" in mountaineering and minimal knowledge about the Himalayan terrain. Some initial reconnaissance regarding the Kanchenjunga range and potential routes up the massif was of limited benefit to the IHE. [11] The only regional map available was a 1922 one produced under India's Surveyor General. To help guide them, the IHE purchased several, each for a little over a rupee. [12] One hangs on my study wall today, resembling a fine Indian print in its grace and intricacies. Curving lines approximate contours and elevations; thicker lines show railway, camel and mule tracks and the map's heavy lines mark district, state and country boundaries. Also indicated are monasteries, temples, forts, suspension bridges, tea gardens, temporary huts, grazing camps and glaciers. It speaks of history along with geography.

Over the next three weeks the expedition passed through miniscule villages with indigenous populations. It is hard to imagine who appeared stranger: the invading Europeans with their seemingly inexplicable goals or the local lamas (high priests), monks, herders and villagers with their seemingly inexplicable lives. At one monastery, the expedition delighted in a devil dance, although they were unclear as to whether the frenzied dancing, complete with grotesque animal masks and elaborate costumes, was intended to ward off Kanchenjunga's evil spirits or drive away the Europeans themselves. Later on a band of monks played instruments, measuring eight to fifteen feet long and amazingly akin to the alpine horns of mountain dwellers in Europe. In return, the IHE played German cabaret songs music from a gramophone, amusing local audiences with this puzzling example of Western ingenuity.

High priests playing their long horns at the Pemayangste monastery.

**The strains of cabaret music from the European expedition's gramophone
entertain Nepalese villagers**

When the IHE finally reached base camp some 10,000 feet below the
summit, the mountaineers saw the unique challenges of the Himalayas.
In the words of Smythe, "to compare Kanchenjunga with the Alps is like
comparing a pygmy with a giant." The behemoth seemed brilliantly fortified
by impossibly steep walls of ice and relentless avalanches that thundered
down day and night. The IHE's doctor counted sixty-four avalanches one
day between 8 in the morning and 10 in the evening, that is, one avalanche
every thirteen minutes. [13] Following the chosen assault route meant the
climbers needed to scale a vertical, at times overhanging 900 foot ice cliff.
It is never an easy task to chip and hack away at the ice to cut steps large
enough to accommodate load-carrying porters; when one is at an altitude
of 21,000 feet it is especially grueling. After seven days of alternating task
among themselves, the team was almost finished. Then disaster struck. A
large portion of ice split away, crashing down and setting off an avalanche
that just missed several of the climbing party, miraculously causing only one
fatality, Chettan, a much-valued porter. He had been Schneider's personal
sherpa [14] and the two of them had been only a few feet apart. At first it
appeared both had been lost, but Schneider was lucky.

Following a somber burial ceremony, Dyhrenfurth convened the badly shaken team to discuss future strategies. The porters were also unhinged, fearful that the gods were taking revenge on their errant followers. Several climbers had decided that approaching Kantsch from their current position was futile; particularly vocal was the irascible Smythe. However Dyhrenfurth, his autocratic leanings coming to the fore, was not to be deterred. A man who routinely roused sleeping climbers with a bugle call to action, the expedition's leader felt this was a time for attack, not retreat. The next morning Hoerlin, Wieland and Smythe attempted another ridge via a steep snow covered couloir squeezed between a jumble of rock and ice pinnacles. My father led the last stage of the climb and after reaching the couloir's top was rewarded with a depressing scene of broken and loose rocks leading nowhere. Traversing briefly onto a crumbling promontory, he turned to Smythe, and declared in perfect English, "This rock is shit." My father's use of profanity was almost non-existent throughout his life but this situation seemed to call for it. The route was unclimbable. That evening when a snow blizzard furiously hit the IHE encampment, any further thoughts of conquering Kanchenjunga were abandoned. Instead, in the next few days, members of the expedition bagged two peaks over 7000 meters high,[15] the highest any of them had ever climbed.

The hostile terrain of the world's third highest mountain, Kanchenjunga.

To explore the area further, the expedition then moved its base camp, skirting around Kanchenjunga via a perilous glacier and the high Jongsong La pass. Again the porters and climbing party divided into small groups and proceeded in relays. Memsahb was the last to leave, initially leading 20 porters who then went ahead with their loads, while she advanced more slowly because of stomach cramps. Accompanied only by a 17-year-old coolie and braving a ferocious snowstorm, the 38 year old "*Hausfrau*" (housewife) fought her way over the 6120 meter (20,000 feet) pass.[16] In doing so, she set an altitude record by climbing higher than any previous woman in the Himalayas.[17] Four years later, Hettie Dyhrenfurth set a summit record, the first woman to exceed 7000 meters when she climbed Kashmir's Sia Kangri (7442 meters; 24,370 feet), a record that stood for twenty years.

Hettie Dyhrenfurth.

Memsahb hardly looked like a mountaineering heroine: she was small and trim, with features more suited to the intellectual salons of her hometown Breslau than to expedition rigors. After the expedition was over, she talked of her delight in returning to hot baths and soft beds.[18] A tennis champion from a prominent family of Jewish industrialists, Hettie was fearless in her willingness to stretch social conventions and tolerate the physical demands and discomforts of a Himalayan expedition. Leaving behind three young children to accompany her husband on his life-long dream to climb in the Himalayas certainly was viewed askance by many, but it was not until the end of the expedition that Memsahb knew how negatively the English had viewed her inclusion. Smythe had been repeatedly warned that Frau Dyhrenfurth would be nothing but trouble, a sole woman not up to the rigors of expedition life. Gradually, she disabused him. Other expedition members respected her enormously as well, benefiting from her considerable organizational skills, ones she attributed to mastering daily maternal and household routines.[19] Pallas was among her strongest supporters; he found her warm and cheerful.

From their second base camp, the expedition had access to a number of unclimbed peaks, the highest of which was Jongsong (7461 meters; 24,482 feet). Its summit straddled the boundaries of Tibet, Nepal and Sikkim and the mountain had its own challenges: strong winds, hanging glaciers, ice walls and soft glacier snows in which climbers and porters alike sank up to their waists. With pending monsoons, disgruntled porters and dwindling supplies, there was pressure to ascend quickly. For a few nights, set back by raging storms, the lead party of Schneider, Hoerlin, Smythe and another climber had no fuel whatsoever, even for making tea. They subsisted on chocolates and plum pudding. On June 3, the weather broke and four of them started their final assault from Camp 3. Soon only Pallas and Erwin had the strength to go on, subsequently setting a world record for the highest mountain ever climbed to the top.

As my father wrote, "It is difficult to describe the feeling of stepping on top; first there is the joy of having made it but soon one is overcome by the wonders of the view and the belief of mountain people, as it was with the Greeks and Romans, that this is the home of the gods." The two Hall boys, my 27-year-old father from Hall in Germany and the 24-year-old Schneider from Hall in Austria, planted their respective state flags, Swabian and Tyrolian, firmly on the peak. Five days afterwards these flags greeted four additional IHE climbers. Five years later, in a poisonous letter written by a major mountaineer who was a Nazi, my father was vilified for not having the "courage" to hoist the German flag on that pinnacle of victory.[20] Clearly my father's and Schneider's gesture of fun and friendliness flew pointedly in the face of Germany's rampant nationalism in 1935.

In 1930, the proud flags of Swabia and Tyrol flutter on the summit of highest peak ever scaled.

A tired Hoerlin and Schneider after their record-breaking ascent of Jongsong.

At base camp, Pallas and Erwin's record-breaking climb was celebrated with several rounds of rum and the jubilant pair immediately plotted to climb another peak, Dodang Nyima (7150 meters; 22,700 feet), which although lower in altitude than Jongsong was more difficult technically.[21] After two days of rest following Jongsong, they set out for Dodang, living up to their repute as "insatiable," [22] a pair with ". . . indefatigable energy." [23] Again their complementary skills put them in good stead and their different styles balanced each other: Erwin's impetuosity and agility with Hoerlin's thoughtfulness and stability. At one critical point while tackling a difficult ice overhang on Dodang, Erwin calmly quipped, "Careful Pallas, soon I will be flying."[24] The tense moment passed, my father firmly holding the rope that secured his partner. Schneider did not fly, but on both ascent and descent the two narrowly escaped several avalanches. With typical modesty that deluded no one, the exhausted pair understated their close calls when they returned to base camp and related their successful feat to those assembled, who toasted them with tea and biscuits.

It was time for the expedition to pack up. Anxious to see yet another kingdom, their return trip to Darjeeling was through Sikkim. As they neared its capital, Gangtok, they were greeted at an overlook by the Maharajah's servants. In tow were racing ponies from the ruler's stable, which swiftly and precipitously carried the climbers down to the town, an adventure more terrifying for them than rappelling from any cliff. That evening the Maharajah entertained them with an elaborate dinner at the palace. There was much to be celebrated. Pallas and Schneider had set a world summit record. Hettie had broken a woman's altitude record. And of the eight peaks over 7000 meters that had ever been climbed, four of them were climbed by the IHE. The expedition had discovered a previously uncharted glacier and collected an interesting set of scientific findings. Another first to its credit was the completion of a movie, "Himatschal—Thron der Goetter (Himalayas: The Throne of the Gods)," regarded as a historically important mountaineering and cultural documentary. Never before had a film camera accompanied climbers to the summit, bearing witness to their every breathe and step.[25] It was a classic for its time. Concurrently, the expedition had negative aspects: a life had been lost, mistakes made and all had not gone smoothly. Most notably, Kantsch remained unconquered.

Smythe was particularly venomous in his feelings toward the mountain: "Kanchenjunga is more than unfriendly, it is imbued with a blind unreasoning hatred toward mountaineers . . . . (it) is a law unto itself . . . among the most desperately dangerous mountainsides in the world." Its degree of difficulty did not diminish over time. In 1953 the leader of the triumphant conquest of Mt. Everest, Sir John Hunt, was asked, "What next?" and Hunt replied, "Kanchenjunga . . . the technical climbing problems and objective dangers are of an order even higher than those we encountered on Everest." Two years later, twenty-five years after the IHE attempt, Kantsch was conquered by a British expedition who, in deference to local spiritual beliefs, stopped a few yards short of the summit. The gods were momentarily appeased.

Chapter 3

IN HUMBOLDT'S FOOTSTEPS

The climbers returned from the Himalayas amidst accolades from the press, government officials, friends and family for their achievements. Germans were transfixed by the dangers and glory of mountaineering, akin to America's fascination with space exploration in the 1960's, and in the midst of hard economic times and lingering malaise from World War I, the country was hungry for heroes. Now Germany found them. The mountaineers engaged in a whirlwind of interviews, public lectures and appearances, with fans anxious to hear about what it was like on top (or almost so) of the world. The film "Himatschal," a critically acclaimed sensation released in March 1931, contributed to the buzz when it was shown throughout Germany, Switzerland and Austria to packed cinema houses. The film opened new vistas to them, distinguished by exotic cultures, impossible heights, and monstrous snow and ice formations. Enthralled audiences felt as though they too had stood on Himalayan summits. The German-Austrian Alpine Club, proud of the success of three of its members—Hoerlin and Schneider who made the first ascent of Jongsong and Wieland the second—honored them with special rings, engraved on the inside *Jongsong, 1930*. I never remember seeing my father wear the ring (nor any other), but I know he treasured it. Years later, when my first-born got married, I gave him the modest trophy featuring a greenish-gray opal, a color reminiscent of his grandfather's hazel eyes.

On the trip home Hoerlin and Schneider had traveled to Egypt, where they engaged in a different kind of climbing: ascending the pyramids, the highest structures on the earth for thousands of years. From there they went to Palestine, where they visited the Dead Sea, 394 meters (1388 feet) below sea level. And once they disembarked from their voyage back to Europe, landing in Venice, they made a small detour before returning to Germany. For good measure, they climbed Switzerland's highest mountain, Monte Rosa, from the Italian side via its towering east wall. Described by the legendary mountaineer Reinhold Messner as unparalleled in height, grandeur and danger, [1] it is often called "Europe's Himalayan face." Pallas and Schneider, having stood on one of the earth's highest elevations and a few weeks later, at one of its lowest, now added one of the world's tallest mountain faces to their outstanding exploits.

After all these adventures, it was time for Hoerlin to buckle down. He had matured, certainly through his travels, but also from carrying the mantle of a record-holder. In his expedition lectures, several to standing-room-only audiences, his emphasis was more on the beauty of the mountains, rather than their conquest, and the grandeur of the forces of nature, rather than individual heroics. [2] At the same time, he spoke about the traits of a good mountaineer—being responsible, seeking challenges, and attaining goals. These are the qualities he now applied to a serious career in physics, resuming his studies at Stuttgart Technical University. The carefree days of undergraduate life gave way to working steadily toward an advanced degree. Well . . . maybe there would be some time for climbing and skiing excursions with old friends.

Hoerlin joined the science laboratory of his favorite professor from undergraduate days, Erich Regener, a noted experimental physicist. Belying the stereotypical aloofness and formality of German professors of that period, Regener was approachable and friendly. He and his wife welcomed students to dinners at his home, joined by their son and foster daughter, or on Sunday walks in the neighboring hills. My father became close to this appealing family.

Regener was one of Germany's leading experts [3] in an especially exciting field of research, "cosmic rays." Scientists in America, Switzerland, Holland, Austria, Sweden and Germany were all competing to explain the origin and nature of these very high energy particles, observed moving through the Earth's atmosphere. Where did they come from and how were they formed? Some type of radiation had been known for decades to be present in the air and, after the 1895 discovery of radioactivity, most physicists thought a similar kind of radiation emitted by the Earth was the probable source of cosmic rays, a hypothesis soon proved wrong. In 1912, a balloon carrying scientific apparatus showed that radiation at 16,000 feet was four times more intense than at sea level, conclusively proving the Earth was not the source of the radiation. Nor was the Sun, a deduction reached by observing that the flux of rays was undiminished during a solar eclipse. [4]

After a lull in research caused by WW I, the theory that the rays originated in the atmosphere was also rejected. In 1922 Robert A. Millikan,[5] an American who coined the term "cosmic rays," posited they were extra-terrestrial, particles from outer space; he concluded further that they bombarded the earth with energies great enough to shatter atoms. This dramatic finding brought greater urgency and additional prominent physicists to the research table. Combined with Rutherford's 1911 discovery of the atomic nucleus and the mystery of what held it together, the nature of cosmic rays made it increasingly clear that previously unimagined sources of energy existed. Although it took several years, eventually these conclusions led to the nuclear age—an age exemplified by both unprecedented horrors of destruction and undisputed advances in medicine and technology.

The period from 1927 to 1937 was one of intense research on a worldwide scale to study the nature of cosmic ray bombardment and its origins. The fact that the rays were extra-terrestrial and absorbed by the Earth's atmosphere made their study at high altitudes imperative, an added attraction for my father. As he articulated, "It was useless to study cosmic rays in laboratories, so physicists started to travel all over the world. Their results were contradictory, so it was a golden opportunity for even more travel for physicists."[6] In a highly competitive field studded with Nobel Prize winners, Regener and his group were described as having ". . . brought to an unprecedented degree of perfection . . ." [7] the design and construction of instruments to measure ray intensity at various altitudes and were widely admired for their ". . . far-reaching experiments . . . ." [8]

Shortly after receiving his Master's Degree [9] in 1931, my father was contacted by Philipp Borchers,[10] one of that breed of academics who combined scientific interests with love of mountaineering. An active member of the German and Austrian Alpine Club, Borchers was a strong proponent of the Club's dual goals of furthering "alpinism" and science and their sponsoring expeditions that pursued both.[11] To Borchers, an expedition to the Andes, more specifically the Cordillera Blanca in northern Peru, was a perfect opportunity to do so.[12] Its mountains, lying just south of the Equator and stretching over 3400 kilometers, make up the highest and longest tropical mountain range in the world. The highest peak of the range and the highest in Peru is Huascaran, not quite 7000 meters high (22,205 feet). With two peaks, the higher one (6,768 meters) had never been summitted. Borchers submitted a convincing proposal to the Alpine Club that specified carrying out geological and glaciological studies as well as surveying and mapping the region. And, as Borchers added, "Moreover, there is the question of measurement of cosmic rays." [13]

Initially my father was tentative about accepting Borchers' invitation to join the 1932 Expedition, but it became obvious that the respective agendas of Borchers, Regener and Hoerlin's could be combined to everyone's advantage. Borchers sought outstanding climbers on his team and concurrently, wished to foster scientific inquiries. Regener wanted to hang on to his diligent assistant and saw a chance to advance cosmic ray research through high altitude observations near the Equator. My father was just getting started on a serious career that he did not want to abandon and yet there was the call of the mountains. Additionally, South America was especially intriguing: a childhood hero of his, Alexander von Humboldt, was famous for his early explorations there. Was this a chance to follow Humboldt's scientific and climbing footprints?

The timing was perfect and so was the fit. Around the world there was a raging scientific debate regarding the essence of cosmic rays—were they photons or protons? Protons, the nuclei of hydrogen atoms, are particles with positive electrical charges, fundamental components of larger nuclei; photons, by contrast, are essential units of electromagnetic radiation, e.g. light, carrying no electric charge. One of the field's leading physicists, Millikan, an intensely religious man, argued cosmic rays were photons. Using a phrase that captured the public's imagination, he described them as "birth cries" of atoms and maintained they were divinely produced to counteract the Universe's increase of entropy. This view was challenged by other scientists, notably fellow American Arthur Compton, also a Nobel Prize winner. [14] It was a battle between the Nobel giants that glaringly illustrated enduring tensions between religion and science, tensions that continue to this day.

The answer to the cosmic ray puzzle lay in understanding the effect of the Earth's magnetic field on cosmic rays. A critical difference between photons and protons is that the latter, because of their electric charge, feel the influence of the Earth's magnetic field while photons, with no charge, do not. The latitudinal variation of the strength of the Earth's magnetic field meant that in one case the cosmic ray flux would change in moving toward the Equator and in the other it would not. In summary, cosmic rays would behave differently not only because of altitude, such as differences between the Alps and Lake Constance (where Regener conducted experiments), but also because of latitude—differences between Stuttgart and Lima. In 1932, three different teams searched for the latitude effect: Compton and his group spread to five continents, Millikan went to the Artic Circle and sent a young Ph.D. student to South America, and Regener sent Hoerlin to Peru.

For the fifteen months prior to the expedition's departure on March 31, 1932, my father toiled over the construction of equipment trying to make it tough enough to survive the long voyage, the heat and humidity of the tropics, transport by mules and then porters and finally, the ravages of winter snowstorms at high altitudes. Although Borchers was fully supportive of his research, he was left somewhat breathless when my father's "luggage" arrived at dockside in Bremen: 1,200 pounds of equipment, two cubic meters large. "You surely have taken the Kaaba from Mecca!", [15] Borchers exclaimed.

During the five-week voyage, the climbers—including Pallas' climbing partner Schneider—wiled away the days by playing shuffleboard on deck and the evenings by learning Spanish. The only person who worked "ceaselessly" was Hoerlin, busy collecting measurements for hours in the stifling hot room of the ship's hold, permeated by diesel oil fumes of the boat's engines, where his equipment was installed. [16] Conditions became unbearable when the boat reached the heat and humidity of the Panama Canal zone.

While crossing the 48 mile canal, everyone's attention turned to this awesome triumph of engineering ingenuity. An intricate system of three massive sets of locks, one lifting ships up to 85 feet, allowed passage between the great oceans, the Atlantic and Pacific. The freighter reached the Pacific at the end of April, when under a full moon and a sea of stars, it was greeted by a pod of dolphins, self-appointed escorts to a friendly country. The magic of the group's introduction to South America was reinforced at sunrise upon seeing from the boat the glow of early sunlight on the snow-covered expanse of the Cordillera range. Schneider was inspired enough to proclaim it "God's country," a description he still used thirty-five years later.[17]

The bonds between Germany and South America were historic. Germany's version of a universal man and my father's inspiration, the scientist, explorer and naturalist Humboldt (1769-1859), had spent several years in South America. Like his celebrated literary counterpart and friend, Goethe, Humboldt's fame spread beyond borders; among his acquaintances and admirers were Napoleon, Simon Bolivar and Thomas Jefferson. In addition to laying the foundations of modern geography and meteorology, Humboldt was a pioneer in the study of the Earth's magnetic field. He was also a climber, setting a world altitude record on Ecuador's Chimborazo in 1802. [18] He fell short of reaching its peak, but set a world altitude record (5878 meters; 19,286 feet) in 1802. His booklet, descriptively called "An Attempt to Scale the Summit of Chimborazo" [19] had been given to my father when he was twelve years old by his father. The small volume accompanied Pallas on his trip to Peru and now sits on my bookshelf, its worn pages indicative of my father's many readings of it, no doubt dreaming of following in Humboldt's footsteps. Throughout his life, Hoerlin was an admirer of how Humboldt joined his exploits with scientific contributions.[20] It gave him particular pleasure to think that studying the effects of magnetism at high altitudes combined two of Humboldt's major legacies.

Spanish translations of Humboldt's writings were available in 1822 and helped permanently fix his reputation; further relations between Germany and South America were cemented by trade agreements, German settlements and, most surprisingly, two sections of the German and Austrian Alpine Club in Chile. With these strong ties, the locals eagerly anticipated the 1932 Expedition's arrival in Peru. When the group landed at the small port city of Casma on May 2, the Peruvian government waived custom duties and speedily transported them (and their supplies) to Huaraz, the capital city of the province. Their arrival was celebrated with an official party, lasting until the early morning, attended by government dignitaries, the chief magistrate, the Bishop, and military officers. A sobering antidote to the festive event was news of unrest in Peru, presaging a brewing anti-imperialist uprising.[21]

My father was struck with how he was, for the second time, arriving in a country on the brink of revolution, first India and now Peru. For the next month the expedition explored the Cordillera Negra (a front range of the Cordillera Blanca) and the countryside seemed peaceful. However, as they approached Yungay, the village serving as an operations base for a Huascaran assault, bursts of gunfire repeatedly echoed through the foothills. On July 13th, an uprising of reformists closed Yungay down while the expedition was in the midst of selecting porters and gathering horses and mules for their trek to Husacaran's snowline. They almost had to abort their plans. An order had been issued to confiscate all beasts of burden in the region, a decree that would essentially paralyze the expedition. The group was much relieved when a deputy in the revolutionary forces whispered to Borchers that if the animals left town, he would not be able to carry out the orders. "We were happy to oblige," remarked the expedition leader, leaving swiftly with his climbers, nine porters, six horses and seven mules.[22]

The valleys of the Cordillera Blanca range in the Andes.

Over the next six months the Cordillera Blanca team climbed five summits over 6000 meters, fourteen peaks between 5000 and 6000 meters and studied many others, including the Matterhorn-like Alpamayo, a stunning pyramid considered by many as the most beautiful mountain in the world.[23]

Alpamayo, the perfect mountain.

Of their conquests, the most notable was Huascaran, named after an Inca chieftain who was a legitimate heir to the Inca empire. It boasted two prominent tops: the ascent of the lower north peak, claimed to have been reached by Annie Peck in 1908, was questionable, [24] fueled by a bitter controversy as to whether Peck or her rival, Fannie Bullock Workman held the world record for women in mountain climbing. Peck insisted that she was the champion, asserting that Huascaran was taller than Pinnacle Peak (6930 meters; 22, 736 feet), the height of Bullock's 1906 Himalayan conquest. The very public dispute was particularly unfortunate because the two women had much in common. Both born to well to do American families, they were accomplished climbers and strong supporters of women's suffrage, often coping with disdain and ridicule from male climbers.[25] In a pointed jab, Peck had even painted a mustache on her face before climbing Huascaran.

Against this background and amidst continuing rumors that Peck had not really reached the slightly lower summit, the 1932 Expedition took the position that their aim was the higher southern summit, a summit Peck had not attempted, while giving her credit for a climb that she at age 58, accompanied by two capable Swiss guides, had attempted six times. Huascaran has enormous crevasses, rotten snow bridges and harrowing seracs, huge chunks of glacial ice, blocking the route to the *Garganta,* a saddle separating the north and south summits.

Climbing through teetering jumbles of ice and snow blocks on Huascaran.

After weaving their way through the labyrinth, the 1932 team of four Germans and one Austrian [26] headed to the south peak, wading through deep snow and trying to distract themselves from the tedium by first counting steps and then, at the suggestion of expedition's physician, their pulse rates. By 5 p.m., all of them had reached the summit. Working quickly, they assembled a fifty-two foot pole, hauling it up in sections and then raising the Peruvian flag ". . . as a mark of courtesy" on the country's highest mountain. [27] A few days later, back in Yungay, circulating a telescope to skeptical villagers who still harbored doubts about Annie Peck's claim,[28] the expedition was able to provide proof positive. The flag, twelve miles away, was visible and stayed in place for five weeks. The villagers seemed more jubilant about seeing their country's flag waving on the summit than about the successful ascent of the "crazy gringos." It is sad to think that in 1970 an earthquake broke off a block of Huascaran causing a huge landslide of ice and rock, obliterating Yungay and its inhabitants.

Huascaran, Peru's highest summit.

After the Huascaran conquest, the group split up, making first ascents of several unclimbed peaks [29] and pursuing their respective topographical, geographical and cultural studies. In terms of mapping the area, it was the beginning of a long process involving Schneider, a budding cartographer, who returned to Peru in 1936, 1939, 1950 and 1954. [30] Today his photographs and measurements clearly demonstrate dramatic glacial recession over time and his meticulously drawn maps are still in use, praised by Peruvian mountain guides. My son Noah and his fiancée Kathrine discovered this when they went climbing in Peru during the fall of 2006. When Noah mentioned that his grandfather had been on the 1932 expedition, his guide was thrilled, showing him the map he was using—a map developed by Schneider and the German—Austrian Alpine Club. My father's copy of it hangs handsomely framed in the bedroom of Noah and Kathrine's toddler son.

As for Hoerlin's scientific experiments, he had started cosmic ray readings in the Cordillera highlands, assisted in setting up his heavy equipment by a remarkable porter. Nestor Montez, according to my father, was ". . . an intelligent man who surprised me with his knowledge about the solar system, the planets and his political conversations." [31]

Nestor Montez with Hoerlin's cosmic ray equipment.

The shortest among the porters, Nestor [32] had voracious curiosity about cosmic ray research; my father educated him about it and Nestor reciprocated by educating him about the APRA (American Popular Revolutionary Alliance) movement, a populist group made up primarily of poor peasants fighting the Peruvian army. Again, as in India, my father found himself in sympathy with the revolution. It continued for 10 years, finally claiming Nestor's life.

Transporting Hoerlin's bulky apparatus was no trouble on mule-back, but carrying it to a 6000 meter observation cosmic ray observation point, the highest ever, was another matter. The ray-measuring equipment alone, weighing 300 kg (over 600 pounds), was dismantled and carried by porters up

Hualcan, one of the easiest but nonetheless risky peaks. Hoerlin established a series of cosmic ray stations there, staying alone at each several days: the first at 4700 meters for twenty days, the next at 5500 meters for fifteen days and the last at 6100 meters for six days. The last, on a snowy knoll, made it easy for him to climb to mountain's summit several times over the course of his stay.

Although relatively easy to ascend, Hualcan (6122 meters; 20,085 feet) turned out to be an unfortunate choice in other respects. Because of its position on the mountain range and its relationship to valleys below, it continually attracted cloud cover, violent thunder and lightening storms, and howling winds. Alone and under these frightening circumstances, days for Pallas were tortuously long and all too often the weather impeded any possibility of conducting research. On some days the solitary mountaineer-researcher had no recourse other than to stay in his tent; his only companion was attractive, sleek and—to some eyes—overweight, equipment that unapologetically hogged the tight space leaving him barely enough room to squeeze in his sleeping bag. On the other hand, it served as a reassuring anchor during times of gale force winds that threatened to blow him off the mountain. In the worst moments of electrical storms, Pallas retreated to a snow cave he had built, fearing the tent and its contents would attract lightening. Occasionally there would be a break in the weather, allowing him to break the monotony by climbing the nearby south peak of Hualcan and admire the spectacular surrounding mountains: "Then I could sit content and happy in front of the tent and relish the beauty of mountain scenery and the wide world. I could sit there for hours…"[33]

On those rare days, a handful of porters—most often including Nestor—and accompanied by the forty-seven year old Borchers, would trudge up the mountain with supplies, also helping move the cosmic ray equipment furthur up Hualcan. Much to Hoerlin's appreciation, they brought letters from family and friends, surely creating one of the world's highest postal delivery services. These welcome respites, determined more by weather than by scientific scheduling, broke Hoerlin's solitude briefly, but otherwise he was by himself for a total of forty-one days. Pallas may have set a different kind of record: the longest stretch of time a single person had been that high. My father certainly broke the record for staking and staffing the highest cosmic ray station in the world.

The world's highest cosmic ray station: Hoerlin's tent with the summit of Hualcan in the distance.

There was much joy on Pallas's return to base camp. Members of the expedition had become highly invested in the success of his research. The cosmic ray equipment had become integral to the whole venture, a shared logistical challenge that engaged the team's physical and emotional support. Borchers had set a tone of facilitation and caring, earning Pallas' references to him as "my mountain father." [34] My father was elated by his results and his return to "civilization," but he appeared to have aged at least thirty years. He looked wrinkled and thin, his smooth youthful complexion has suffered from the ravages of rough weather and dehydration in high altitude. When he sent a photograph of himself to his family, he received the following reply from his sister: "Mother looked at it and said, 'Is that my boy? No, it is not. Or is it? No, no, it is not him.'" [35] She was not able to recognize her own son. After life at a more accommodating altitude, my father's age-appropriate and familiar looks were restored.

The basic objectives of the expedition had been filled and its members separated, some staying for further geological explorations, others for more climbing, [36] and Hoerlin for more measurements. In addition to those taken at sea level during the five-week voyage from Germany to Peru, then on the one-week boat trip from Peru to Chile, he gathered more on a nine-week-long crossing through the Magellan Straits back to Germany.

Hoerlin prior to his extensive cosmic ray studies on Hualcan

A dehydrated, weather-beaten and happy Hoerlin after his solitary stint at 19,000 feet on Hualcan

The Straits, 40 degrees south of the Equator, were almost exactly as far—but in the opposite direction—from the Equator as was Hamburg, 40 degrees north of the Equator. By showing sea level data at both locations, he was able to calibrate the Equatorial effect of cosmic rays and test the accuracy of his equipment. His elegant results, charted on a graph, showed an almost perfectly symmetrical relationship.

An amusing aspect of the international competition to study latitude effects on cosmic rays occurred in early December 1932, while Hoerlin was waiting in Lima for a freighter to Europe. He encountered the assistants of Millikan and Compton, the two rival efforts. Although the timing was amazing, it was not completely coincidental that these analogous undertakings converged in the southern hemisphere. Millikan's assistant had been in the mountains of southern Peru and Compton's had readings from the rooftop of a Lima hotel. The three of them exchanged experiences in an impromptu cosmic ray conference. Neither one of the researchers had Hoerlin's wealth or depth of data about cosmic rays in the Andes, but they were both part of larger projects scattered around the globe. It was my father's introduction to American science, which was beginning to assert itself boldly in a field that had been dominated by Europeans. A new age of big science was dawning and the sun was rising in the United States. Five years later Hoerlin would be part of that American scene.

At the Christmas 1932 meetings of the American Association for the Advancement of Science, when my father was still on the freighter to Germany, Millikan and Compton participated in a symposium on cosmic rays. The two scientists were barely civil to one another, refusing to shake hands at the end of the session. Their acrimonious debate was latched onto by the press, who quickly dispensed with the image of scientists as "... hardheaded, factual, cautious, accurate, and, as such worth listening to ... Now here were two Nobel Prize winners displaying all the passion and fallibility of ordinary men."[37] By February 1933, Compton's findings prevailed: the latitude effect was indisputable and cosmic rays were definitely photons. In Kevles' words, "(Millikan) said no more about the birth cries of atoms and left it up to the clergy to decide whether the Creator was still on the job."

It was not until March that my father completed his voyage and landed back in Germany. His research, agreeing with Compton's, was not published until July 1933, in the prestigious journal, *Nature*. Compton had already published his in the March 1933 issue of the *Physical Review*. Given Compton's high profile as well as the size and scope of his operation—approximately sixty collaborators and eight expeditions around the globe—it is not surprising that he is given primary credit for ascertaining the geomagnetic effect on cosmic rays. However, as with much of science, discoveries rest upon many shoulders. One of them was my father's.

Chapter 4

WHERE BOOKS ARE BURNED

When Hoerlin disembarked on March 3, 1933 from the freighter in Bremen, near Hamburg, all his cosmic ray equipment was fully functioning and intact. Some had almost been lost in the Andes, jettisoned by porters at over 20,000 feet above sea level during a sudden wild storm on Hualcan. The next morning, conscientious researcher that he was, my father had rescued it, digging parts out of the snow and carefully hauling them to his cosmic ray roost. The equipment miraculously survived a host of traumas, enduring freezing temperatures, high altitudes, mule rides, humidity, sea voyages, and . . . even abandonment. But now everything was safely home. Welcomed by his appreciative and smiling Stuttgart professor Regener, Hoerlin carried two packages down the gangplank, souvenirs from Peru. He handed one, a handsome alpaca poncho knit by a Huaraz villager, to Regener. The larger package, which Hoerlin continued to cradle, contained a silky and soft blanket made from vicuna, the world's finest and most costly natural fleece. Vicunas, small and graceful creatures, possessed a mystical presence in the soul of Peru; my father, not usually a superstitious man, intuited that someday the blanket would find a good home.

Although the 1932 Cordillera Blanca Expedition had made several first ascents, Germans did not treat it with the same fanfare as they had the 1930 Himalayan Expedition when Hoerlin set a world climbing record. It was true that the 1932 endeavor had ". . . inaugurated modern climbing in the Andes and . . . made Peru's ranges known to the mountaineering world,"[1] but the Andes did not have the panache of the Himalaya's 8000 meter peaks, a more dramatic framing for German heroics. And heroics were what

Germany prized with the resurgence of nationalism and assertions of racial superiority.

After a year's absence, my father's re-entry into Germany was a rude shock. A few days beforehand in Berlin, on February 27, the German Parliament—the Reichstag—had burned to the ground. [2] Hitler seized the opportunity to use the disaster as irrefutable evidence that Communists were plotting to overthrow the government. The next day he signed a decree "for the Protection of the People and the State," essentially negating the country's constitutional guarantees of civil liberties. Rights of free expression (including freedom of the press), assembly, property and privacy were restricted or suspended. My father had just left one country, Peru, in the midst of a rebellion instigated by the need to adopt social reforms and democratic ideals, only to return to another country—his own—where a newly installed party was rapidly shedding those very same ideals.

Hoerlin had been away for seven months when he participated in the 1930 Himalayan Expedition and for a full year during the 1932 Cordillera Blanca Expedition, returning each time from these long absences to discover the state of affairs in Germany had seriously deteriorated. A worldwide economic depression had hit the country especially hard with high unemployment rates creating misery and unrest. Bitter feuding between the major political parties had rendered Parliament ineffective and the continuing instability of government created a climate of uncertainty. Communists, moderate Social Democrats and strident National Socialists (abbreviated as Nazis) vied for power in a series of elections, but it was not until March 1933 that Hitler squeaked by a splintered electorate to become President, establishing himself as one of the most evil tyrants of all time. My father had seen it coming. As he once explained to me, "Being away for extended periods gave me the benefit of fresh perspectives; I saw the erosion of trust and Hitler's persistence in plotting how to fill the void."

The new Nazi government moved with lightning speed to infiltrate all aspects of German life: its intellectual and cultural underpinnings, scientific communities, and even sports. On March 23, the Reichstag passed the Enabling Act, the "Law for Removing the Distress of People and Reich," which created the legal basis for Hitler's dictatorship, giving him unchecked powers. [3] Communists, radicals, Jews, gypsies and people with disabilities were systematically marginalized and endangered. Anti-Semitism, which had existed over time in varying degrees throughout much of Europe, was now fueled in Germany by Hitler's rhetorical rants, soon underscored by the enactment of laws intended to rid the country of Jewish influence, and ultimately of the Jews themselves. A total of 525,000 Jews lived in Germany in 1933, less than one percent of the population, but they became scapegoated as a curse for the whole country. According to a renowned historian of the period, a ". . . sense of urgency, but no panic" [4] prevailed; however warning signals were flashing. Thirty seven thousand Jews fled Germany in 1933, the largest exodus of any year between then and 1937.

While others turned a blind eye toward the ominous manifestations of a totalitarian takeover, my father bore witness to increased abuses and injustices. In the months following the election, "Heil Hitler" became the standard greeting and turmoil was rampant. Anti-Semitic pamphlets and racist graffiti were ubiquitous in Germany's cities. Jews were jeered, insulted, and physically manhandled when they walked the streets. Hoerlin was profoundly and irrevocably affected by what has been described as ". . . a world altogether grotesque and chilling under the veneer of an even more chilling normality." [5] Life was changing not only for those in harm's way, but also for full-fledged Aryans. In the first year of Hitler's regime, there were immediate repercussions on Hoerlin's work setting, hometown, and beloved domain of mountaineering. Life under the Nazis became increasingly horrendous after 1933, but the roots of these horrors surfaced early on.

A Nazi flag waving over the Stuttgart Institute of Technology was the none-too-subtle communiqué that greeted the returning mountaineer/ scientist at the Physics Institute, where colleagues cheered Hoerlin's Peruvian accomplishments with champagne. While a "chilling normality" may have existed on the surface, the underlying milieu of the Institute with its relatively high percentage of Jews was decidedly tense. In the spring of 1933, Hitler passed a plethora of laws beyond the initial Enabling Act that tightened the vise of his powers. The first, approved in April, was the only openly anti-Semitic law enacted in Germany since 1871. Called the Civil Service Law, it legally sanctioned exclusion of citizens based on a formal definition of race, determined in this case by the existence of a single Jewish grandparent. [6] Since the university system was state run, all employees were regarded as civil servants and required to provide proof of their Aryan heritage. In effect the law purged Jews from universities, bastions of intellectual discourse held in contempt by Hitler. With little resistance from these bastions, it is estimated that in 1933 alone 1200 Jews holding university positions were dismissed.[7]

After Hoerlin submitted extensive documentation of his family background, he was certified on May 29, 1933 as a full-blooded German and a Christian.[8] However, this brought him little joy. Colleagues and dear friends did not share the classification. The University's highest official was the physicist Peter Paul Ewald,[9] who had a Jewish mother and a half Jewish father. Ewald, one of Hoerlin's most respected professors, had founded the Physics Institute before being appointed Rector of the University in 1932, a position he no longer could hold with the passage of the Civil Service Law. The April law, which first applied to Jews, was expanded in June to Aryans who were married to Jews. A fellow doctoral student of Hoerlin's was labeled "politically incorrect" because of his Jewish spouse and leftist tendencies. He happened to have married the foster daughter of Regener, Hoerlin's thesis advisor. Regener himself was affected since his wife was Jewish. Naively hoping the worst was over, Regener could not imagine this as just the beginning of Jewish persecution and the destruction of German academic life.

Most university students, in general enthusiastic about this regime change, welcomed National Socialism in spite of its threat to the worldwide reputation of German academic excellence. With the strategic brilliance that often marked their political empire building, the Nazis had been busy since 1926 establishing a vigorous student division. Wearing brown shirts with swastikas, the National Socialist German Students' League led boisterous pro-Nazi rallies inevitably stirred up by anti-Semitic slogans, more often than not disintegrating into the humiliation and beatings of Jews.

In the spring of 1933, the League orchestrated a book burning campaign to cleanse Germany of Jewish and other foreign or treasonous literature. Launched in April with the announcement of an "Action Against the Un-German Spirit," the agenda for the May ceremonies consisted of torchlight processions, marching bands, Nazi songs, speeches by Nazi leaders and most dramatically, huge bonfires onto which books deemed un-German were thrown. These included books by such Jewish authors as Sigmund Freud, Albert Einstein and Leon Trotsky, but also non-Jewish ones such as Helen Keller, Ernest Hemingway and Jack London. At the Berlin book burning of May 10, 1933, the Reich Minister for Public Enlightenment and Propaganda, Joseph Goebbels, proclaimed, *"German men and women! The age of arrogant Jewish intellectualism is now at an end! You are doing the right thing at this midnight hour—to consign to the flames the unclean spirit of the past. This is a great, powerful and symbolic act ... Out of these ashes the phoenix of a new age will arise ..."* [10]

Goebbels was right about it being a new age. Over 25,000 books were burned, the movement spreading from university towns to cities all over Germany. It was a frightening precursor of the censorship the Nazi government would practice in the future. Over a hundred years earlier, the German-Jewish poet, Heinrich Heine, had eerily intoned,

"Where books are burned, human beings are destined to be burned too."

In Stuttgart, marauding crowds of students were persuaded at the last minute not to harass the University's Jewish librarian, viewed by them as the devil's assistant in procuring questionable books. The 'politically incorrect' Regener was rumored to be another target; when Hoerlin heard this, he instantly appointed himself as guardian of the Regener family. Armed with his wooden ice axe, the intrepid mountaineer moved into their apartment located above the physics lecture hall, sleeping on the floor behind the front door, ready to resist aggressive intrusions by young thugs. Over six feet tall and known around the university for his climbing feats, he was a formidable deterrent to any provocations. The Regener home was secure. Fifty years later, Regener's son would repay my father's kindness.

Shortly after returning from Peru, Hoerlin was reunited with his own family in Schwaebisch Hall, who were relieved to have him back. His father, having great faith in his son's mountaineering skills, had been more concerned about the dangers of Peru's bloody rebellion than those that came from scaling its highest peaks.[11] His sister, recently diagnosed with tuberculosis, was particularly happy to see him. She too had been worried. In her extensive correspondence with her brother in Peru, she informed him that the German Zepplin, the pride of the nation, had cancelled its scheduled August 15th trip to South America because of political "Wirren" ("confusion"). His mother, thinking of food as a balm against most anxieties, prepared his favorite fare: Baerlauch suppe (wild leek soup), Spaetzle (noodle dumplings), Rotkraut (red cabbage) and sausages with lots of mustard. The dinner conversation made my father acutely aware of how the new Nazi regime had reached Schwaebisch Hall, eclipsing any dangers he encountered in South America. The typically Swabian meal—albeit delicious—had provided only temporary reprieve from the swirl of disturbing political developments.

Adolf Hoerlin, age 68

The Hoerlin household was liberal in outlook. On the day that Hitler's April 1933 official boycott of Jewish shops and businesses took effect, Adolf Hoerlin demonstrated his displeasure by dressing in his Sunday best and resolutely walking across Schwaebisch Hall's historic Marktplatz to call on his fellow merchants who were Jewish. Politically active, the distinguished looking merchant was elected as a City Supervisor (the equivalent of a City Councilman) for ten years between 1920 and 1930 and was also a prominent member of the business community. His show of support to Jewish merchants delivered an unmistakable message to the townspeople. At the time even a public handshake between Aryans and Jews was looked at askance. Regrettably, my grandfather was in a minority of Hall's 10,000 residents, many of whom cheered when books were burned in an enormous bonfire on the town's square in May, leaving behind a blackened scar. Today a Jewish star embedded in the cobblestones acknowledges the destructive act.

Once Hitler was elected, it became commonplace to see Nazi uniforms on Schwaebisch Hall's walkways, flags with swastikas along the homes overlooking its picturesque river and National Socialism's geometric graffiti

**Schwaebisch Hall with flying Nazi flags, barely visible
in this 1934 photograph**

on old stonewalls. [12] Anti-Semitism inevitably grabbed hold; the poisons of
animosity and loathing began to saturate the atmosphere to the point where
Jews were branded as "parasites of the people." [13] Nazi functionaries, who had
focused on intimidating gentiles who associated with Jews, began to enforce
sanctions and laws giving legitimacy to religious hatred. With frightening
alacrity, National Socialism was overtaking all aspects of society. Although
Hoerlin himself was not the target of violence, intolerance and/or injustice, the
workings of the Nazi government shook to the core his central values regarding
the dignity and rights of humankind. The university where he studied had
been decimated, his hometown tarnished and the world of mountaineering
was being invaded. In a process translated commonly as "coordination" and
more literally as "marching together," the Nazi goal *Gleichschaltung* gathered
private and public entities under the malevolent umbrella of a synchronized

and centralized state structure. The resulting loss of identity and integrity for clubs, professional bodies, organizations and institutions meant the Nazis were in complete control of the arts, labor unions, the church and recreational and sports clubs. The word *Gleichschaltung* became anathema in Germany to many, ". . . a word so cryptic and impersonal that it conveys no sense of the injustice, the terror, and the bloodshed it embraced." [14]

The Nazis viewed the prestigious German and Austrian Alpine Club with its 240,000 members [15] as a particularly desirable jewel to add to a crown of *Gleichschaltung*. Founded in 1869, the *Alpenverein* emulated the British Alpine Club instituted in 1857. However, whereas the British Club was an exclusive society restrictive in membership only to people of means with a certified record of climbing achievements, [16] the German—Austrian version welcomed men and women alike who were interested in mountains and mountaineering, regardless of skill level, class background or political persuasion. It was unique among Alpine Clubs (such as those in Italy, France or Switzerland) in its universalistic approach, making it the largest alpine organization in the world. [17] While in Peru, Hoerlin had been elected to the Executive Committee of the club, thereby serving during a tumultuous period when the Verein's very existence was threatened.

The history of the *Alpenverein* is replete with debates revolving around preserving the purity of nature and whether building and maintaining mountain huts was consistent with that goal. Its leaders bitterly fought the "mechanization, materialization, capitalization and industrialization of the mountains"[18] in their attempt to stem the impact of tourism enabled by the infringement of trains, cable cars, roads and hotels on the alpine landscape. In the early 1900's another hotly contested issue surfaced: anti-Semitism. Some sections of the club, particularly Austrian ones, prohibited Jewish applicants from membership. In 1924, the leadership of the Verein, citing its longstanding open door policy and abstention from political dogma, did not take a stand, although it advised Jewish applicants to seek membership in sections without the so-called Aryan clauses. [19] Meanwhile, anti-Semitism in the Alps was all too common. Spiteful signs on trails and huts warded off Jewish climbers and permission to use *Alpenverein* huts was often not granted. The *Neue Deutsche Alpenzeitung* of Munich was appropriately outraged:

"... you ask questions about heritage and blood at the doorsteps
of your shelters and forget those about spirit and feeling! You
search for heritage and the shape of a skull and overlook the
beating of the heart and the sound of the soul. What is the point
and how will things end?" [20]

The issue had landed on the Verein's doorstep after the formation in
1921 of new section, "Donauland," based in Vienna and consisting primarily
of Jewish members. It had a short life span. In 1924, at the Verein's annual
joint meeting, 89% of the representatives from Germany and Austria voted
in favor of expelling Donauland. Under the threat of Austrian sections pulling
out of the organization if Donauland was not disbanded, the *Alpenverein's*
governing committee had made the recommendation for ejection to preserve
accord between the German and Austrian mountaineering brotherhood.
They hoped to play a political role in a unification that went beyond
mountaineering and feared that further quarreling would divert the Verein
from its focus on protecting the Alps from tourism. [21] Concurrently, the Verein
feared anti-Semitism would spread and officially declared a moratorium on
the question of Jewish membership for the next eight years.

The *Alpenverein* of today considers the 1924 meeting as the
darkest chapter of its history.[22] It was widely perceived as a resounding
denouncement of Jews, although the club's stance was more nuanced.
The question regarding Jews as members was stayed until 1933 when it
again surfaced because of the advent of the Third Reich. Although Hitler's
election was cheered by some sections of the Verein, the majority of sections
remained silent. Some signaled their acquiescence. The Munich section
recommended that the Nazi flag be flown from their mountain huts as often
as possible. [23] This nod to the Nazis was hardly enough to stave off the new
bureaucracy from further intrusions. Hitler appointed a new Sports Minister
(*Reichssportfuehrer*), Hans von Tschammer und Osten, and charged him
with prompt implementation of *Gleichschaltung,* incorporating all organized
forms of physical exercise into the Nazi state apparatus. Initially an exception
was made for the *Alpenverein.* Due to its highly visible national stature and
a membership that included powerful officials within the Nazi party, it
was—momentarily—cosseted. However, there were some conditions. When
the Sports Minister met with representatives of the Verein in June 1933,
he assured them the club would not be dissolved if it came into line with

National Socialist doctrine on the Jewish question.[24] Simply put, the price of independence for Germany's largest mountaineering club was adoption of exclusive Aryan membership. [25]

Adding insult to injury, the Sports Minister was putting his side-kick Paul Bauer—and my father's nemesis—in positions of greater authority by creating Nazi organizations such as the German Mountaineering and Hiking Association (*Deutscher Bergsteiger und Wanderverband*) and putting Bauer in charge. Bauer, who had attempted Kanchenjunga the year before Dyhrenfurth's 1930 International Expedition, was a reputable climber whose approach to mountaineering resembled a re-enactment of WW I, except for the altered scenario that Germany would emerge victorious. Germany, still stung by its defeat, had latched onto mountaineering as key to German efforts at recovery, as noted in the 1919 principles of the *Alpenverein*: "Alpinism . . . is one of the most important means in rebuilding the ethics and morale of the German people." [26]

No one took this dictate more seriously or applied it more militaristically than Bauer. Looking more like a bespectacled professor than a field commander, Bauer's full beard did not hide his tight-lipped mouth that barked orders requiring "unconditional, military obedience" [27] from his climbing team. His expedition reports were saturated with terms like attack, fight, columns, shock troops, and siege, [28] emphasizing political triumph rather than any particular love for the mountains. Both he and the Sports Minister appealed to climbers to inspire German youth to be fearless and prepare for any struggles.

The tensions between the *Alpenverein* and Bauer's group were immediate and accelerated over time. As Bauer's influence grew, threats to the club's autonomy intensified and created major factions within the club itself, with its contingent of fiercely individualistic alpinists. It was a trait the Nazis had not fully assessed; as observed by a leading expert, "Most good climbers hated obedience . . . and the strong mountaineering brotherhoods had a definite anarchistic streak." [29] The *Alpenverein's* leadership walked a delicate line internally, between the rebels and their more conservative counterparts and externally, between independence from and appeasement to the National Socialists. In constant negotiations with Bauer and the Sports Minister, the Verein's Executive Committee attempted to save some degree of sovereignty and resist *Gleichschaltung.* In these talks, Hoerlin staunchly opposed any form of nazification. He was a thorn in Bauer's side.

While Verein politics absorbed much of his time, the aspiring doctoral student continued his cosmic ray research. In the summer of 1933, Hoerlin traveled to northern Norway where the ". . . land of the midnight sun and of icebergs dwarfed the ice falls of the Himalayas." [30] and then onto Switzerland, accompanied on the latter leg of the trip by Regener's son, the 21 year old Victor who would later become a physicist himself. [31] Their destination was the international high altitude research station, located slightly below the Jungfrau, one of the world's best known mountains. A far cry from my father's highest cosmic ray tent in Peru at 20,000 feet, the building of the laboratory at less than 12,000 feet was achieved by transporting heavy construction materials via Europe's highest railroad. The Jungfraujochbahn train, inaugurated in 1912, was an engineering marvel that ushered in the kind of tourism opposed by the Verein. Eighteen years later it was judged differently: the train had made possible the type of scientific research encouraged by the Verein: studies in physiology, meteorology, glaciology, astronomy and—of course—cosmic rays. [32] These areas also comprised the scientific agendas of most Himalayan excursions of the time.

On the way back from one of his research trips to the High Altitude study center, Hoerlin stopped in Zurich to visit his old Bara Sahb [33] Gunter Dyhrenfurth, leader of the 1930 Kanchenjunga expedition, who was organizing another international climb in the Karakorum range, an impressive cluster of peaks over 8000 meters. [34] Dyhrenfurth had spoken about moving ". . . heaven and hell to launch the Expedition" and hoped to be joined by Pallas, Erwin Schneider and possibly Uli Wieland.[35] Four days prior to Dyhrenfurth's letter, Hoerlin had received a letter from another eminent climber, Willy Merkl, who was forming a team of German climbers for an expedition to Nanga Parbat, another 8000er located about 100 miles southeast of the Karakorum across the Indus river valley.

Both these large expeditions, slated to leave in early spring 1934, sought the support of the Verein and the presence of Hoerlin, Wieland and Schneider, all first rate climbers with Himalayan experience. Each of the expeditions, in different ways, was shaped by the politics of the Nazi era. Schneider was convinced that the Karakorum expedition had virtually no chance in obtaining backing from Germany because of its international, rather than national, emphasis and because of Dyhrenfurth himself. Dyhrenfurth, although his family had been assimilated for generations, was considered Jewish or as Schneider adamantly stated, ". . . the accident of his birth means he will no longer be able to win a flower pot in the 3rd Reich."[36] In addition, his wife Hettie came from a prominent Jewish family.

Both Merkl and Dyrenfurth independently pressured Pallas, Schneider and Wieland—who referred to themselves as ". . . the bad boys from the Third Reich" [37]—to join their respective expeditions. Merkl in his invitation to Hoerlin [38] added the extra lure of welcoming Hoerlin's extensive research instruments. Although they had never met, Merkl pursued this tact doggedly: in late July he came to meet with Hoerlin and Professor Regener in Stuttgart[39] and in September Merkl visited Hoerlin's research operation at the Jungfraujoch.[40] He knew that the physicist's scientific pursuits would give the expedition extra credibility with the *Alpenverein*. It was not clear whether Hoerlin's participation in the expedition was attractive to Merkl because of his climbing skills, his scientific work, or his position in the Verein. Most probably, the politically agile Merkl wanted him for all these reasons.

Merkl was also trying to recruit Schneider, who was not receptive to his overtures, and argued for joining Dyhrenfurth: ". . . we know Dyhrenfurth well, he is nobody's fool, we can surely influence him and get along well. NONE OF THIS IS CERTAIN WITH RESPECT TO MERKL!" (Schneider's emphasis) [41] "Merkl, although he is certainly a nice guy," Schneider continued, "is vain, arrogant and pig-headed." [42] This seemed like three serious strikes against a "nice guy," but as the expedition later unfolded, Erwin turned out to be correct. Schneider also brought into question Merkl's reputation; his 1932 Nanga Expedition had been badly organized and plagued by sherpa discontent. Team interaction had disintegrated, leading to finger pointing and a breakdown of cohesiveness. Would this lapse in leadership be repeated in 1934?

A major consideration for Schneider was which one of the expeditions his most trusted companions, Pallas and Wieland, would join. Although a less experienced mountaineer than either Schneider or my father, Wieland's steady cheerfulness, imperturbability and drive would be valuable assets to the expedition. The quiet man had been holding off from any commitment, not knowing which direction to turn, [43] but by August was favorably disposed to Merkl after climbing with him in Switzerland. [44] But what irreversibly tilted Wieland's decision was a call from Sports Minister Tschammer und Osten prodding him to sign onto Merkl's group. [45] It was difficult to turn down a request generated from the highest levels of your country's government.

Hoerlin continued to waiver, torn not only between the two expeditions but also his desire to wrap up his doctoral research. Futhermore, the family situation in Schwaebisch Hall was worrisome; his father had become ill again in September and his sister and mother were overwhelmed by the responsibility of running the family business. The always impatient Schneider asked Pallas in letter after letter, with poetic salutations of "lazy pig" (faules Schwein) or "sweetie" (Suesser) or "old turnip" (alte Ruebe), to make up his mind: "Let everything be weighed by that knucklehead of yours and write me as soon as possible your opinion, which is always valuable to me." [46] To see one's dignified father addressed in such terms was amusing to me, almost eighty years later.

In November, Hoerlin made his decision. Although appreciative of Merkl's putative interest in scientific research, my father questioned the quality of his leadership and was unsettled by the rising nationalistic tone of the Nanga Expedition. Conversely he was nervous that Dyhrenfurth would repeat organizational shortcomings of Kanchenjunga in the Karakorum. But the final answer came on November 10, when Hoerlin's father died at age 69. The man who, more than anyone else, had encouraged him to seek unknown horizons was gone. When my father wrote, "It is an old urge . . . the urge to explore, a longing for the wide world," [47] he echoed the feelings of his own father who never had been able to act on that urge. Adolf Julius Hoerlin had been given the gift of vicariously enjoying his son's exploratory, mountaineering and scientific achievements on three continents. But now was a time for the son to respect his father's memory by filling responsibilities on the home front, helping out his mother and sister with the store and making sure to complete his studies. Temporarily at least, the conquest of a 8000er was off Pallas' agenda.

Chapter 5

MOUNTAIN OF FATE, MOUNTAIN OF DESTINY

With the death of his father, letters of sympathy—marked by traditional black borders—consoled my father. One of them was from Merkl, who after expressing his condolences added: "... I simply can't imagine your not being with us {on the Nanga Expedition} and I only hope that your participation still will be possible ... it would be my greatest joy if you left with us in March." [1] Such pleas failed to convince Pallas. As things turned out, his absence was probably life-saving and definitely life-changing. Because of Nanga Parbat, he met my mother. But that was months later.

On March 25, 1934, to the cheers of friends and relatives, the train carrying the advance team for the expedition—Merkl, Wieland, Schneider and his fellow Austrian, Aschenbrenner—pulled out of the Munich station heading to Genoa where they boarded the steamer, "Victoria." Sixteen days later the main party left Munich and on April 13 boarded the "Conte Verde" in Venice. Surprisingly, they shared the vessel with Dyhrenfurth's International Expedition to the Karakorum. Although newspaper reports at the time played up animosities between the respective Nanga and Karakorum groups, these do not correspond to actual accounts of the sailing. [2] Friendly rivalries over a shipboard game, quoits, occupied the climbers' time. Quoits, the inspiration for American horseshoe pitching, was played by throwing rope rings onto a peg. If the ring landed on a peg, it was called a ringer. Obviously both expeditions wished for a "ringer" around a 8000er.

Although each of the expeditions had been outfitted with the latest mountaineering gear by a Munich sports store, commonalities ended there. As reported in the *Alpenverein's* June 1934 newsletter, the Karakorum expedition was under the "Leitung" of Dyhrenfurth and the Nanga Parbat expedition under the "Fuehrung" of Merkl. [3] Both words, translated from the German, mean leadership, but Leitung has a connotation of "guidance" whereas Fuehrung has the implication of "command," reflecting a subtle difference in style between the two men. Hettie and Gunter Dyhrenfurth's deliberate emphasis on mountaineering as an international endeavor and their negative feelings against the Third Reich, compounded by their Jewish backgrounds, contrasted with Merkl's commitment to an all-German effort and his strong feelings about pleasing the Third Reich. But such matters are seldom so straightforward. On the one hand, the supposedly "all-German" Nanga team included two Austrians, Schneider and Aschenbrenner; Schneider was outspoken against Hitler.[4] Also along was a young geologist, Peter Misch who was of Jewish ancestry and under the Civil Service Law's Aryan clause should have been barred from the Nanga expedition. [5] On the other hand, Dyhrenfurth's team included the self-promoting climber and filmmaker Hans Ertl who later became known as "Hitler's photographer," a key figure in the Nazi film propaganda machine. [6] For both teams, the stew was an ethnic and political mishmash.

While both Dyhrenfurth and Merkl were committed to large-scale expeditions with hundreds of porters, their goals were not the same. Merkl was single-minded: his overriding aim was the conquest of Nanga Parbat; geological research and film documentation were lesser objectives. Dyhrenfurth espoused a broader approach: to explore and climb unconquered peaks in the Karakorum and to produce the first dramatized film shot in the Himalayas. Called "Der Daemon des Himalaya" ("The Demon of the Himalaya"), the film script featured melodramatic heroes and dangerous mythical forces battling each other in the environs of majestic peaks.[7] As reported by Schneider, "They [the Dyhrenfurth group] want to hop onto an "easy" 8000er in the vicinity of K2 and make a film . . . the script of which I saw . . . and it made me feel faint." [8] It was understandable why Schneider was feeling weak-kneed. The film later was dismissed as "high-kitsch," demeaning to the dignity of mountaineering.

The two expeditions diverged in financial backing as well, which colored their objectives. The majority of Merkl's funding was from the German National Railroad Association (Reichsbahn), whereas Dyhrenfurth's came from India-Ton, a small Berlin production company that had wanted to produce the feature film. [9] The involvement of film-makers and actors in the Karakorum Expedition later led to tensions. The investment of the Reichsbahn also led to complexities. The railroad association was certain their support of the high-profile Nanga Expedition would do them proud. In a letter of thanks, Willy Merkl pledged to them: "Something like this is only possible in Germany. We will fight for Germany and devote everything toward the conquest for Germany of the first eight-thousander . . . Heil Hitler!" [10] This bravado was not sustained when Merkl wrote Hoerlin, more modestly stating: "Hopefully, something will come of it." [11] His short message was written on Himalayan penny ("Himalaya-Pfennig") postcard featuring a photograph of Nanga Parbat, part of a countrywide campaign to publicize and raise funds for the expedition. With such visible sponsorship, the pressure to succeed was intense.

In Germany, Nanga had become a national fixation. Just as Everest had been claimed by the British, Germans considered Nanga "their" mountain, based on its discovery by three German brothers in 1854. An unsuccessful expedition led by Merkl in 1932 had piqued German interest. The National Socialists latched onto the prospect of a successful Nanga expedition as a highly visible proxy for Teutonic superiority and competitive rebirth in the aftermath of WW1. In the words of the Sports Minister: "The conquest of the summit is expected for the glory of Germany." [12] Others viewed the expedition differently. Members of the *Alpenverein* asserted the importance of its scientific research along with its mountaineering objectives.[13] Still others stressed the "spiritual values" of mountaineering, its primal connection to nature, and its basically apolitical standing. [14] These varying constructs—political, scientific and spiritual—with their inherent conflicts, tragically played out on the steep and icy stage of the world's 9th tallest mountain.

The 1934 expedition attracted the attention of multitudes of Germans, a contemporary version for the quest of the Holy Grail. Media coverage had sparked popular interest, making it ". . . by far the most publicized mountaineering event in German history." [15] The *Alpenverein* planned to cover it fully in their monthly newsletter and asked Hoerlin to be its point person for all press releases disseminated to the German, as well as the worldwide press. [16] The expedition's designated press secretary was Dr. Willi Schmid, an eminent music critic at the *Muenchner Neueste Nachrichten* (the "Munich Latest News"), one of the highest circulation newspapers in Germany.

Although an unlikely choice in some respects, Schmid had done considerable free-lance work and would be ably assisted by his wife Kate. [17] To tend to the expedition's many details, an office had been set up in a room of the Schmid's spacious apartment, which became a central gathering place for meetings. The couple was close to Merkl, whom Willi had met through mutual friends. Kate's relationship to Merkl resembled that of a slightly older (by one year) sister: bossy, warm and critical. In her expedition-related letters to Merkl, Kate alternatively chides him for missteps ("The fault lies with you" [18]), cares for him ("Make sure you get enough sleep"[19]), and advises him ("dear boy, that's the crux of it, to be a good leader one must first and foremost be a good psychologist" [20]). The cache of letters spans the time from early preparations until July 2, when the Nanga climbers had started their second, and final, assault.

Kate and Willi Schmid, the Nanga Parbat press team (unidentified woman in the middle), at a send-off party for the expedition at their home. Reproduced with permission of the German Alpine Club.

Kate Schmid and expedition leader Willi Merkl in the Nanga Parbat office in the Schmid's apartment. Reproduced with permission of the German Alpine Club.

The first stage of the expedition began early in May, when the Nanga advance and main teams united in Kasmir. An army of almost 600 porters made the long and tedious trek to the mountain's base, carrying provisions and equipment over deep gorges, rushing rivers, high passes, and large glaciers. With only 400 pairs of sun goggles to distribute among them, several porters developed cases of snow blindness even before May 26th when they reached base camp. [21] Although there had been glimpses of Nanga at various points, it was revealed in its full glory the next morning. In awe, one of the sahibs (the name for European climbers) exclaimed: "The summit (8125 meters/26,600 feet) directly above us, glowed in the first light of the day. Slowly the blinding brightness cascaded over its mighty walls down towards the glaciers. We gazed up at the mountain, as if it were something totally unreal." [22]

There seemed to be little opportunity to admire or reflect quietly on the beauty of the mountain. Messengers bearing encouraging letters decorated by multi-imaged stamps from around the world, streamed regularly into Nanga's base camp. Almost daily reports about the expedition's progress were sent via short wave radio, telegrams, and press releases. The news media gave blow by blow accounts, sometimes exaggerating situations, other times focusing on bad weather or porter troubles, but regularly crafting a narrative of courage and camaraderie. The expedition had all the ingredients for gripping news:

a daunting challenge, dangers, triumphs, individual heroics and national honor.

Regrettably, the media tended to describe the expedition and its goals in nationalistic terms, fervently hoping the Nazi flag would fly from Nanga's summit. By 1934 the integrity of the German press had been co-opted with the hiring of reporters sympathetic to National Socialism who had taken the

Nanga Parbat, the German "Mountain of Fate."

jobs of Jews expelled by Hitler's dictates. [23] As with the dismissal of Jewish teachers and scientists, the expulsion of Jewish members of the press was accepted without protest; there was a readiness of others to benefit from their departures, a circumstance that constituted "... a profound moral lapse" [24] among Germans. With missionary zeal, these 'replacement' reporters put a relentlessly positive, if not inflated, bent on German deeds making several readers and listeners suspect the reliability of their releases, including those about the Nanga expedition. Erwin Schneider was among those most critical and, as usual, did not mince words: "I'm sure you're hooked to German radio and otherwise you will probably read the usual toilet (filthy) rumors and scare stories that the Third Reich feeds to the journalists. It's enough to make one throw up." [25]

After reaching base camp the bulk of the 600 porters, no longer needed, were paid off and discharged, leaving behind a more manageable group of 60 porters. Taking a few porters with them, a three-man scientific contingent set out to circle the Nanga Parbat massif to produce a detailed topographical map.[26] The onerous task of organizing porters for the assault fell to Wieland, who had recruited most of them and who they trusted. Often fielding the porter's complaints, the logistics were wearing on Wieland, as he conveyed to Pallas: "Big expeditions are terrible. It's always the baggage loads that hold things up. If God so wishes, the three of us (Wieland, Schneider and Hoerlin) will again participate in a small Expedition, but one with an important goal."[27] Schneider had voiced similar longings in a prior letter, suggesting next year the three close friends go to Peru's Cordillera again.[28]

Approaching Camp 2 through Nanga's challenging seracs.

One of Wieland's letters was particularly unsettling. Occasioned by his imminent departure from base camp, the considerate man wrote to send warm wishes to my father, well in advance of his July 5th birthday: "I may never again see this glorious place, [since I will be] leaving it . . . for a few days in any case and hopefully for at least four, at the most six weeks . . . and therefore congratulate you beforehand for your birthday." [29] Wieland added that a motivating motto of the Nanga expedition was: "One must sacrifice everything for progress [in reaching the summit]!"[30] The sacrifices became more drastic than he could have envisioned. A little over a month later, Wieland was dead.

By June 7th, the team was preparing for the final assault, having secured Camps 1, 2, 3 and 4 on the mountain. But letters to my father, while sounding optimistic about reaching the top, do not radiate a sense of happiness. Organizational problems delayed setting up Camp 4 and Merkl's leadership ability in solving them was in question.[31] Even an official book on the expedition, an uncritical account, referred to the authoritative and grim demeanor of Merkl. [32] Conflicts were brought to a head by the death of a climber. On June 8, Alfred Drexel suddenly contracted pulmonary edema at Camp 3 and efforts to save him failed. Merkl summoned the whole team back to base camp, where they re-assembled in shock and sorrow for Drexel's burial. On the afternoon of June 11th, a long solemn procession of men laid Drexel to rest; Merkl at the graveside ceremony, which had the trappings of a soldier's funeral, spoke of continuing to "fight on . . . with the iron determination of our dear comrade." [33] In a subsequent letter to Hoerlin, Wieland sadly recounted the passing of Drexel, relaying that "Frau Dr. Schmid will send you a release for the *Alpenverein's* newsletter; please take care of it right away." [34]

Photographs of Drexel's body, wrapped in a Nazi flag, were sent around the world and became an instant and vivid image of the nazification of German mountaineering.[35] Merkl had insisted on taking photographs and rolling films that showed the retrieval of Drexel's body down the mountain and his subsequent burial.

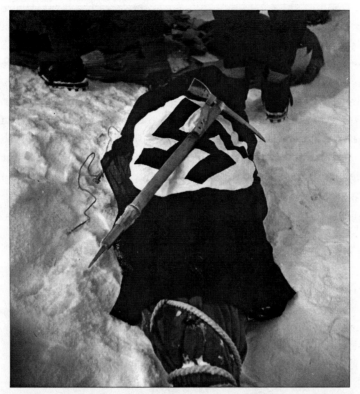

The body of Alfred Drexel swathed in a Nazi flag and topped with an ice axe, a lasting symbol of the politicalization of mountaineering. Reproduced with permission from the German Alpine Club.

This public and political treatment of Drexel's death incensed Schneider. Strongly reproaching Merkl for what he regarded as disrespect, Schneider spoke for other members of the expedition as well. His direct affront to Merkl's authority enraged the expedition leader to the point where he threatened to banish Schneider from the mountain. Schneider's anger also spilled over by questioning whether Merkl wanted to film Drexel's death for commercial purposes, given that Merkl had promised an inspirational documentary to the Nazis.[36] Like most of the Nanga climbers, Schneider disapproved of Nazism but tolerated the nationalistic trimmings of the expedition in deference to mountaineering aspirations.[37] But for him this overstepped that fragile line of tolerability.

The mood of the expedition did not improve with a delay of almost a month between when they were positioned for the first assault (June 7th) and set out for second assault (July 1st) on Nanga from Camp 4. The ostensible cause for the reprieve at base camp was waiting for tsampa, flour made from roasted barley, an indispensable staple of the sherpa diet. One of several drawbacks of a huge expedition was assuring adequate provisions for everyone, not to speak of the corresponding transport logistics. The tsampa supply had run low and the sherpas were not budging until it was replenished. It took 17 days until tsampa was conveyed to base camp, an interval during which feelings against Merkl's leadership festered. The weather was sunny and clear; valuable time was being wasted.

At Camp 4, the sherpas were smiling, Later, they would be among the expedition's casualties.

Tensions between Schneider and Merkl persisted. And in confidential letters home, the deputy leader of the expedition, Willo Welzenbach, wrote of deep aggravations regarding Merkl: "Merkl increasingly acts like a dictator who allows no criticism. He appears to really believe that a stern and uncompromising demeanor serves to establish his authority and suppress the inferiority complex which he obviously feels as someone who is up and coming." [38] Concluding his diatribe, Welzenbach made the damning observation, "[Merkl] is emotionally unworthy of his position as leader."[39] Starting a major assault of any kind, much less a second one, under this kind of cloud does not bode well for the future. Nonetheless, during the first week of July, Camps 5, 6 and 7 were progressively sited on the mountain.

Traversing the Rakoit glacier, a route of deep crevasses and fragile ice bridges.

This was the time to test, as Kate Schmid wrote in her July 2 letter to Merkl, ". . . whether or not it is humanly possible to reach the peak." [40] At Camp 7, a total of nineteen men—13 sherpas and 6 sahibs—crowded together on the narrow ledge at an altitude of 23,570 feet (7184 meters). When two sherpas fell ill, sahib Bechtold reluctantly accompanied them down the mountain while the others prepared for a final ascent spearheaded the next day, July 6th, by the two Austrians, Schneider and Aschenbrenner. They reached 7900 meters, less than 250 meters beneath the summit, with relative ease and deferentially waited first there and then a bit lower for a total of four hours. Feeling no sense of fatigue, the yodeling and cavorting Tyroleans were certain of conquering Nanga's peak. They were tantalizingly close, but in the spirit of teamwork refrained from pushing onward. Schneider had already rankled Merkl's authority, but this time obediently waited as the rest of the climbing party, three sahibs and eleven sherpas, carrying supplies, ascended slowly.

Merkl had made clear to everyone the Nazis government's wishes for as many climbers as possible to summit together for the glory of Germany.[41] Such a plan, antithetical to the custom of two strong climbers making a first summit attempt, already had been disparaged by Welzenbach: "One cannot bring together a club of 10 to 12 people on an eight-thousander. It means no one will get to the top. But all preaching is in vain here. Willy knows what is best." [42] When the weary second group finally neared Schneider and Aschenbrenner, Merkl decided to establish Camp 8 (7480 meters/24,540 feet) with the full expectation that the mountain would be vanquished the next day. All sixteen spent the night there, putting themselves in a high risk position, essentially cut off from necessary back-up support, supplies or help as well as suffering exhaustion from the toll of climbing at extreme altitudes.

During that night, hurricane force winds and a blinding blizzard of snow descended on the camp, making it out of the question to consider a morning assault. Bad weather had already hit the lower reaches of the mountain, but the climbing party was oblivious. The scientific team, trekking back from their mapping tasks, described Nanga from below as ". . . an island above a sea of clouds." [43] Hoping the weather would improve, the sixteen men at Camp 8 held out there between July 7th and 8th, when it was decided to temporarily retreat from the mountain until the brutal storm had cleared. The Austrians, who were fittest, were asked by Merkl to lead the way down just as they had been directed to lead the ascent and departed with three sherpas. The others planned to follow promptly.

With near zero visibility and deep powdered snow, the five roped men zigzagged their way down between false turns and treacherous ridges. After several close calls, one of the sherpas slipped, pushed over an edge by gale force winds, but was saved by Aschenbrenner and another sherpa. However the wind had torn a rucksack, containing one of the group's two sleeping bags, off the back of the sherpa: "it sailed away like a balloon before our eyes."[44] Gradually the airborne bag disappeared like a deflated dream of conquering a 8000er. Only one sleeping bag remained for 5 people, the day was getting late and everyone was drained and discouraged. Schneider and Aschenbrenner, feeling they had to move quickly, unroped themselves from the three sherpas, assuming they would follow in their tracks and/or be picked up by the second team close behind them. The two sahibs proceeded to Camp 7, which was abandoned with no supplies and then to Camp 6, which was completely covered by snow. After a short stop at Camp 5, where there was a bit of food, Schneider and Aschenbrenner continued down to where they knew there were people and provisions: Camp 4.

With the storm bearing in, the three climbers at Camp 4 had attempted to bring supplies to the higher camps but had been repelled by the terrible weather. Joined now by their exhausted colleagues, the group at Camp 4 waited with growing anxiety for the others. The storm continued to rage but clouds briefly parted late the next morning, and they caught sight of a fairly large group still disturbingly high on the mountain but descending with a solitary straggler wandering behind them. A tragedy now unfolded, the proportions of which have been described as ". . . for sheer protracted agony, there is no parallel in mountaineering history." [45] Wieland, later identified as the lone straggler, died on July 9th just above Camp 7,[46] Welzenbach at Camp 7 between July 12th-13th, Merkl together with his sherpa near Camp 6 sometime between July 15th and 16th. Early on the 15th the latter two were still alive, their plaintive cries for help still audible to those at Camp 4. Five severely frost bitten sherpas somehow managed at various times to stagger to Camp 4, and gave horrific accounts in excruciating detail of the expedition members, slowly and painfully perishing. Rescue attempts for the three remaining sahibs and six sherpas had proved futile; the swirling storm and "bottomless snow"[47] made it impossible to move, virtually imprisoning those at Camp 4. It was a gruesome nightmare that lasted a week: ghost-like sightings of those descending, calls of distress within hearing distance, uncertainties about who was alive or dead, and the anguish of being totally powerless. At the time, it was the greatest disaster in the chronicles of Himalayan mountaineering.

With inevitable communication time lags, "Frau Dr." Schmid (aka Kate Schmid) had written Hoerlin in Stuttgart on July 15th that according to a telegram received the preceding day, there were serious issues for the expedition. She closed by saying, "Now is definitely the time to think of the men and wish them well."[48] On July 18th the *Muenchner Neueste Nachrichten* had printed an article with a banner headline alluding to the gravity of the situation and reported that Merkl, Wieland and Welzenbach were missing[49], unaware that by that time they were dead. Lingering hopes that at least Merkl and Welzenbach would somehow survive were based on their remarkable stamina, having been trapped in a bivouac for sixty hours amidst violent storms on a hazardous mountain face in 1931.[50] This time, however, luck was not with them.

In 1938, another German expedition found Merkl's body. In the pocket of his jacket was a July 10, 1934 note from Welzenbach written from Camp 7 to the sahibs between Camp 6 and Camp 4. It was a final plea for help, ending in this heart—wrenching manner, ". . . We have both had nothing warm to eat and practically nothing to drink for 6 days. Please help us <u>soon</u> in C.7. Willo and Willy."[51] From July 9th to the 13th, Merkl and Welzenbach—too weak and frostbitten to move—shared a tent at Camp 7 waiting for rescue from Camp 4 in sight below, observing attempts to try and reach them. One wonders how, or if, during those last days their mutual resentments were disclosed. Merkl must have known the extent of the disaster.

Kate Schmid's July 2nd letter to Merkl never reached him. While he was fighting for his life in the Himalayas, she was ". . . going through the worst days of my life" in Munich. Two days beforehand, her husband had been carted away by Hitler's henchmen and she had no idea about his fate. Trying to protect Merkl from her feelings of despair and dread, she spares him details and assures him that ". . . the work {for the expedition} will be carried on . . . You must not worry that I'll leave it in a lurch. Definitely not."[52] In her two page missive, Kate goes over expedition finances, press requests for photos, and asks Merkl to send postcards to her favorite nephews. The mundane nature of the correspondence contrasts with the unforeseen tragedies that were unfolding.

On the day after she wrote her letter to Merkl, Kate Schmid was notified that her husband was dead. True to her promise to carry on the work of the expedition, she continued to release the increasingly ominous press releases and stay in touch with the *Alpenverein's* contact person, Hermann Hoerlin. [53] However, when conflicting reports of deaths overwhelmed her, she asked for expert help . . . and help, by way of Hoerlin, came. Hoerlin had rushed to Munich shortly after receiving the following telegram on July 17th:

HIMALAYAN EXPEDITION IN EXTREME DANGER.
CAN YOU IMMEDIATELY COME TO FRAU DR. SCHMID . . . [54]

Hoerlin, along with most of Germany, knew that Frau Dr. Schmid was coping with a personal tragedy. The news of Willi's death had even traveled to the Himalayas, where the remaining members of the expedition read through the piles of mail waiting for them at base camp. As Fritz Bechtold wrote: "Among the letters, there was one I had to read three or four times before I could grasp it. Willi Schmid, our dear, happy and intelligent comrade, in charge of our press headquarters in Munich, who along with his wife tackled our enormous workload in their home, who always knew how to inspire us—is dead . . . Fate and tragedy have transpired here on the mountain and at home."[55] Bechtold, who had pro-Nazi leanings, could not comprehend how Hitler, the newly installed leader of their country, could have been responsible for the murder of Willi Schmid: "It is so monstrous that something believed in for so long, as something great, was capable of erring." [56] This awkwardly couched criticism foreshadowed the many monstrous acts of a supposedly infallible dictator in the days to come.

Telegramming that "all of the expedition members want their return unnoticed," [57] the surviving climbers sailed home in early September. Letters from Bechtold and Schneider had commended my father for assisting Kate and spoke about how pleased everyone was that he was by her side. In the words of Schneider, "At least you could help the poor woman." [58] Bechtold, who had never met my father, thanked him profusely on behalf of the expedition for ". . . stepping in for us in these dark days . . . ." [59] Noting the enormous load of work carried by Frau Dr. Kate Schmid, Bechtold added: "What this woman in such a short timeframe must endure and accomplish is indescribable . . ."

News about Nanga reached Dyhrenfurth when the Karakorum group was on its way home, this time on a different boat than the Nanga survivors. It seemed like an eternity since members of the respective expeditions had played quoits on deck and wished each other well as they disembarked in Bombay. Neither party had netted an eight-thousander, although Hettie Dyhrenfurth had set a women's world record by summiting Sia Kangri (7442 meters / 24,350 feet), a record she held for forty years. The Nanga group, at great cost, had gotten closer to 8000 meters than any other attempt, but that summit feat was not attained until 1950 and then it was the French, not the Germans, who made history. [60] The Germans kept on attempting to conquer Nanga, but of their five expeditions in the 1930's, none of them would prove successful.

The word Nanga Parbat in Urdu is paraphrased into "naked mountain," but in Germany it was called the "Schicksals Berg." The dictionary offers two translations of Schicksal: fate or destiny. In the case of Kate and Hoerlin, Nanga was both a Mountain of Fate and a Mountain of Destiny. My father mused in those first days after the tragedy, "what if he had gone on the expedition . . . ?" "what if he had brought his skills to bear . . . ?", "what if he had been able to temper Merkl's overzealous desire to please the Fuehrer?" "what if he could not have changed anything and had died . . . ? The one "what if" he could answer concerned meeting Kate. If there had been no Nanga, it is dubious there would have been Kate and Hoerlin.

Chapter 6

LOVING KATE

By 1934, my father had conquered some of the world's highest mountains, crossed its two most famous canals, chanced upon the birth of revolutions in India and Peru, and risked the wrath of the Nazis by his political stances. However, none of this prepared him for Kate. As he later expressed, "You are totally different from any other women . . . I have ever known." [1] They first met on July 18th in Munich, the day after Hoerlin had received the urgent telegram beckoning him there. Immediately dropping his doctoral research in Stuttgart, Hoerlin took the train to Munich. By the time he arrived, everyone's worst fears were concerned: ten mountaineers, four elite German alpinists and six experienced sherpas, had perished.

Ordinarily Hoerlin, fit and athletic, would have bounded up the steps to Kate's apartment. But there was nothing ordinary about this visit. The gravitas of the situation slowed his pace. When he reached the third floor landing, Hoerlin made sure his tie was straight and his suit jacket buttoned before he rang the doorbell. Instinctively, he withdrew his hand, realizing that a few weeks beforehand members of Hitler's specialized police force must have—without warning—rung the same bell. They had seized Kate Schmid's husband and subsequently murdered him. But this time, on July 18th, Kate was expecting someone. She swung the door wide open, revealing a stunning woman fashionably dressed in a simple blouse and straight skirt, her proud posture making her seem taller than average in height. Raven black hair was pulled back from a finely featured face and her large brown eyes, radiating warmth and intelligence, immediately locked onto his grayish green ones. Their reciprocal gaze was interrupted when he shyly glanced down and expressed his condolences.

Hermann Hoerlin   **Kate Tietz Schmid**

In an environment charged with emotional turmoil, the two people who would become my parents met. The rawness of the tragedies undoubtedly pulled them together quickly but on a simpler level, each of them was enormously attractive with their own brands of magnetism. My father, tall and handsome, had just turned thirty-one; my mother, a real beauty, was thirty-five. Kate ushered him through the spacious apartment. He noticed her walk—nimble and flowing—as he followed her past rooms graced with Biedermeier furniture, typical for current bourgeois sensibilities, its refined functionality accented by light fruitwood designs. Scattered Oriental rugs on parquet floors, tasteful paintings on the walls, and windows open to summer breezes spoke of a comfortable home. But a void was evident in one of the rooms, a book-lined library with a cello leaning against the corner. It was Willi Schmid's study.

When Kate and Hoerlin reached the far end of the apartment, they entered a neatly organized office with piles of correspondence displaying the letterhead of the 1934 German Expedition. Pinned to the walls were spectacular photos with small black dots against a background of enormous white peaks. Wondering whom among those dots had died, his thoughts were interrupted by his hostess beckoning him to be seated. "So you are Hermann Hoerlin," she said, looking intently at him. She had corresponded with him about Nanga Parbat, but never laid eyes on him. Admittedly, he was very good looking but she fixated on his hands, strongly sculpted, large and generous, open to the world.

The office had been a gathering place for the Nanga climbers and they dropped by frequently—finalizing plans, tending to details, coming and going with alacrity and interacting easily with Kate and Willi plus their exuberant children. Intermingling daily were sounds of children's laughter, Willi's cello playing, the frequent ringing of the expedition's phone and the fast clickety-clack of Kate's typing. When the time came for the expedition's final send-off, the apartment was the setting for a festive gathering with everyone's spirits—and expectations—high. A few months later, the apartment filled a sadder function: a refuge for families and relatives of the deceased. In June, when Nanga claimed its first casualty, Kate had spent the day there with Drexel's father. Now the parents of Wieland, Welzenbach and Merkl were beginning to gravitate to an environment they found comforting. Even in her own grief, Kate was empathetic.

The extent of the Nanga disaster was reverberating throughout Europe as well as abroad and Kate and Hoerlin quickly set themselves to the tasks at hand: answering hundreds of inquiries, scheduling radio interviews and disseminating press releases. After a few hours of concentrated work, they retired to Kate's living room where she, always hospitable, offered him a piece of Sandtorte pound cake. With it he drank black tea and she black coffee—different preferences they chuckled about. It was only then that she spoke about her husband's death.

On June 30th Willi, Kate, and their three children (ages two, seven and nine) had been home, along with Kate's elderly mother, a nursemaid and a cook. Shortly before dinner, the doorbell rang and when the cook opened it, the four SS men standing there asked for Dr. Willi Schmid. Interrupting his playing of a Bach cello suite, Schmid came to the door and was arrested without explanation or the presentation of a warrant. Kate's efforts to give her husband his identification papers were rebuffed and he was taken away.

In the next few days, Kate desperately attempted to unravel the mystery of what had happened to him. She heard nothing until the intervention of a friend, the Board President of the *Muenchner Neuste Nachrichten* (MNN), [2] Munich's largest newspaper where Willi Schmid was employed as a music critic. Late in the afternoon of July 3rd, the Gestapo gave notice of her husband's death. The body, in a sealed coffin, was turned over to two MNN representatives under a railroad bridge near Dachau on July 4th; the Gestapo warned Kate that the coffin should not be opened under any circumstances. [3] Kate complied. On July 7th an official conveyed the following message to her: "Dr. Willi Schmid was arrested because he was suspected of participating in subversive machinations against the State. Transferred to Dachau Concentration Camp, he met his death through an unfortunate accident." [4]

Hoerlin was deeply shaken by Kate's account of the tragedy, eliciting his intrinsic protective instincts. By then he and other Germans had become aware of the full extent of the Night of the Long Knives, also known as the "*Roehm Putsch.*" [5] At least 90 people were executed and over 1000 "suspects" arrested in the period from June 30th to July 2nd. Using the excuse of an impending attempt to overthrow the new government, Hitler's SS (*Schutzstaffel*) corps and Gestapo squads rounded up the so-called perpetrators in an operation dubbed with the code name Hummingbird (*Kolibri*). The Third Reich asserted that in an emergency, the national interest must be protected from terrorist threats. There were no arrest warrants, no depositions, no trials. Immediate executions were legal.

Most of those murdered were members of the *Sturmabteilung* (SA) or Brownshirts, a notoriously brutish arm of the National Socialist party led by Ernest Roehm. Hitler regarded the SA as the last obstacle to his achieving absolute power but also killed others perceived as impediments: Communists, political dissenters or Jews. Public reaction in Germany to the Night of the Long Knives was astonishingly subdued. Most people were too frightened to speak out while others felt the intervention was warranted, given the SA's rowdiness, and that by curbing the SA, Hitler was bringing about order and preventing further unruliness.[6] In retrospect, June 30, 1934 marked the Nazi's abnegation of any pretense of moral behavior. That day's callous murders foreshadowed atrocities in years to come.

The Nazi's justification of the murders could not extend to people mistakenly slaughtered in the frenzied purge. Schmid was one of them. The "unfortunate accident" referred to earlier was that he had been confused with the SA leader, Wilhelm Schmidt. Since Willi Schmid had a considerable reputation at home and abroad as a musical scholar, the death was extensively reported in English, Swiss and of course German newspapers . . . much to the discomfort of the Nazis, who wanted no publicity about it. They continued to claim the "*Roehm Putsch*" was warranted and did not want to weaken that position by the revelation of erroneous killings. The Nazis were already under attack by foreigners, who were outraged by ". . . the horror at the butchery, even more so at the gangster methods by the State's leaders." [7]

During this period of anguish, Kate was coping as best she could. Good friends of the Schmids from Switzerland had come immediately to Munich when they heard about Willi's death, whisking away the older children, Duscha and Thomi, to their beautiful estate in Aarau where the Schmids had spent several vacations. Hedi, the youngest, stayed at home. Kate continued to handle the press coverage of Nanga Parbat but when the expedition collapsed, the thirty-five year old widow felt overwhelmed.

The Alpine Club's choice of sending Hoerlin was both fitting and complicated. In his role as an experienced mountaineer, it made sense. On the other hand, he was troubled by the expedition's increasingly political tenor. Based on letters from his good friends Wieland and Schneider, he was aware of how Merkl had caved to Nazi pressures, even to the detriment of sound mountaineering principles. But Hoerlin was not about to lay blame, wishing to avoid a frenzy of finger pointing. The Schmids' friendship with Merkl was all the more reason not to pass harsh judgment.

The Schmids had also known Wieland and both Kate and Hoerlin mourned the death of this modest and fun-loving man, whose mother had written them, "He was not meant for this cruel world." [8] Hoerlin and Wieland had climbed in the Alps together and been part of the 1930 Kanchenjunga Expedition to the Himalayas. Now he was among the Nanga fatalities whose deaths were cast into a propagandistic mold. Hitler hailed the mountaineers as national heroes honored to sacrifice their lives for Germany. In Munich, city officials gathered under an enormous swastika to proclaim the climbers had strived to ". . . promote the prestige of Germany." [9] Large memorial services underscored this theme, headlines [10] heralded it, and articles and commentaries echoed it further. The newsletter of the national railroad was more direct in its adulation: "What these heroes did, was only for the honor of Germany, was only for Germany's glory and greatness."[11]

Similarly, Kate had been pressed by the Nazis to "...think of her husband's death as the death of a martyr for a great cause." [12] It was impossible for her to do so. Dying "by mistake" hardly qualified as martyrdom and "the cause" was heinous, not great. Such blatant exploitation infuriated her. When the SS sent her a lump sum of money, a crude attempt to hush her, she rejected it. Even when Heinrich Himmler—its notorious and fearful head—telephoned and told her to take the money and be silent, [13] she refused. Kate was not easily intimidated.

Hoerlin was awed by this woman's unique inner strength and fearlessness. As the days progressed and they worked side by side at the Nanga Parbat office in her apartment, they had chatted amicably about their respective backgrounds. Nothing she told him accounted for her intrepidity. She, like he, had grown up in a small town in a bourgeois household. Schwerin, where she was born, mirrored Hoerlin's hometown of Schwaebisch Hall in many ways. Each boasted an exquisite town square, castle and church. Both cities lay in the heart of glorious natural landscapes. Schwerin, in northern Germany, was surrounded by lakes not far from the Baltic Sea; Schwaebisch Hall, in the south, was set in the hills not far from the mountain ranges of the Schwaebisch Alb. Hoerlin and Kate had each been well educated in the local schools. My father—not a diligent student until he began his doctoral degree—showed early propensities toward math and physics; my mother showed considerable aptitude in math as well but was particularly talented in languages, with an ability to recite long passages of poems and plays in German or in English. In keeping with the times, Kate had not gone on to university studies, but was sent at age 16 to a finishing school in Dresden. And finally, Kate's family and Hoerlin's lived above the stores they owned and where they, as children, had been expected to help out. Perhaps it was this common work ethic and small town diligence that allowed them to effectively complete the tasks at hand.

During the seven days Hoerlin spent in Munich, Kate and he sought respite from their labors by taking advantage of the summer days. They walked in Munich's favorite park, the English Garden, and went for excursions in the countryside, sometimes swimming in nearby lakes. Occasionally little Hedi accompanied them, charming them with her antics and cheer. Just as some pleasant rhythms were beginning to form, life's flow was interrupted by another blow to Kate. Her much beloved mother—Hedwig—passed away after a long illness. A formidable woman who exuded elegance and culture, "Mutti" brought her daughter up with an appreciation of both. She also imbued Kate with a love of music; an amateur singer herself, Hedwig was frequently sought as a soprano soloist at regional concerts. In later years, after her husband died, she often visited the Schmids for long periods, particularly during bouts of acute asthma. When Willi was killed, she been staying with the family for six weeks. Distraught by the death of someone she regarded as a son, she had proclaimed, "That is my death too." A few days later she returned to her home in Schwerin and eerily, after a week her prophecy came true.

Kate immediately left for Schwerin. Compared to the deaths of her husband and the young Nanga Parbat climbers, Kate viewed this as a 'good' death, ending a rich life of 71 years. Nonetheless she felt a new vulnerability as she parted from Hoerlin, who had given her such feelings of security. She realized how important he had become to her, how his concern and tenderness instilled in her a sense of trust. Enough time had been spent together for their relationship to deepen; conversations had become more intimate and feelings stronger. Her departure for Schwerin and his for Stuttgart marked the beginning of a remarkable correspondence that tracked their romance over the next four years. Between July and December of 1934 alone, Kate wrote Hoerlin seventy letters; he was not quite as prolific as she and wrote her a mere forty. Among her first letters was one saying how much Hedi and she missed him: ". . . {with your absence} we are a little more orphaned but you would not have been here at all if life had gone otherwise for us." [14]

The fact that life was going "otherwise" for Kate had never been personally acknowledged by the Third Reich, nor had any apology been extended for their killing her husband. That changed on August 1st when Hitler's deputy, Rudolf Hess, visited her home. The dark haired, intense-looking deputy was known to be shy and insecure unless he was introducing his Fuehrer, whom he worshipped with fanatical fervor, declaring, "Hitler is Germany and Germany is Hitler." On his visit to Kate, however, his demeanor was restrained and empathetic. She immediately wrote Hoerlin about it: "I told Hess that he was the first <u>person</u> who has met with me and that I have waited for four weeks for such a person. Hess expressed his official and deep sympathy, also in the name of the Fuehrer, and was so deeply stirred and shaken that it really did me good and gave me ground under my feet. When he left he could not utter a sound. He simply bent for a long time—ever so deeply—over my hand." [15]

It is difficult to imagine Hess in a positive light, but allegedly he had a few decent instincts, considered by some as the "conscience of the party." [16] By 1941 that perception had changed: he was deemed emotionally unstable after a solo flight to England that he termed a peace-making mission.[17] But on August 1, 1934, he went through the right motions; his assistant, Fritz Wiedemann, who a few weeks later became Hitler's Personal Adjutant in Berlin, was there as well. In follow-up to his visit, Hess wrote a letter stating ". . . your husband was not shot because he was connected with the Roehm revolt or was otherwise guilty of something. In fact he is the victim of an accident." [18] Kate wanted it on the record, especially for the sake of the children, that their father was cleared of any implication of being subversive. She was also determined to procure a compensatory stipend from the government for the children and herself for his wrongful death. She would not accept money from the Nazi party, but wanted to hold the Third Reich accountable. Accepting money from the SS, a paramilitary organization founded by Hitler, was repulsive to Kate. She insisted that it be paid by the Reich, a standing governmental entity. Unfortunately, the distinction between the two soon became moot.

Following Hess' apology, Kate felt she could leave Munich and reunite with her older children in Switzerland. She invited Hoerlin to meet her there. "It would give me joy if you would come to Aarau," she wrote. "Joy—that word has become a rarity and sounds foreign to me. But still—it would give me joy if you would come." [19] Hoerlin responded instantly: "I consider it the greatest gift and blessing, that you permit me to visit you. Since those days together in July {in Munich} I am closer to God, than I have perhaps have ever been." [20] For my father, basically an atheist, discovering Kate had shades of spirituality.

Whether it was getting away from Munich, the Swiss air or scenery, or Kate's obvious delight in being with her children—or a combination of these factors—Hoerlin and Kate's time in Aarau was magical. Hoerlin, already approved of by Hedi, was welcomed by Thomi and Duscha and they bestowed on him the honorary title of "Uncle". The children ushered him around the grounds of the grand estate, showing off its extensive gardens, farm animals and—with great excitement—the two live crocodiles, Caesar and Mussolini, who graced the greenhouse. Kate delighted in another side of Hoerlin, a less serious one, not "so German," as Kate put it. Hoerlin had fun with mischievous little jokes, triggering giggles from Kate and the children. He too would laugh, a full body experience for him with shoulders shaking, setting off more rounds of merriment.

Although Nanga Parbat, far away in the Himalayas, had initially brought Hoerlin and Kate together, it was gentle foothills of Switzerland that hosted the beginning of their romance. The two of them took long walks, strolling through Aarau's quaint streets and along its meandering river. Observers could have mistaken them for a married couple. They must have looked wonderful: my father, fair-haired and with attractively chiseled features, walking in a steady gait next to Kate, dark-haired, with a special glow to her loveliness. On the last day of Hoerlin's visit, they went hiking in the Jura mountain range. The day was glorious, alternatively sunny and stormy . . . a perfect backdrop for the unfolding drama of their love. As Kate wrote a few days later ". . . it is as if a storm passed over me that tore my arms apart . . . although my arms stretch out, they still cannot embrace the heavenliness of the day, the night and the morning." [21]

The depth of their emotions and intensity of their passion dazed both of them. After they parted, Kate—slowly absorbing the impact of newfound love—reminisced to Hoerlin ". . . how I walked over the fields by your side, the wind and you taking turns kissing me and how good the rain felt on our hot skin. Since the wonder of that one day," she continued, "I again see the clouds wander, see the green and blues of the trees, can breathe deeply again . . . So it stands, it is still possible now that I have the strength to give and I am not constrained by my sadness . . ." [22] For my mother it was a rebirth, for my father an emotional awakening: "A deep happiness accompanies me, so deep, that it almost . . . paralyzes me, a feeling I've never had."[23]

Kate returned to Munich with the children in mid September, hesitant to leave the sheltered and idyllic estate of her Swiss friends, its proximity to nature and its association with a new love. She wrote Hoerlin, "Having to go back is no homecoming for me—I go forth in a very dark, starless night but in the knowledge that somewhere the light still shines and always will."[24] The light of Hoerlin's love enveloped her, but the Munich apartment only underscored the absence of Willi—or as she called him—"Pitsch." Nights were the roughest times: ". . . in the middle of working in these quiet, quiet evenings I still expect to hear a key, one that no longer turns." [25] Now she was a single parent, carrying the weight of *mater familias* alone.

At age 19 Kate had met Willi, while accompanying a friend on a hospital visit. They had fallen in love "bed-side," he recovering from multiple shrapnel wounds suffered during WW I. Three years later in 1921, they married. It was a happy union, blessed by three delightful children and filled with an extraordinary circle of friends. Willi, sturdily built and of medium height, was a devout Catholic whose contemplative leanings were balanced out by his Bavarian sense of fun. Bespectacled and balding, he was scholarly in appearance and in practice, fitting easily into Munich's intellectual scene. With Willi's death and the almost coincident appearance of Hoerlin, Kate was struggling to find her way between two profound loves—one marked by death and the other by life. She did not hide this emotional tug from Hoerlin: "Do you accept me as I am—amid two worlds?" She relayed a dream she had, replete with guilt about her rapid attachment to Hoerlin. In the dream Pitsch was calling out to her to follow him. [26]

Since returning to Munich, Kate was busy helping prepare a book about the Nanga expedition. But her most absorbing project was one near and dear to her. The Schmid's close friend, Oswald Spengler had suggested compiling a book of Willi's poems, letters, concert reviews and musical essays. My mother was thrilled with this idea, particularly coming from a European cultural icon, the author of the widely read and influential tome, <u>The Decline of the West.</u> Another friend, Paul Reusch, a leading German industrialist, guaranteed money for its publication. And most remarkably, Kate got permission from Nazi headquarters in Munich, the Brown House (Braunes Haus), for its distribution. She had effectively argued that Willi's writings were devoid of any political overtones. Nevertheless, the Nazis insisted on reviewing the manuscript, reluctant to have anything published about Schmid at all since it would remind people of their "mistake."

Kate worked almost daily with Spengler on selecting pieces for the book, a process leading her to vividly and poignantly revisit her previous marriage: "... in these intense hours with Spengler it has again become abundantly clear that I am both chained, and inextricably belong, to Pitsch's world." Caught by the pull of the past and the promise of the present, she pondered: "I cannot yet decide, who I am: a wife who carries on {with her former life} ... or a person who begins anew." [27] Beginning anew was literally and figuratively embodied by my father and my mother was grateful for his ability to guide her toward the future: "You—my beloved, young person—it is wonderful and life giving when you extend your hands toward me and pull me forth and into your world." [28] Her letters attest to a powerful physical attraction between them, a non negligible force in their relationship: "... my lips between the lines on your forehead, the curve of your brow, the arc of your mouth ... and then you bend over me and look at me, I can barely reach to stroke your hair. And then my soul is torn asunder and blissfully, blissfully opens up. And then I cannot do anything other than be <u>there</u>." [29]

The closer they became, the more Kate and Hoerlin became aware of what distinct worlds they inhabited, in spite of similarities of their background. Forever gregarious, Kate was enmeshed in the flurry of Munich's social and intellectual life, numbering among her friends writers, poets, musicians, academics and some of Germany's top industrialists. It was a life filled with gaiety, afternoon coffees and teas, concerts and operas, and spirited conversations. The social highlight of the year was Fasching, Munich's annual carnival celebrated with public partying and masquerade balls. Kate was always among the revelers, a ritual that had little appeal for my father who came from a more sober tradition. He was immersed in the challenges of exploration, mountaineering and science. Both his vocation and avocation steered toward solitary endeavors, as recognized by Kate: "I thought about ... what kind of person you are. And that your profession, your inner calling, has not been restricted in the least. And that he who once looked out at the expanse of the world can never nor should ever forget it. Furthermore, I thought how well you can tolerate what only very few people could: weeks, actually months, of solitude (and) thought about how you travel through foreign lands in this earnest, not at all superficial, carefree way . . . it would be sad, if you no longer had space for this in your life." [30] In this letter, she referred to his breaking the world mountain climbing record in the Himalayas, his almost six week stint alone high in the Andes to measure cosmic rays and his implicit independence.

For both Hoerlin and Kate, compromises would have to be made if they blended their lives. Their relationship was a mix of the familiar and the unknown. Although Hoerlin had seen more of the world, Kate was more 'worldly' than he, having lived in Munich's urbane milieu for the past thirteen years. She affectionately called him "Bub", an endearment for "boy" both because he was four years her junior and because he was far less sophisticated than she. Kate was a far cry from the earnest and dutiful Protestant ethics of Hoerlin's upbringing and he acknowledged as much: ". . . {with you} I have certainly been torn from what I'm used to. And I thank God for it." Explaining his desire to change, he spoke of his old girlfriend, "Why did I leave Lisel; because {the relationship} had become mundane . . . a monotonous flow of things hateful to me, because in the last analysis she wanted me to be thoroughly middle class." [31]

Hoerlin, a model of rationality even with his predilection for physical adventure and risk, was unhinged that his emotions for Kate managed to even divert him from work: "sometimes I am like a captive, captured by a confusing, restless love, that will not let me get around to anything else. [32] You pull me away, you do not mean to, but I want it to be so." [33] And Kate, a bundle of spontaneity, had nothing but admiration for his typical level-headedness: "It is wonderful to observe you, because you think so clearly. I've known it and have experienced it often, but then I am still always astonished, how charmingly you can do it, this essence of logical thinking." [34] On one of her visits to him in Stuttgart, she had seen him in his white lab coat, more eye-catching than ever, and right then and there approved of his physics career. She consistently encouraged him to complete his doctoral studies. Also, amidst the upheavals of her life, she had found in him a peacefulness for which she was thankful: "You have intoxicated me with the quietest things," she wrote, "Let it always be so, let me through your longings and desire partake in your very clear inner peace, that is a balm for me in which my love finds refuge." [35]

The two lovers met as frequently as possible and in the interim, their letters were full of longing. Kate's were impassioned: "Why does destiny force me so incredibly close to you? That I have no breath unless I blend it with yours, that your heart beats with mine . . . because I must attest with my whole being, that I love you. [36] Hoerlin's were no less ardent: "I burn for you, do not let me be reduced to ashes . . . I cannot help it, that I have this desire . . . quell my blood—for me a 1000 nights are not enough." [37] Hoerlin wrote of how he loved looking deep into her eyes and liked her hair down; Kate loved to stroke his hair and forehead and feel his strong hands around her. And happily, of key importance to Kate, "Uncle Hoerlin" and the children got along: "I believe there is no better absolute proof of our closeness, for the veracity and intensity of my feelings, than the love of my children for you. You are, of the many people who come and go, the most beloved for them. That is the most beautiful and clearest confirmation that I can give you {for our future}." [38]

Loving Kate, however, was not always easy for my father. In an era when flirtatiousness reigned, Kate was Queen. For her it was an art carefully cultivated, a game of charm and wit. However, the young man from Schwaebisch Hall was hurt and miserable over her behavior. As she tried to convey to Hoerlin, who did not hide his pain from her: "Oh, Bub, there have been men who wait for me and court me—for years, many years. Pitsch observed this calmly and with the wonderful security of our love. {He said} 'If one wanted to separate you from your love of people, one would take away the air you breathe.' That he knew. He never suffered because of me. The mere thought that you—whom I love—could suffer, paralyzes me." [39] Hoerlin, not quite sanguine with this explanation that blurred the lines between social and more personal relationships, reminded her, "I have a young and deep love for you, full of desire and longing. Do it no harm. There is hardly anything else in the world for me, other than you."[40] The issue of jealousy did not disappear, occasionally threatening to fray their tightly woven fabric of love, but each time they were able to mend the threads.

As Christmas neared, Kate had almost finished with the Willi Schmid book, titling it "Unfinished Symphony" ("Unvollendete Symphonie"). It had been sent to the Brown House for final approval. In the preface, written by Spengler, there is no mention of the circumstances of Willi's death and . . . true to Willi Schmid's apolitical persona, no references to the politics of the times. The book was completed and Kate had found a version of closure to her ongoing struggles about loving two men. She had reached a place of reconciliation between staying true to Willi and committing herself to Hoerlin. In her words, ". . . I have an immediate sense of Pitsch's wishes—indeed, how could have this {love} happened to me without his wanting it? I know that, aside from the children, the blessing of my life is that you appeared." [41]

When 1934 drew to a close, a year both horrible and miraculous, Kate focused on the holidays, presents for the children and getting together with Hoerlin. And what could she possibly give <u>him</u> for Christmas? She found the perfect gift: "{My} heart and arms are heavily laden with the many things I have for you, what I bring to you, since it belongs to you and wants to come to you—my life." [42] Hoerlin's devotion was no less: ". . . my heart, my blood, <u>everything</u> is yours . . ." [43] and he entrusted her with his most precious possession. The vicuna blanket, which he had purchased in Peru in 1932, whose fine soft wool rivaled no other, which he so carefully cradled when disembarking from his voyage back to Germany, was given to Kate. She appreciated its import: "I have spread your blanket on the ottoman in the library. No one other than me is permitted to lie on it. The fleece is immeasurably stunning . . . it invites me to stroke it with my hand, to press my face against it and to thank you . . . proximal to the wonder of its intrinsic beauty is its immediate association with you, it has your light warmth, my beloved."[44] After two years, the vicuna had finally found the good home.

Chapter 7

DANCING AMONG WOLVES

Kate always loved to dance. As she once wrote a friend about Fasching, a Mardi Gras-like revelry, ". . . we danced and danced, endlessly and still not enough! . . . why am I so crazy over dancing?" [1] She was swift on her feet, a vision of elegance and beauty. Hoerlin was a good dancer too, his lead firm and his style deliberate, moving smoothly across the dance floor. At the start of the 1935, Kate and Hoerlin's courtship was in full swing. Theirs was a dance of love, practiced with passion. But they watched their steps carefully . . . they had to. They were dancing among wolves of several species, wolves that nipped at their heels. Wolves appeared in the portals of universities, on the doorstep of organized mountaineering, in homes, on the streets, and especially in the lives of those Germans the Nazi government considered "politically unreliable."

One might think that someone who was prototypically Aryan, a reputable mountaineer and a promising physicist would be immune from the cancer of National Socialism. Such was not the case. Nazism penetrated all facets of society, even those typically considered asocial and apolitical. When Hitler came to power, the dismissal of Jewish physicists from university positions ". . . constituted one of the first state applications of racial hygiene . . . as if to purify the body of science and technology of a dangerous virus." [2] Germany's most famous physicist and arguably the world's most celebrated scientist, was well known to be Jewish. He knew immediately that he had to emigrate. Albert Einstein's judicious decision was based on his conviction that ". . . civil liberty, tolerance and equality of all citizens before the law" had vanished in Germany. [3]

In the years that followed, the ideological racial beliefs of the Third Reich transformed German science from a world-renowned mecca of research into an increasingly isolated and nationalistic enterprise. No longer was it enough to purge Jews from its ranks; the Nazis maintained all of German science needed to be freed from findings associated with Jewish scientists, such as Einstein's relativity theory. At a meeting with Hitler, one of Germany's leading mainstream physicists warned that this mindset was destroying the preeminence of the country's scientific reputation. He was strongly rebuked by the Fuehrer: "Our national policies will not be revoked or modified. Even for scientists. If {this} means the annihilation of contemporary German science, then we shall do without science for a few years!" [4]

"Aryan physics" became touted as the only true German physics. By 1936 articles in the scientific literature extolled "Aryan physics" over what was dubbed "Jewish physics," insisting that theories like relativity and quantum mechanics should no longer be taught. [5] My father strongly objected to this prejudicial labeling and its explicit rejection of progress. He also bemoaned the oppressive atmosphere that permeated German physics, usurping its former conviviality and research independence. Physics, along with other disciplines, was being recast to march lock step with Nazi dictates.

Hoerlin was finding it tremendously stressful to operate in a mileau buffeted by political winds in a profession already imbued with more than its share of ups and downs, as experiments and theories were proven or unproven. He confided to Kate: "I need peace and quiet to be able to work. "[6] Echoing the support he lent during her difficulties, she in turn encouraged Hoerlin onward toward his doctorate and he responded: "You wrote me about my capabilities, in which you believe. There are some—it would be false modesty to dispute that; (however) I must try hard to recognize my talents correctly and to use them correctly. This became especially clear in the last couple of years, when I aspired to a great deal but achieved little that I was satisfied with. I cannot permit myself to be scattered, least of all because I am not a quick worker." [7] A day before Christmas Eve in 1935, he apologized to Kate for not yet completing his dissertation: "It pains me a great deal that I can not give you and my patiently waiting mother a Christmas gift of my finalized research results of the past year. The one thing I can say with total faith and certainty is that I have made good progress ... and that I will become a very respectable physicist." [8] A career in Germany, however, was becoming more problematic and Hoerlin was hardly in the Nazi's good graces, having spoken out against an Aryan interpretation of physics and protected his dissertation advisor from anti-Semitic rants.

Under National Socialism, mountaineering was faring no better than science. Leading the pack of hostile wolves was Paul Bauer, who did not hide his ambitions to put the *Alpenverein* under his thumb. Working directly for the Sports Minister, he already had considerable authority but increased his domain by establishing a state-sponsored entity, the Reich League of German Mountaineers, designed to "lead German mountaineers to a consciousness of their high calling, to guide the rising generation that they may learn to be fearless . . . ." At a meeting of the *Alpenverein,* Bauer conveyed his vision of the new organization as ". . . the breakthrough of the heroic world view for which our Fuehrer Adolf Hitler has fought throws our mountaineering activities into the proper light before the eyes of the public." [9] Bauer's objectives were clear: 1) absorb the *Alpenverein,* with its approximately 240,000 members into the Nazi state structure of *Gleichschaltung*; 2) rid all sports clubs of Jews; and 3) establish the right to determine all future expeditions outside of Germany.

My father vehemently opposed each of these objectives. He also had a strong personal dislike of the conniving Bauer. Their mutual animosity dated back to 1928, when Bauer off-handedly rejected Hoerlin's inquiry about joining his 1929 Kanchenjunga expedition. Hoerlin, with a reputation as an independent thinker, was not welcomed by the group of climbers cultivated by Bauer. Two years later, when Hoerlin accepted Dyhrenfurth's invitation to join his 1930 expedition, Bauer treated it as a major affront. Not only had Dyhrenfurth the gall to set his sights on a mountain claimed by Bauer, but Hoerlin—one of Germany's star climbers—had the audacity to join a international expedition with a Swiss leader (by that time Dyhrenfurth, although German-born, had lived in Zurich a number of years). To those more level-headed than Bauer, it made no sense and the *Alpenverein* promptly came to the defense of young Pallas, whose integrity and honesty they praised. [10]

Hoerlin came under attack from Bauer again after the 1934 Nanga catastrophe. This time Bauer's motivations emanated from his obsession with

Germany's conquest of a 8000er and ensuring a pivotal role for himself in making that happen. Undoubtedly, another attempt on the mountain would be undertaken, the recent tragedy having only added to the country's resolve: "The expectations . . . were too high and its fall . . . too deep not to expect consequences regarding further German undertakings in the Himalayas."[11] When Schneider announced his intentions to lead a 1936 Nanga expedition and his hope of recruiting his favorite partner—Pallas—to his team, Bauer went ballistic. In a nine page letter to the Sports Minister, Bauer denounced Schneider and Hoerlin: ". . . {they} had no understanding that (Nanga) was a matter of national concern. They built their 1930, 31, and 32 plans with the participation of well heeled foreign mountaineers—Schneider and Hoerlin had gone to the Himalayas with Dyhrenfurth, belonging to the Jewish tribe." [12] Hoerlin and Schneider's willingness to associate with a Jewish climber combined with their non-nationalistic stance on mountaineering irrevocably condemned them in Bauer's eyes.

Bauer had never forgiven the twosome for their "cowardice" in not flying the German flag on Jongsong Peak in the Himalayas when they broke the world summit record in 1930. He held Hoerlin responsible for again not raising it on the 1932 first ascent of Huascaran in the Andes and insisted that Schneider apologize for an impertinent remark he made in Peru about the Fuehrer. With his usual sardonic humor, Schneider had described the expedition's attempts to find the best route up Huascaran. Having first explored left of a giant ice field, he derisively reported: "Crying, we backtracked and then tried to come to our senses and follow the demands of our time by heading toward the right (Hail Adolf! Germany awake!)." [13] Schneider considered it ridiculous to be asked to make amends.

In his missive to the Sports Minister, Bauer not only attacked Hoerlin and Schneider but also the climbers who died on Nanga Parbat for not understanding the imperialistic purposes of climbing. His insensitivity was astonishing, exemplified by a letter to the brother of one of the fallen. Expecting Bauer to offer his sympathy, Hans Wieland opened a six page missive in which Bauer extolled his own virtues and scolded the young man for spreading rumors about Bauer's arrogance. Bauer had heard that Wieland said ". . . {Bauer} acts like he owns the Himalayas." [14] Other climbers frequently complained about Bauer's exclusionary possessiveness, particularly regarding Kanchenjunga and Nanga Parbat. He was nicknamed "Paulchen" (little Paul) in climbing circles—a name that did not match his aspirations but put him in proper perspective, at least according to them.

Unbeknownst to anyone other than Paulchen's disciples, Bauer himself was making plans for a 1936 Nanga Parbat expedition led by either him or someone from his inner circle. This put him in direct conflict with the *Alpenverein* and their support of Schneider for leading the next attempt. Bauer, whose jealousy of Schneider's acclaim could barely be contained, seized upon a way to discredit the feted alpinist who had reached heights never before achieved. Bauer hooked on an issue that revolved around Schneider and his fellow Austrian Aschenbrenner leaving their sherpas behind in a snowstorm on their descent from Nanga Parbat. In righteous tones, Bauer asserted: "It is a firm rule that in blinding weather a team must stay together . . . Those who, like Schneider and Aschenbrenner, continue on . . . cannot be regarded as good mountain comrades. It is dangerous when people of such questionable actions are elevated to heroes . . ." [15] For good measure, Bauer added his concern that setting such a bad example would corrupt generations of mountaineers to come.

Schneider's decision to unrope from the sherpas was questionable, but it obscured the immediate basis for Bauer's skullduggery: who would lead the next Nanga expedition? In his continuing efforts to disgrace Schneider, Bauer convinced the Sports Minister to convene a Court of Honor to put Schneider and Aschenbrenner on trial and make a judgment. While the annals of mountaineering are replete with mistakes and accidents, the formation of such a court was unprecedented. The Verein, strongly opposed to such a trial, held their own inquiry, acquitted the climbers and stuck to their endorsement of Schneider as leader of a 1936 Nanga expedition. This enraged Bauer and much of his venom was now directed at Hoerlin. Bauer wrote his faithful climbing friend, Karl Wien, decrying Hoerlin's influential position on the Verein's Executive Committee, "It is impossible to have him{on the Committee}. He appears to me as someone who cannot get beyond his preconceived opinion, his personal anger and hatred . . ." [16] Bauer was correct in his assessment of my father. When Hoerlin perceived an injustice, he stubbornly sought to amend it. Bauer was condemning Pallas' best friend, trying to destroy the Verein, and legitimizing anti-Semitism. Yes, Hoerlin was angry.

Kate had not yet seen this combative side of Hoerlin but she applauded his steadfastness and resolve: "That is excellent, how you stand up for Schneider and Aschenbrenner and don't yield a hair's breadth." [17] However, she and Hoerlin were unaware that Bauer had somehow learned of their liaison and was poised to use it against Hoerlin. Writing to Wien, Bauer revealed: "Today I discovered something about him {Hoerlin} that can perhaps be a reason for taking action against him..." Wien responded instantly voicing his agreement that, as he proposed twice in the letter, Hoerlin should "disappear."[18] If Bauer could tarnish Hoerlin's otherwise sterling reputation with the fact that he had taken up with a woman who was Jewish in background, it could harm Pallas' position within the Verein. Although the Nuremberg Laws had not yet passed, romances between Aryans and non-Aryans were most assuredly frowned on.

In March, the Sport Minister's Court of Honor preceded, its neutrality a farce and the harshness of its verdict spiteful. Declaring the two Austrians "without honor," the ruling specified ". . . the interest of the Reich and the prestige of German mountaineering demanded an exact choice of participants for a possible new expedition." [19] Schneider was in effect banned from future German Himalayan expeditions. The *Alpenverein's* response was to file an objection, presented by Hoerlin, to the edict and proclaim their continued plans for a 1936 Nanga expedition. The decision of who should lead it hung in the balance. By the end of August, the Verein had met and Hoerlin wrote Bauer of their conclusion. In curt language that must have given him inner satisfaction, my father informed Bauer that the leader of the next Nanga expedition would be Dr. Philipp Borchers, who had led the 1932 Andes expedition in which Hoerlin had participated. The Committee's vote for Borchers had been overwhelming: 32 to 4 in his favor, based on the criteria that ". . . a leader must have the (kind of) character that in every respect enjoys the trust of the . . . *Alpenverein.*"[20] It was a stunning statement of no confidence in Bauer. Writing on behalf of the Verein, my father's letter did not close with the customary sign off "with a German climber's greeting" ("Mit deutschem Bergsteigergruss")—but instead with "Heil Hitler," no doubt, meant mockingly. I am not aware of any other time that my father ended a letter that way.

Over the spring and into the summer, my father had been at the forefront of a series of dizzying moves, trying to outsmart Bauer and save the integrity of the Verein. In all too familiar Nazi fashion Bauer took every opportunity to intimidate and denigrate people, including sending around a six page single-spaced lawyerly letter challenging Hoerlin's comments (made two months beforehand) about the physical fitness of Bechtold, who was Nanga's obstensible leader after the death of Merkl. [21] Hoerlin was tired of such pettiness. If Bauer had known how disillusioned he was and how close Hoerlin was to quitting the Verein, Paulchen may not have been pushing as hard to get rid of Pallas. The politicalization of mountaineering was demoralizing, as he wrote to Kate, "I am no longer capable of participating as I had beforehand. One group sits there with their brown SA uniforms . . . . others in black SS uniforms. Many are totally pig-headed. What do I want with them?" [22] The meetings were consuming significant amounts of time and energy; in his scientific fashion, Hoerlin had calculated that he had spent 50 days out of the year on Verein business. [23]

Separately from Hoerlin and several months earlier, Kate too had become embroiled in the Nanga controversy, although unwittingly so. Since the survivors of the expedition returned to Germany in early fall 1934, Kate had been working feverishly with Bechtold on an official Nanga Parbat book to be published in German and English, guaranteed to be an international best seller. She sorted through masses of dramatic photographs (111 of them ended up in the book) and diaries of respective climbers. Soon, a bitter schism between Bechtold and Schneider developed over the book's narrative. Bechtold approached it as an opportunity to immortalize the feats and sacrifices of German mountaineering, portray mountaineers as dedicated to the Fatherland's glory, and Merkl as a "born leader of men." [24] By contrast, Schneider did not wish to conceal the discord in base camp, the inexcusable delays, nor the shortcomings of Merkl's leadership. Bechtold's version won out, since it had immediate appeal to Nazi ideology, although ultimately it would entail a "disservice to mountaineering history." [25]

Kate attempted to bring peace between Schneider and Bechtold, but to no avail. "Strange," she observed to Hoerlin, "how much is buried between these men. They themselves are so disturbed by it, that they don't even see <u>my</u> exhaustion and because of their own stress continue to make demands." [26] Unquestionably, tensions were fed by the two climbers' competing designs for another Nanga expedition, although Bechtold was hiding his close collaboration with Bauer on achieving that. Little did Kate know that Bechtold, the man she worked with on an almost daily basis, was conspiring against Schneider, the Verein, and ultimately, her lover Hoerlin. In fact, I believe Bechtold was Bauer's source for the potentially harmful rumor about Kate and Hoerlin. Embroiled in a cat's cradle of conflicts, Kate was even accused of having contributed to ongoing rifts. [27] As the book became more and more geared toward political ends, Kate only wished for her work to be over. Although never reticent about her accomplishments, Kate never discussed her role in the book's completion with anyone, most probably uncomfortable with its tenor.

"Nanga Parbat", a collection of carefully screened diary excerpts and a glowing text, evolved into a book of fact and fiction. Kate had written a straightforward preface (although not attributed to her), hoping to keep the book quietly out of the political arena, but that was not possible. Bechtold notified her that the Sports Minister wished to write a foreword and then added ". . . it would be valuable for his name to be mentioned in one or preferably more places." [28] Although on a fast track for publication, the book's release was delayed until it could be sanctioned with an official imprimatur. The Sports Minister's introduction set the tone by challenging German youth to emulate the conquering spirit of their fallen countrymen. Released in January 1935, the book became an immediate national(istic) best seller and a persuasive platform for launching another German attempt on their mountain of destiny.

Concurrent with the Nanga complications, Kate was dancing among additional wolves. These wolves dwelled in the top echelons of the Third Reich's bureaucracies and the National Socialist party. The Brown House, Nazi headquarters in Munich, had become regrettably familiar to Kate. She had first gone there because of Willi's disappearance, next to plead her case for a stipend for herself and the children, and then to pave the way for publication of Willi's book. For each visit, she braced herself to speak up clearly and forcefully. After one visit, she was asked out for dinner by SS officers and in disbelief at the thoughtlessness of the invitation, issued by the very group responsible for her husband's death, exclaimed to Hoerlin—"Oh . . . what kind of a world is this?" [29] Kate also wanted to distance herself from the Nazis in regard to a stipend, arguing for payment to come through the Reich and not the party. In early November, after a series of meetings at the Brown House during which she swayed the assembled officials to her viewpoint, she reported, ". . . the gentlemen definitely want to take things into their own hands and plead with the Reich. A noble competition broke out among them regarding <u>who</u> would present my situation in Berlin. Don't you find that sweet?!! I am under the protection of the Brown House—a play of tragicomedy." [30] The winner of that competition was Hess's assistant—Wiedemann—who would argue her case in the nation's capital.

Hoerlin had offered to go with her to the Brown House, but Kate was fierce in wanting to fight her own battles. Yet his support was omnipresent: "This morning I sensed in the Brown House," she wrote him, ". . . your calm strength." [31] She valued his devotion and his political acumen, his ability to assess the environment and look toward the future. At the same time, she was keenly aware of the power of her presence and was not averse to capitalizing on it, often mixing it with her usual flirtatiousness. The gravity of the Brown House did not compromise her charisma; appearing alone must have accentuated her plight. While she should be fully credited with her bravery, she also was strategic in employing her feminine wiles.

Kate met numerous times with top political and administrative headquarters first in Munich and then Berlin; her ability to weather these appearances was a surprise even to her: "Sometimes I myself cannot explain it . . . a deep inner calm overcomes me in that moment when it's necessary to really fight and assert oneself." [32] Pulling herself together after a three hour ordeal at the Brown House (BH) and attempting to relay it in neither under-dramatic nor over-dramatic terms, Kate described a February meeting to Hoerlin: "This morning I was again summoned to the BH. There are terrible bullies there who are completely against me. I knew they would appear and therefore was prepared, even more so since now I have gained the favor of the highest officials. However, this did not stop the underlings (and their very bad consciences) . . . I fought there not for me, since I stand as I am and stand firmly—but for the three children. It is strange: but now I have real friends there—where my enemies allegedly sit. They paid attention to me . . . especially Wiedemann. I remarked to those in the BH: "Maybe what is demanded of me is to love Germany in spite of everything . . ." [33] Even under these draconian circumstances the Nazis persisted in wanting declarations of loyalty to country.

Undoubtedly, in dealing with government officials, Kate was emboldened by knowing Wiedemann. He had been closely tied to the Fuehrer since World War I when he was Hitler's company commander; his appointment in early January 1935 as Hitler's adjutant in Berlin put him in a powerful position in relationship to local political underlings. Wiedemann did not hide the fact that he was Kate's ally, having met with her individually several times. "He is definitely the Best, whom I could absolutely encounter," she had written Hoerlin, "an active officer who was at the front four years, courtly and taking a personal interest in me and my misfortune."[34]

With decisions regarding the compensation claim stalled, Kate enlisted the services of a lawyer who represented her and accompanied her to a series of meetings in Berlin over the spring and summer of 1935. The lawyer, Wilhelm Diess, was a well-calculated choice: Diess had been an officer (*Gerichtsoffizier*) in the 16th Reserve in WWI, the same Regiment in which Hitler and Wiedemann served. Now he was in the position of arguing, on Kate's behalf, that the Reich rather than the party should pay a stipend. Diess and Kate proceeded to meet with some of Hitler's closest colleagues, men on whom the Fuehrer depended on for reaching his twin goals of making Germany a dominant world power and, eventually, carrying out a mass extermination of Jews.

Kate's skill in judging people did not always extend into the political realm. "It is a kind of cowardice," she admitted to my father, "that I never read the newspapers."[35] This lack of political context, plus her soft spot for powerful men when they treated her deferentially, seemed to muddle Kate's typically finely tuned judgments. She had already met Himmler and Hess by the time she was introduced to Franz Schlegelberger, the State Secretary in the Reich's Ministry of Justice, describing him to Hoerlin as ". . . most agreeable, a jurist of the old school, precise, clever, conciliatory." [36] Schlegelberger later would become Justice Minister and in the 1947 Nuremberg Nazi Judge's Trial, the highest ranking defendant. He was found guilty of ". . . instituting and supporting procedures that led to the wholesale persecution of Jews and Poles." Himmler was scheduled to stand trial as well but committed suicide beforehand. Otherwise he surely would have been found guilty of mass killings of Jews, Poles, Gypsies, Communists and prisoners of war. At the trials, Hess, who had carried the title of Deputy Fuehrer, was found guilty of crimes against peace and conspiracy to commit crimes. Kate was indeed in a den of wolves.

On the morning before she met with Schlegelberger, just as she was leaving her hotel, the porter handed her a letter from Hoerlin. It gave her enormous comfort, as she later wrote him: "I was feeling secure, peaceful, almost happy driving to Wilhelmstrasse (Justice headquarters), composed and strengthened by your faithfulness. You should know how warm and strong and helpful your love was to me again and again in these days." [37] She felt things had gone well and were definitely in good hands: "In Berlin I was in good form, neither said nor did anything wrong, and everything went, as I—often unconsciously—wished it would. This much is certain, this whole thing will definitely fall out of the domain of the SS to a place where it will be judged in an absolutely honest, trustworthy and considerate way. I will not be mistaken in this good and certain feeling." [38]

Again, Kate's assessment was faulty; perhaps she did not comprehend how cumbersome government bureaucracies could be, especially amoral ones. For a year, from September 1934 to September 1935, internal letters among Wiedemann, Hess, Himmler and Schlegelberger plus external letters between them and Kate's lawyers went back and forth. [39] In keeping with Germanic propensities to document everything, the letters detailed meetings, their legal implications and political consequences. Schlegelberger conceded in a letter to Wiedemann that he felt that because of the delays, Frau Schmid would lodge a complaint and it was in the interest of the Third Reich to avoid that. [40] They were certain that the public would sympathize with the young widow and that their efforts to keep the death of Schmid relatively quiet would boomerang. But still there was no decision, only more meetings, questions, clarifications, and forms. Kate vacillated between despair and defiance, writing to Hoerlin: "I have come to this decision: I <u>will</u> no longer let myself agonize, otherwise I will be totally useless and incompetent. I must learn to bear the uncertainty and the unknown as an ongoing condition of mine—if I have to torment myself for another 6 months (or perhaps even longer) I am done for, Hoerlin, and only letters and photos will attest as to who I was." [41] After four calls in one day from Berlin, Kate wrote: "Only I am aware of how close I am to capitulating. But I certainly know this, the stronger the pressure, the harder the metal. Perhaps this is an erroneous theory for a scientist. For me it is valid and works." [42] Hoerlin was frustrated and angry by the way his beloved was being shunted aside. "Not even the worst bureaucracy", he exclaimed, "can go this far. Are there men at all left in this _____?" [43] The blank was left either because he was ready to use an obscenity or knew that letters were routinely opened in the Third Reich . . . or both. In either case, the 'worst bureaucracy" was only in its infancy.

In July Kate was again in Berlin, hoping Hitler's personal Adjutant would push things forward. Her meeting with Wiedemann was held in Hitler's private office. They were ushered there by armed guards, the sound of their tall heavy black boots muted by the thick carpeting. "We actually had our discussion with a gentleman from the Interior Affairs in the room of the Fuehrer, a wonderful, quiet, splendid room where a pair of magnificent, old Italians {paintings} are hung and the linden trees sway outside the window," Kate reported. "It now really appears that a settlement directly from the Reich is imminent, although I am skeptical . . ." [44] It is hard to reconcile my mother's obvious admiration of Hitler's office with the horrendous ideas that were hatched there.

In mid-September, the Reich finally notified her that she had been awarded a stipend. [45] As she had insisted, payment would come through the Reich and not the SS; it was a generous settlement, providing each of the children with an allowance until age 25 and Kate with one unless her circumstances changed. [46] Reaching the agreement had involved Kate meeting with the Ministries of Justice, Internal Affairs and Finance along with the head of the SS, Hitler's Deputy and his Adjutant. However, the notification seemed like an anti-climax in that it had taken so long to achieve. It left her with feelings of mistrust; ". . . after 15 months of waiting, this does not assuage in me any sense of peaceful security and in truth, the reality of the document seems utterly unreal to me." [47]

Surely, Kate's reaction was fed by jolting news she received within hours of the pension notification. Without warning or explanation, Willi Schmid's book, "Unfinished Symphony" had been confiscated from bookstores throughout Germany a few days after its release. Having received permission for publication from the Brown House and Wiedemann himself and even submitting the book for pre-publication review, Kate was understandably infuriated: "No time since the death (of Willi) has been more torturous than this. I <u>could</u> not allow this to happen without a fight—in spite of or exactly because of my situation. For now there are only about 300 examples of impounding . . . So I turned to the Reichs Justice Ministry and the Reichs

Chancellery and today received notification from Wiedemann that he sought clarification from the Gestapo . . . Therefore because of the book I must yet again go to Berlin." [48]

Kate had never liked Berlin and she called it "the most alien city" ("*die fremdeste Stadt*"). Although she had many relatives there, she seldom stayed with them, preferring to come to and leave town as quickly as possible. Most of her meetings had been in the offices of the Reich, but this time Kate headed to the national headquarters of the SS and Gestapo on Prinz Albrechtstrasse, which later became known as a "house of terror" where prisoners were tortured and held in the basement. [49] There she confronted the authorities, demanding to know on what grounds "Unfinished Symphony" was removed from bookstores, stressing her former husband's apolitical character, and pointing out that the book contained not a single critical word against the government. [50] Although the book did not mention the circumstances of Willi Schmid's death, the Nazis most probably did not want anyone to be reminded of the grievous "accident."

A lengthy introduction to "Unfinished Symphony" by Oswald Spengler did not help her cause. The prominent historian had fallen out of favor with Hitler. His best selling 1918 book, "The Decline of the West," had once been adopted by Hitler as an intellectual forbearer of Nazism; the admiration had been mutual at first, with Spengler voting for the National Socialists in 1932 and hanging a swastika flag outside his Munich home. However, after a 1933 meeting with the Fuehrer, Spengler was quickly disillusioned and came to hold Hitler in contempt: ". . . a numbskull . . . in a word—stupid."[51] The Nazis retaliated, deploring Spengler's refusal to support ideas about racial superiority. Spengler's 1934 book "The Hour of Decision" was banned and by 1935 he had been fully ostracized by the Nazis. None of this deterred my mother from insisting on the publication of Willi's book with Spengler's introduction; finally "Unfinished Symphony" was released (again), placed back on bookstore shelves, and enjoyed the critical acclaim it deserved.

Wiedemann had once again played a central role in helping Kate. If there was such a thing as "a good Nazi," Wiedemann was a contender, certainly with respect to his support of Kate. Tall, dark and handsome, Wiedemann was also a notorious ladies man and, unquestionably, was attracted by Kate's beauty and vivaciousness. He had met her first, tragically widowed, when he came to her home with Hess, then in Munich's Brown House and now at meetings in Berlin. She had no idea how indebted she would become to him. He was a wolf of a different shading. Rather than threatening her, he was protecting her.

Chapter 8

"WHERE DO I BELONG?"

Of all the roaming wolves of the Third Reich, by far the most menacing was anti-Semitism. This wolf stalked Kate, the woman who would become my mother, with stealth and tenacity. Kate was Jewish. As with most things about her, my mother's Judaism was complicated. To begin with, almost no one knew of her Jewish background. Even I did not until I was 14, and then, learned of it only inadvertently.

Kate grew up in an assimilated Jewish household in Schwerin, where Adolf and Hedwig Tietz—like many German Jews of that time—attended synagogue on high holidays, made regular contributions and yet lived secular lives. Adolf was related to the prominent Tietz merchant family, [1] well known for establishing the first department stores in Germany, offering their customers a new and exciting shopping experience. The Jewishness of the Tietz's was best described as in the "liberal tradition." [2] In Schwerin, Hedwig and Adolf identified loosely with the small Jewish community; Adolf, the more observant of the couple, held a regional office in the synagogue hierarchy. Both Adolf and Hedwig were buried in the Jewish cemetery in Schwerin, along with one of their two sons. Kate's birth certificate duly recorded the Jewish lineage of both parents. However, documents are only as reliable as their primary source of information. In this case, they protected the family from certain scandal. Kate Tietz was an illegitimate child. Whether this was successfully concealed from Adolf is unknown, but one can imagine it contributing—at the very least—to tensions. It may account for Kate's lack of any photos of Adolf.

Kate was the love child of a long-term affair her mother had with a Prussian count, Freiherr von Alvensleben, a member of a large Junker (landed nobility) family. Although Kate called Adolf Tietz "father," she maintained she was aware of her paternal roots at an early age. On those scant occasions when my mother spoke to me about her past, she described spending time during the summer with von Alvensleben on his estate in Pomerania, not far from Schwerin, and meeting with him over the years on travels with her mother. Some recollections were particularly vivid. She told me of one that stayed with her. When still a young girl, she had been on a morning walk with her mother. Von Alvensleben suddenly appeared on horseback, bending down to give her a precious doll. That was the day she was convinced he was her real father.

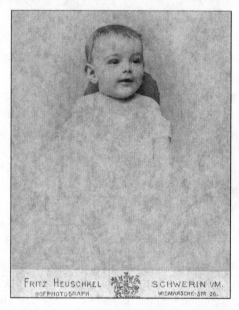

Kate as a baby

I do not believe there was a confirmation of this paternity until Kate was about to marry in 1920. When Kate became engaged to Willi Schmid, a devout Catholic, Hedwig Tietz had a frank talk with her daughter about "the event that brought you about." [3] Perhaps knowing about von Alvensleben's Christian heritage was a way to ease Kate's marriage outside of the Jewish faith. Hedwig was totally supportive of the relationship, Adolf indubitably less so, given Willi's Catholicism. During Willi's two and a half year courtship of Kate, he had made several trips to Schwerin to get to know her family. Willi was all the more curious about Kate's biological paternal roots after

Kate told him about von Alvensleben: "I am sure your father contributed to you as much as your mother. That's one reason why I would like to know some day what he was like, his personality, nature and life. It's just because of our children, who will inherit qualities from him as much as from us."[4] For a description of the Count, Willi needed to rely on Kate's memories since von Alvensleben had died a few years prior to then. Allegedly, he had left a letter confirming his paternity of Kate.[5]

Kate as a young girl, age 15, by Schwerin Lake with the town in the distance.

With the definition of "Jew" becoming a legal matter during the Nazi era, this lineage played an increasingly significant role. [6] However, both these facts, her status as a Jew and as a 'bastard' child, were deep secrets, kept from almost everyone. My siblings and I were ignorant about them for years. However, wanting honesty and openness in their relationship, she shared these confidences early on with Hoerlin. As she wrote, "Since my lips first touched your forehead, I have hidden nothing from you . . . neither the shiver of bliss nor the many questions, whose resolution can occur only gradually with a high degree of determination, decisiveness, and clarity." [7]

Kate, age 19, around the time she met Willi Schmid.

Kate's mother, Hedwig Pinner Tietz, in 1921.

Kate's conversion to Catholicism in 1921 had been motivated by romantic and practical reasons: she was deeply in love with Willi and he had told her he would not be able to retain his status as a teacher in the Bavarian civil service system unless he remained a Catholic and was married to one. [8] While Willi was in general open-minded, he too was influenced by widespread anti-Jewish sentiments, writing to Kate of his "instinctive" revulsion for "average" Jews. He also reproved Kate for attending synagogue with her parents while visiting Schwerin during the period when she was being tutored in Catholicism in Munich. Kate did not take organized religion as seriously as Willi; her connection to Judaism appeared to be more cultural than spiritual.

Kate neither acknowledged her Jewish background nor seemed to miss it. On the other hand, her impatience with prejudicial remarks such as "but you're different," was apparent when she was 20. In a rare instance of Jewish identification, she remarked to Willi in 1919: "... the more someone considers me an exception from the rest of my people, the more actively my sympathy grows for those hated and slandered people. At that point I am indifferent to the fact that I never felt the manifestations of enmity—everything within me tenses with absolute readiness to resist the effort to degrade the people from whom I am descended to second-class citizens .... the majority of my people are not quite foreign to me and yet I am considered an outsider by my family ... *where do I belong?*" [9]

"*Where do I belong?*" became an ongoing thematic for Kate. To what family did she belong? To what heritage and what religion? And—with increasing apprehension—to what country? Kate had fully embraced Christian customs, the three children had been baptized and Catholicism was integral to Schmid family life, so she must have been deeply disturbed by the prospect of being exposed as "Jewish." Although she continued to hope to be considered a Catholic, every day of Hitler's regime eroded that fantasy.

In the early days of his regime, Hitler was careful not to speak publicly of "... the Jewish peril" [10] but one does not have to look far back in his history to affirm the Fuehrer's hatred of the Jews. In my mother's birthplace—Schwerin—Hitler gave a rousing speech on May 5, 1924 that, according to the local paper, was "... a hail of furious insults and threats against the Jews." [11] Once he became chancellor in 1933, Hitler's rhetoric was tempered somewhat since he was intent on not antagonizing public opinion outside of Germany and projecting to the world press an image of reform and stability especially prior to the Winter and Summer Olympics. Instead, he let anti-Semitism take its noxious course, fueling it tactically with boycotts, policies, and laws.

With the entrenchment of anti-Semitism, Kate harbored fears that if her Jewish roots were revealed, it could impact negatively on Hoerlin and have consequences on their relationship—not because of his personal feelings, but because of the political milieu. Mixed marriages and sexual relations between Ayrans and Jews were targets of unceasing, often violent party attacks. [12] Aryans who were married to Jews—like Hoerlin's Stuttgart doctoral advisor Regener—were being pilloried, even those dating Jews seriously harassed. The April 1935 edition of the SS periodical *Das Schwarze Korps* called for punishment up to 15 years imprisonment for intimate relations between Germans of any gender and Jews.[13]

Anything that had the slightest association with Jews was suspect. When the feature film "The Demon of the Himalayas" ("Der Daemon des Himalaja"), shot during Dyhrenfurth's 1934 Himalayan expedition to the Karkakorum, was released in 1935 the Sports Leader of German Mountaineering filed a petition with the Reich Film Office to have it removed at once from theaters. His rationale was that the film was a Jewish product beneath the dignity of German mountain climbing: ". . . it is not necessary to tolerate the Jewish businessmen who try to bring their shady deals into the Reich . . ."[14] The author was the villainous Paul Bauer, who for years abhorred Dyhrenfurth, disparaging his Jewish roots and Jewish wife. When Dyhrenfurth dedicated his film to the fallen heroes of the 1934 Nanga Parbat Expedition, Bauer was furious. Bauer's position was at least consistent: mountaineering films as well as mountaineering organizations should be free of any connection to Jews.

With anti-Semitism rapidly spreading, Hoerlin knew the risks of his love affair with Kate. Beginning in the fall of 1934, Kate repeatedly warned him of what it meant to tie himself to her, she who was "fettered by her fate" ("gebunden an mein Schicksal"). In November, she wrote, ". . . now I sometimes think I <u>must</u> remove myself from your happy and clearly planned life. I <u>must</u> depart from you—soon—immediately." [15] A month later she contemplated the consequences of future bonds ". . . then, then . . . don't you have to measure what happens?"[16] And a few days after that, my mother was more overt: "Do you know, how it feels, when one is not permitted to have a child in today's Germany? Now I know it." [17]

Kate's fears were warranted. Any child born to Kate would defy the Nazi's maniacal drive toward a pure blooded Aryan nation. Germans had become obsessed with racial "cleansing," employing biology as a way to "scientifically" identify Jews. A variety of genetic laws were passed ostensibly to upgrade racial quality, beginning with the 1933 Law for the Prevention of Genetically Diseased Offspring. It made sterilization compulsory for persons with hereditary diseases, habitual criminals, and person with mental retardation or mental illness. [18] Rumors were rampant that these sterilization laws would be extended to Jews. [19] In the name of "racial protection" and "German purity," there was a clamor for preventing further Jewish-racial poisoning and pollution of German blood. [20] The many public discussions about the issue spurred Kate to ask Hoerlin his opinion about the so-called race question. As a true scientist, rather than a politically motivated pseudo-scientist, he answered: "I believe race can be given many definitions, none of them correct, because examples fail to be representative. Either there are a thousand races among us or none at all. Nothing good can follow from our being categorized according to blood; that premise can be maintained only by people who—to put it mildly—are thick-headed. You can understand why I must put this to rest once and for all, especially today, where only rubbish is spoken and blindly believed in this field." [21] Kate answered immediately. She clearly had been nervous and had read his letter—over and over again—with, as she reported, shaking hands. As she exclaimed, "the sun shone upon me, I lay down quietly under {the import of} these words. I lay by the open window and longed for the outside." [22]

Others may have been deterred by the prevailing winds of eugenics and unrelenting policies intent on separating Jews from Aryans, but neither my father nor my mother shrank from their goal to find a way to spend the rest of their lives together. "Only the question of <u>how</u> {it can happen}" Kate opined, "remains unanswered." [23] Hoerlin, no stranger to formidable tasks, acknowledged: ". . . we will have to fight hard against a powerful foe but the primacy of our love is a strong cohesive link." Further responding to Kate's unease over what he was undertaking, Hoerlin chided her: ". . . never talk again about my being burdened; nothing will be gained, if one is passive. To force the issue, we must stand united." [24] This attitude of willed optimism was crucial in facing the challenges before them.

Kate and Hoerlin had their work cut out for them because the situation was rapidly deteriorating. In February 1935 *Deutsche Justiz*, the Nazi jurisprudence journal, called for a legal ban on marriage between Aryans and Jews. Soon afterward, authorities advised marriage registrars, on moral grounds, to cease permitting such marriages. [25] Seven months later, on July 15, 1935, a policy that had started piecemeal across Germany became the law of the land. The Law for the Defense of German Blood and Honor (abbreviated to Blood Law) ushered in the Nuremberg Laws, a set of three laws. One proclaimed the swastika flag as the national flag (forbidding Jews to hoist it) and another articulated who exactly was entitled to the rights of citizenship (depriving Jews of political and civil rights). The third part of the legislation, banning intermarriage and outlawing sexual relations between Jews and Aryans, was the most pointed in terms of enforcing apartheid and the drive for racial purity. [26]

It was a serious blow for Kate and Hoerlin. Their relationship had been intimate for months, already breaking the bonds of social conventions: "I know that for today I cannot think about tomorrow—its bourgeois rules, its continuing legal restraints," my mother writes. "What unfathomable luck, that the times let me give to you, what is mine. I drink in and bless every minute with you, as if it were the last—what can we know about tomorrow? And you should know, that I am blissful . . . blissful." [27] Had those who pressed for the Nuremberg Laws read the following letter, my father would have been punished for the crime of *Rassenschande* (racial defilement): "My physical desire is stronger than ever in these months; with all my senses there is an impetuous yearning and craving for you that I've never experienced before. And you have (happily) hot blood." [28]

Blood, in fact, was the basis of the so-called "Jewish question." With the goal of assuring the purity of German blood, Hitler had ordered the drafting of four versions of the Blood law, each carrying penalties of varying severity. Hitler chose a version not restricted to "full Jews," leaving open the question of how a Jew is defined. No one could agree. Amidst bureaucratic infighting, Rudolf Hess was made responsible for overseeing a supplementary decree to the Nuremberg laws promulgated in November 1935. Hess, the very man who had bowed so deeply to Kate when he apologized on behalf of the Reich about Willi Schmid's murder, pushed for a more encompassing definition of Jew, one that included *Mischlinge* (those of mixed descent). This viewpoint finally prevailed but the debate continued within Nazi ranks about *Mischlinge*. The Reich's Justice Minister, Schlegelberg, with whom Kate had met in his Berlin office, took a more nuanced position than Hess. He even pleaded for leniency in the post-war Nuremberg trails, maintaining his rulings were more liberal than other judges; he professed to have given *Mischlinge* the choice between being deported or being sterilized. Had <u>he</u> known my mother's Jewish roots and had <u>she</u> known about his turpitude in destroying the German legal system, their 1935 meetings would certainly have been less cordial. During that same period, Kate's encounters with

Himmler and Hess would have been equally impossible to fathom, had they known of her Judaism.

Convoluted and insanely detailed, the Nuremberg laws often had ridiculous contradictions—vacillating in their explanations between religious and racial criteria. [29] However, the dominant criteria were bloodlines. A Jew was any person descended from at least three Jewish grandparents. *Mischlinge* had two categories. A *"Mischling* of the first degree" included any person with two Jewish grandparents who did not belong to the Jewish religion and was not married to a Jewish spouse. If a person had one Jewish grandparent, he/she was classified as a *"Mischling* of the second degree." Marriage regulations for each category were different. For a *Mischling* of the first degree, official consent to marry a German Aryan was required; a *Mischling* of the second degree, on the other hand, did not require special permission to marry a German Aryan, but was prohibited from marrying a Jew. The complexity of the racial laws inspired one municipality to create a user-friendly illustrated version of them.

The laws created havoc. Jews were now alien subjects, no longer allowed to call themselves German citizens. Families who had long believed themselves to be Christians were treated otherwise. Even if one's Jewish grandparents had converted to Christianity, one was not a Christian. My mother's conversion to Catholicism did not exempt her from being defined by the Nazis as Jewish, even if she did not think herself so. However, based on her birth record, she was a full Jew. Based on her biological father, she was a half Jew. Her children also fell under the rubric of the Nuremberg categorization, considered either *Mischlinge* of First Degree or of Second Degree, depending on Kate's paternity. The final decision regarding racial classification rested with Hess. [30] To ascertain one's identification, it was now required to attain a Certificate of Descent, called an *Ariernachweis* (Aryan certificate), as a precondition of German citizenship. Proof that one was <u>not</u> of Jewish origin ultimately became a matter of life and death. The Nuremberg Laws paved the way to concentration camps.

Kate had few delusions about the implications of the Law. In October of 1935, after its passage, she wrote my father, "There is war in the world. There are laws that intend to stop life in every respect. Death is near . . . you kiss me, you walk with me and it fills me with unspeakable happiness to observe your being and to feel again and again your eyes fixated on me with heavenly love." [31] Jewish members of Kate's family were already in trouble. Kate's half brother, [32] Fredi, a physician living in Hamburg with a wife and two young sons, could no longer earn a living in Germany. Athough Fredi's medical practice had been sharply curtailed since 1933, a supplementary decree to the Nuremberg Laws in December 1935 assured that the medical profession was "free of the Jews"[33] within a year. Fredi's license was cancelled and he lost his job as a state employee. "The Hamburgers," as Kate called her brother's family with a nod to their city of residence, pinned their hopes on starting afresh by emigrating to America and had been dealing for months with bureaucracies on both sides of the ocean. "Is it too late?" Kate asked Hoerlin. "There are calls from Berlin—from the Interior—, Justice—, Finance Ministers, <u>never</u> anything written, not a line, that offers a guarantee or security. Only call after call . . ." [34]

Simultaneously Fredi was scrambling for the $5000 immigration fee which America required as a security guarantee; my mother lent him a significant portion of the money, quite certain it would never be returned to her. Fredi relied heavily on Kate and she was empathetic: "It is one thing for a person to be led, step by step, with open eyes to the abyss. But if one has his wife and children accompanying him on such a walk, it is beyond human strength." [35] As Fredi became semi-paralyzed by anxiety and his needs pressed on Kate more and more, she asked her uncle, married to her mother's sister, to help calm Fredi. Hermann Boehm was also a physician living in Hamburg and, like Fredi, his practice was eviscerated. Boehm, however, had a different response to the situation. He thought things would get better and similar to other German Jews of his age cohort, he felt too old to emigrate. He paid dearly for this decision two years later when he was interned at the Theresienstadt concentration camp.

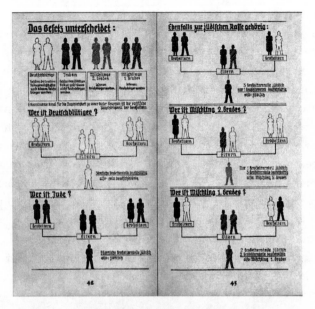

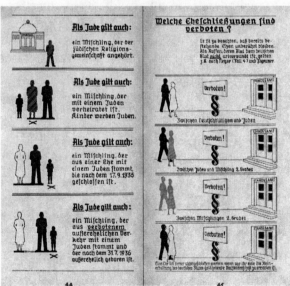

This set of illustrations details the Nuremberg Laws: what differentiates Jews from Aryans, degrees of Judaism (Mischlinge/mixed race of first and second degree), what constitutes belonging to the Jewish race and what marriages are forbidden (Verboten). Note that Jews are depicted as black, Mischlinge as striped and Aryans as white. Reproduced with permission from the Bielefeld Stadtarchiv.

Another uncle of Kate's also decided to stay in Germany. Felix Hausdorff was an eminent mathematician at Bonn University and he and his wife Lotte had a broad range of interests and wide circle of friends, most of them artists and composers. Hausdorff, who wrote a famous and enduring mathematical text, was proud to be the author of literary works as well. Although aware of the dangers of Hitler, he had declined several prestigious positions abroad before, and even after, his forced dismissal from the Bonn faculty. A few weeks afterwards, Kate told Hoerlin of her visit with Uncle Felix and Aunt Lotte; they had been constant and dear to her throughout her childhood and youth and she cared for them deeply: "Things went very well with the Hausdorffs, I experienced them as the same first rate, sensitive and cherished people I have always known. Distress has not contorted them. Felix is so bound to mathematics, that he is in no way distracted—what luck that is!" [36] Unluckily, a few years later, the distractions of math could no longer counter the ugly realities of Nazism for the Hausdorffs.

In addition to medical and academic worlds, the enactment of anti-Jewish measures affected businesses as well. By 1933, Jewish owners and operators of small stores were intimidated and often forced to sell them to Aryans. Some of Germany's large department stores had been Aryanized including that of Kate's extended family: the prosperous Tietz Department store chain with 10 stores and 13,000 employees in Berlin had been seized by the Nazis and its name changed to "Hertie." [37] Kate's much more modest family store in Schwerin, once her mother died, was sold for a fraction of its market value. The details of that transaction were tended to by Kate and involved several trips to Schwerin. Seventy-four years later, the German government paid reparations for this forced sale to Kate's heirs. [38]

The Schwerin visits were painful to Kate, underscoring the loss of her mother and her childhood. "Oh, it is so sad here," she wrote. "I was never as sad as now about my mother. I saw her everywhere, on every corner, in the kitchen, upon her chair. She left and unending love left with her. I am sitting here in the middle of the old household, but things have almost lost their endearing, clean appearance in the midst of the incomprehensible chaos and distortion, which paralyzes one's breath and poisons the air. As I lay in the dark yesterday, the clock of my childhood struck midnight, but it was not soothing to me, as it once was. Peace reigned only over the graves. You must know how beautifully they are situated, just above the large lake.

It is very quiet there, only the trees rustle . . . The guarded caution here is indescribable . . . And I must accept it happening, that the streets, trees, the beloved land of my childhood are taken away from me with no chance of being saved." [39]

Kate was saying farewell to Schwerin, which during the summer of 1935—like almost all of Germany—was besieged by vicious attacks on individuals and violent demonstrations against Jews. Nearby, on the Baltic Sea, resort hotels were closed to Jews, although Kate was able—with her best friend from school—to retreat to the small harbor town of Althagen, the peaceful site of former vacations. There, sleeping under a thatched roof, waking to the sound of shrieking seagulls and strolling among the sandy beaches and dunes, Kate could heal from the trauma of upheaval. Hoerlin could hear her sigh of relief when she relayed to him: "The bad times that took away our homeland in Schwerin, do not appear here." [40]

The refrain of *"Where do I belong?"* pertained not only to Schwerin. With growing distress, Kate was feeling alienated from Munich which in the 30's prided itself as "Capital of the Movement", the birthplace and stronghold of National Socialism. After leaving Schwerin for Munich, the shrill caws of seagulls were exchanged for strident greetings of "Heil Hitler!" Uniformed men, routinely holding boisterous parades and rallies often followed by anti-Semitic incidents, populated Munich's formerly quiet streets. In 1934 Kate observed to my father: "Bub, what sort of days are these? They almost tear my heart out, they force me to ask: where to? where to? It was once my home, this fine city . . . its walls now enclose me in a giant prison. At first I was too close to them, but the more perspective I had, the more able I was to measure their inhumane scale." [41] In 1935, a pro-Hitler demonstration was reported as follows: "The whole of Munich was on its feet. Trust in Hitler's political talent and honest intentions is getting ever greater, just as generally Hitler has again won extraordinary popularity. He is loved by many." [42] The adulation of Hitler rapidly attained cult-status, much to the disgust of my mother. A particularly large celebration occurred in Munich on November 9, commemorating Hitler's failed beer hall putsch of 1923 that attempted to overthrow the Weimar government. Declared a new national holiday by the Nazis, the turnout was huge and when it finally wound down, Kate's comments were scornful: ". . . a ghastly holiday . . . what should I be happy about?!?! The drum beats are muffled, the sound of marching reverberates through the streets, the torches lie in complete darkness." [43]

My mother, having lost her childhood home in Schwerin, was now increasingly anxious about her presence in Munich. My father was also feeling unsettled, albeit in different ways. His home and family store, owned by the Hoerlins for generations in Schwaebisch Hall, was being sold. In September 1935, his 27 year old sister Liesel—after battling TB for years—finally succumbed. She died peacefully in her sleep, her gentle and sweet personality staying with her until the end. Her mother had valiantly carried on the store's business after the death of her husband, consulting regularly with Hoerlin and assisted intermittently by Liesel, depending on her health. But when Liesel passed away, she was quite alone and decided to move back to her hometown, Ludwigsburg, near Stuttgart. The Schwaebisch Hall chapter of her life, and of her son's, was closing.

Hoerlin and Liesel had been close, she always teasing him in sisterly ways, and he—with brotherly affection—was solicitous toward his younger sibling, the fragility of her health having manifested itself early on. When climbing in the Himalayas and the Andes, Hoerlin's correspondence was more often to her than to his parents and she followed his adventures with excitement and pride. As her illness progressed, Hoerlin helped her seek possible remedies, arranging for a visit to the Swiss sanatorium started by Dr. Maximilian Bircher-Benner, whose fame now survives with Bircher Muesli cereal, an uncooked mix of rolled oats, raw fruit and nuts. Liesel adopted the good doctor's credo of optimal health, a balanced diet eaten in the fresh mountain air—preferably in Switzerland. Distraught by his sister's deteriorating condition, Hoerlin made certain that Kate and she met. Kate was already overdue for visit to Schwaebisch Hall, which she knew by reputation, to meet both his mother and sister.

The visit, in the spring of 1935, went wonderfully. Kate was struck by the dignity, bravery and selflessness of Hoerlin's mother and her heart went out to Liesel, who welcomed her warmly and openly. Hoerlin had confided his love of Kate to his sister and while the three were promenading through Schwaebisch Hall's quaint streets, she whispered her approval. Hoerlin also sought his father's "approval" by bringing Kate to his gravesite and that too—more mysteriously—was bestowed on her. Afterwards the young couple ambled over the surrounding hills, prompting Kate's understanding of their formative influence on Hoerlin's appreciation of nature. She and he shared a love of being outside, Hoerlin having experienced that more in the mountains and she by the sea but it was one of their commonalities.

The German definition of home, "Heimat", goes well beyond the boundaries of a specific location. It is a concept that includes memories of positive feelings and associations, a habitat where—if one leaves—one longs to return, a place that welcomes you back. In this sense, both Hoerlin and Kate were homeless but they had found through each other another kind of home, thus expressed by Kate: "Do you know how deeply and intensely you are my home? That in this precious home where my heart belongs, it finds peace and joy. And you know, what you mean to me . . . you as a person, as a man, as my much beloved Heimat." [44] Kate had found the answer to her question, *"Where do I belong?"*

Chapter 9

A SUNLESS YEAR

The word "trembling" ("zittern" in German) appeared repeatedly in my parents' letters early in their courtship: trembling with love, trembling with anticipation, trembling with joy. In 1936, another kind of trembling surfaced: trembling from fear. Kate's situation was precarious. The Third Reich was accelerating its agenda to identify and purge Jews, ". . . the most dangerous enemy of the German people." [1] Anti-Semitism, successfully grafted onto the general discontent of the population, was sprouting a life of its own. It seemed only a matter of time before Kate's Jewish roots would be exposed.

Well into the year, she had written my father: "It makes me tremble . . . in this sunless year, I am frightened." [2] In the beginning days of 1936, she had expressed fear for both herself and Hoerlin, and those feelings persisted: "All of me is trembling—up and down, inside me and surrounding me—everywhere. Hoerlin, go forth, go forth. You must live, where it is peaceful . . . filled with the surety of what is given and what is possible. That is the air you need in order to breathe and is cut off from me." [3] He answered immediately, first holding out hope for a more promising future: "Someday you will find the stability and calm you long for. That is my absolute belief . . . There will again be a time when we walk hand in hand over the hills, absorbing the beauty of the world and forgetting its cruelty."[4] And then Hoerlin, in his self-effacing way, addressed her entreaties for him to leave her: "If a person comes to you, who is more than I am or can be, and means more to you, then I will be on my way without protesting." [5] Barring that unlikely scenario, he stood by her unconditionally. Her response was emphatic: "<u>You</u> are the one who fulfills

119

me, I breathe with you, my hand still has not left yours, my stride still attempts to keep step with yours." [6] Together, Hoerlin and Kate walked forward.

For the past year they had been discussing "the birth of an idea" conceived by my father and welcomed by my mother. In his usual fashion, Hoerlin was plotting survival strategies, in this case not for climbing the world's highest peaks, but for fleeing Germany assuming Nazi tyranny persevered. Kate admired Hoerlin's propensity to think ahead, clearly and wisely, and praised him accordingly: "The birth of an idea is a goal definitely worth exerting all one's energy on—and it is, this I feel with great certainty, no plan out of the blue, no Utopia, no fantasy . . . it is absolutely your plan, your essence and therefore in accordance with your capabilities. I believe that and you should feel that I am totally with you, when your determination can forge a path." [7] The man, four years younger than she, who Kate initially had called *"Bub"* (boy) bore a profound responsibility and had developed several creases on his forehead. These, unlike the dehydration wrinkles earned from his previous high altitude mountain exploits, would not disappear.

Like all good plans, Hoerlin's contained contingencies. In this case, the biggest contingency had been whether the racial dogma and totalitarian tenets of National Socialism would continue to gain ground. By 1936, that was settled: the Nazis were irrevocably entrenched. Early in the year the fervor of National Socialism was fanned by the assassination of the head and founder of the Nazi party in Switzerland, Wilhelm Gustloff. [8] Elevated quickly to martyrdom, Gustloff was—according to Hitler—". . . a good German . . . who did nothing but pledge himself to the loyalty of the homeland." [9] The assassin was Jewish, a young medical student incensed by Gustloff's unbridled hostility toward Jews. Gustloff originally lived in Schwerin and accordingly, my mother's hometown became the setting for a state funeral with Hitler himself delivering the eulogy. In a remarkable and revealing speech, the Fuehrer did not miss the opportunity to remind mourners that Jews were to blame for the downfall of Germany in WWI and that there would be retaliation for this murder:

> "Behind every murder stood the same power [was] responsible . . .
> the hated filled power of our Jewish foe, a foe to whom we had done
> no harm, but who nonetheless sought to subjugate our German
> people and make a slave of it—the foe who is responsible for all

the misfortune that fell upon us in 1918, for all the misfortune which plagued Germany in the years that followed. And now National Socialism has gained its first conscious martyr . . . so our comrade has fallen a victim to that power that wages a fanatical warfare not only against our German people but against every free, autonomous and independent people. We understand the challenge to battle and we take up the glove." [10]

Carried by a special train, Gustloff's coffin wound its way from Switzerland and stopped in several German cities, its route lined with Hitler Youth members, before reaching its final resting place in Schwerin.

On Kate's last visit to Schwerin, her hometown had been swarming with uniformed Nazis and she dreaded returning. Civility had been usurped by intimidation and belligerence. For Kate, the present and the past darkly shadowed the town, filled with ghosts of what had been and no longer was there. But her brother Fredi begged her to go; he and his family needed money to emigrate to the United States; Fredi, among many other Jews, was a victim of the Reichsbank's exchange rate of less than 30% of value for those leaving Germany. [11] He was depending on the Tietz family inheritance, although considerably reduced in value because of the forced sale of the family's home and store. The transactions were in limbo and Fredi, seemingly incapable of closing a deal, asked Kate to take charge. The lawyer representing the Reich in the negotiations was an old high school friend of Kate's, who once assured her that although she was Jewish, she was "different." Now an avowed Nazi, he treated Kate well, still evidently feeling that she was "different."

Kate reluctantly agreed to make the January trip, writing to Hoerlin, "I am <u>afraid</u> about this trip, its loneliness and hopelessness . . . I have not been able to sleep . . ."[12] Intrepid in having faced top Nazis in Munich and Berlin in 1934 and 1935, Kate was feeling shaky by 1936. At a time when strident calls for action on "the Jewish question" resonated throughout Germany, it became more and more problematic to have any Jewish blood whatsoever. The original Nuremberg laws of September 1935 had been revised, strictly defining and subjecting to a test the legal status of *Mischlinge*. [13] Even with these supplementary decrees, the rights of *Mischlinge* continued to be hotly contested within Nazi circles and the laws interpreted and applied patchily across German municipalities and regions, some much more stringently than others. In various localities, Jews were no longer able to lease certain properties,[14] a development that could jeopardize Kate's rental of her Munich apartment. Claiming her inheritance from the family's "Jewish-tainted property"[15] in Schwerin brought further attention to Kate's background, since such transactions were meticulously noted in German records.

Once in the public domain, this information was fodder to organizations such as the *Sicherheitsdienst* (SD), the national security and intelligence arm of the Nazi party. Reporting directly to Himmler, the division was staffed by fiercely anti-Semitic young operatives who made it one of their primary projects to compile a card index of every Jew, as classified by the Nuremberg decrees, living in Germany.[16] Assiduous in their investigations, the SD was convinced that if life could be made economically and socially impossible for Jews, they would leave Germany.[17] Within Germany, a whole new industry was spawned: genealogical researchers (*Sippenforscher*) who painstakingly reviewed records of birth to determine ancestry.[18] It was inevitable that either the party's SD or the government's requirement for proof of Aryan descent would ferret out Kate's Judaism, to whatever degree.

The message of danger, already conveyed by my father, was re-enforced by Kate's early January swing through the northern cities of Hamburg, Schwerin and Berlin in 1936, a bitterly cold winter. Relatives and friends in Hamburg expressed alarm about their future. Legal proceedings in Schwerin, in spite of the favorable involvement of her old friend, underscored the erosion of an equitable society. And the Berlin meeting with Wiedemann broached for the first time a tricky topic: Kate's standing in Nazi Germany. She had grown to trust Hitler's Adjutant and turned to him again for advice. A letter from her biological father, Count (Graf) von Alvensleben[19] attested to her mixed religious parentage. In contrast, her birth certificate and the Schwerin church registry listed both her parents as Jewish. Another document showed her conversion to Catholicism in 1921. How would she be classified—a full Jew or a *Mischling*?

As a full Jew, she would no longer be a German citizen but "a subject of the state" instead. As a *Mischling*, there was the chance that she would be treated less harshly. Could Kate have fabricated the von Alvensleben paternity in order to better protect her children and herself? In researching this book, I tried in vain to find proof of her mixed heritage. According to my older sister,

Kate on one of her many trips to meet with Nazi bureaucracies in Berlin.

Fritz Wiedemann, Kate's protector, who was personal Adjutant to Hitler.
Photo credit: Preston-Steinheimer.

my mother had burned the von Alvensleben letter, along with many others, years later. My mother's account of her biological father was consistent to all of her children, as well as a few friends. And it is highly dubious that Kate would have lied to Wiedemann—or that he would have fallen for it, had it not been true.

Prior to Kate's meeting with Wiedemann, he had every reason to regard her as Christian. Now he knew she was Jewish <u>and</u> a bastard child, or more kindly stated, a love child, related to the large and powerful von Alvensleben family. Some of them were pro-Hitler, others adamantly against him. Three von Alvenslebens were in Hitler's elite SS corps where one, Ludolf-Hermann, [20] was a group leader and later became Himmler's top adjutant. Himmler touted the SS as a bastion of racial purity; members needed to ascertain the Aryan ancestry back to 1750. [21] Any relationship, no matter how remote and how illegitimate, to someone Jewish would be more than embarrassing—it would be ruinous.

With Wiedemann promising to look into the classification process, Kate was anxious to return to some semblance of normal existence. For the past year and a half since Willi's death, she had admirably juggled the competing balls of single parenting, financial security, social life and a new love—each propelled by separate trajectories. By 1936, longing for routines of everyday life, she turned her focus on integrating Hoerlin into the family fold and spending more time with the children. Often they had been left in the loving hands of maids, relatives or close friends. While this was not an unusual childrearing practice of the era, it had been exacerbated by Kate's many trips to Berlin and Schwerin, in addition to being with Hoerlin. Every time she returned to Munich, the children were delighted; as Thomi exclaimed, "Mutti, when you come home it is exactly like Mozart's music—one doesn't know <u>why</u> it is so beautiful!" [22] Thomi, 9 years old, the 3 year old Hedi and 12 year old Duscha had frequently visited Willi Schmid's extensive and caring family in Garmisch-Partenkirchen, nestled in the Bavarian Alps about 50 miles southwest of Munich. The two family maids also doted on the children. When one of them left, she was replaced by Maia, a strikingly pretty young woman from a small farming community. A pious Catholic, Maia had worked previously for a Jewish family but that job came to an end with the Nuremberg laws explicitly prohibiting Aryan women under the age of 45 to be employed by Jews. Forced to seek another position, Maia surely was unaware that her new employer was of Jewish origin.

In spite of her ongoing anxieties and the ominous political environment, Kate was determined to ground herself in the surety of loved ones: family and friends. Hoerlin spent more and more time with the Schmid children, finding a place in their lives and in their hearts. Gradually, he also was woven into Kate's lively social life in Munich, comprised of intellectuals, artists and musicians. She shone in this domain, confidently taking center stage as she entered a room, fully expecting to dominate its space. Years earlier, in 1925, she had attended the novelist and essayist Thomas Mann's 50th birthday party in Munich. When several participants had urged her to toast him, she ostensibly answered, "I am here, isn't that enough?" [23] Never intimidated by prominent people, she sought admiration and usually received it. She also was accustomed to stimulating conversations, characteristic of one of the many parties she described to Hoerlin: "Sunday evening there was an elegant and unique assemblage—possible almost only in Munich—of professors, nobility, doctors and high ranking Reichswehr officers. Everything intellectually interesting..." [24]

Kate also entertained graciously at home, creating a *gemuetlich* setting for friends: "Vossler and Frau Hutchinson and Spengler and Bumke are coming for tea—so, all kinds of important people! Do you actually imagine me in awe of their company?" I cannot remember a time when my mother was in awe of anyone; she saw no reason Hoerlin should be. She reassured him: "... {the conversation} is not about literature, not about the 'intellectual', but rather about very typical and close human relationships and bonds." [25] Karl Vossler was Rector of the University of Munich and he and his wife became friends of the Schmids after Willi had been his student; Frau Hutchinson was a mistress of Wilhelm Furtwaengler,[26] an internationally acclaimed conductor, and lived with their child in Munich; Herr Geheimrat [27] Oswald Bumke was a central figure of German psychiatry in the 20th century, achieving notoriety partly for opposition to Freud and partly for his seven week stay in Russia with Lenin, tending to the revolutionary leader's stress-related illnesses prior to his death in 1924.

These intellectual luminaries did not populate circles Hoerlin frequented, but he swallowed hard and entered the fray. His comparatively unusual profession, physics, and heroic climbing exploits fascinated people and they quickly welcomed him. Many had seen him in the "Himatschal" film, giving him a semi-celebrity status. No doubt his handsome chiseled looks and pleasant demeanor added to the attractive mix. Women were drawn to this man of quiet strength, but he seemed quite oblivious about his appeal. During these congenial occasions, my father was one of the few people who spoke out openly against the Nazis. People still harbored hopes that the vulgarities of the Third Reich would be short-term and appeared to be in denial about indications to the contrary. Sometimes Hoerlin felt he was a voice of gloom in reminding Kate of omnipresent threats. After a particularly difficult conversation, Hoerlin wrote: "I am pleased that when I was with you the other evening, I spoke to you . . . I know it was more agonizing for you than for me. But I was full of anxiety . . ."[28]

Kate's admirer, Bumke, shared his trepidation. Among Kate's friends, he was remarkable in speaking out on political matters. When National Socialism proposed sterilization laws in 1931, Oswald Bumke opposed them, his rationale eerily presaging the future: ". . . if the discussion about sterilization today is carried into the arena of a political contest, then pretty soon we'll no longer hear about the mentally sick but instead about Aryan and non-Aryan, about the blonde Germanic race and the inferior people with round skulls."[29] Hoerlin held in high regard Bumke's political awareness, extraordinary prescience and courage. The approbation was mutual.

Hoerlin's relationship to another friend of Kate's, the eminent historian-philosopher Oswald Spengler, was more tentative. Kate had met Spengler during the revelry of Fasching and brought the intellectual icon home, triumphantly announcing "Look who I found!" A friendship between the lonely and dour man and the vivacious Schmids developed; the harbinger of the West's decline was enchanted by Kate. After Willi's death, Spengler often accompanied Kate to the opera or to museums, sometimes bringing her children alone to the latter. When she detected a hint of romantic interest in her, she deflected it by introducing him to Hoerlin. The two men found commonality in disparaging the Nazi's pseudoscientific racial theories, although their other viewpoints diverged markedly. Spengler had little admiration in general for science and technology, pessimistically professing that they would destroy Germany's cultural underpinnings. Hoerlin, as a physicist and optimist, did not share his perspective. Spengler revered the past, Hoerlin looked toward the future. However, when Spengler died from a heart attack at age 56 in May 1936, both Hoerlin and Kate felt the loss.

Of Kate's friends, there was only one that Hoerlin took an immediate dislike towards: Willy Bogner, dubbed "kleine Willy," a tongue in cheek reference to his youth and his height of well over six feet. "It comes to this," my father admitted, "somehow I do not like young Willy."[30] Bogner was almost ten years younger than Kate, a champion Nordic skier, a bon vivant with a racy life style and an eye for pretty women. My father's judgment of him was tinged with a modicum of jealousy, but he also disapproved of Bogner's political connections and leanings. As the winner of numerous cross-country and ski jumping events, Bogner had won the accolades of Sports Minister von Tschammer und Osten, an outspoken racist and elitist, who proclaimed ". . . sports is the way to weed out the weak, Jewish and other undesirables."[31]

In 1936, the Sports Minister was responsible for organizing both the Winter Olympics in Garmisch-Partenkirchen and the Summer Olympics in Berlin. In a rare instance, one country was hosting both events and Germany seized it as an extraordinary opportunity to showcase its Fuehrer and demonstrate the superiority of the Aryan race. Only Ayrans were permitted to participate on German teams, with the exception of one Jewish hockey player and a few *Mischlinge*. [32] Although there were threats from other countries, especially the United States, to boycott the Games because of Germany's discriminatory practices, both Olympics turned out to be propaganda coups for the Third Reich. The carefully honed image of a peaceful and tolerant nation was enhanced by the temporary removal of anti-Semitic signage, such as "Jews not wanted," commonly posted throughout Germany. The world press and international visitors were led to minimize rumors of officially sanctioned anti-Semitism. According to a New York Times correspondent, "Not the slightest evidence of religious, political or racial prejudice is outwardly visible here . . . In short, politics is being kept out of the sphere in which it has no place . . . Only sports count and nobody thinks of anything else."[33]

Twenty-eight nations participated in the opening ceremonies of the Winter Olympics, the fourth ever held, and by today's standards, the event was modest and simple. Local oxen lugged a cannon into the welcoming arena and as it was set off, the church bells of the Garmisch-Partenkirchen answered in a chorus of chimes. The Olympic flag, with its five Olympic rings representing the five continents flew on one side of a massive ski jump looming over the arena; on the other side, an Olympic torch—used for the first time—spewed flames. Standing on a center podium to open the ceremonies was the Fuehrer. The ritual called for athletes entering the arena to give the Olympic salute, which unfortunately was similar to the Hitler salute, only aiming one's right hand higher. As the athletes marched in, they saluted Hitler with the Olympic version, except for the American teams who feared such a gesture could be mistaken for the Nazi one.[34]

After Hitler made welcoming remarks, Willy Bogner joined him on the podium. The skier had been chosen to recite the traditional Olympic Oath, representing the athletes in their commitment to the *"true spirit of sportsmanship, for the glory of sport and the honour of our teams."* The exclusion of outstanding Jewish competitors apparently did not negate true sportsmanship and honor. Bogner finished the oath with the flourish of a Nazi salute.[35] The Sports Minister had promoted Bogner to this honorific task, anticipating he would be a medalist. But with the Norwegians dominating Nordic events, Bogner did not return to the podium as a victor. His much publicized, high profile appearance with Hitler gave added weight to Hoerlin's dislike for young Willy. And Kate was jarred into reassessing her friendship with the dashing skier who always greeted her with bouquets of flowers.[36] Again, Hoerlin's level-headedness gave ballast to Kate's sporadic tilts toward the seductive winds of charm.

The Summer Olympics, launched by Hitler in front of a huge crowd greeting him with a combination of the disturbingly similar Nazi and Olympic salutes,[37] was a much grander event than its winter counterpart. Filled with pomp and fanfare, it signaled the return of Germany to the world community after the disgrace of their WWI defeat. Germany's goal of displaying Aryan superiority by sweeping gold, silver and bronze medals was thwarted by African-American runner Jesse Owens. A black man had trumped the blue eyed, blond haired *Uebermensch* (Superman). There were a few other glitches as well. The International Olympic Committee had agreed to award the Gold Medal for Alpinism to Hettie and Gunter Dyhrenfurth for ". . . a number of significant ascents and scientific expeditions in the Himalayas."[38] The Dyhrenfurths, who by then were Swiss citizens, were informed of the prize by the head of the Swiss Olympic Committee, which invited them to the award ceremonies.[39] However, an official invitation from Berlin to attend—sent by telegram—did not arrive until August 15th, a day before the official ceremony. Unquestionably, the bumbling way this was handled reflected the awkwardness of the Olympic's Nazi hosts in bestowing such an honor on a Jew (Hettie) and a *Mischling* (Gunter).

Hettie chose to stay home in Zurich for a variety of understandable reasons, ranging from a general disapproval of Germany's demeanor to a specific anti-Semitic incident toward her son Norman. [40] One less obvious rationale for Hettie's absence was that Hans Ertl was in Berlin, working as a cameraman for Leni Riefenstahl's groundbreaking documentary "Olympia" about the 1936 Summer Olympics. Ertl, a renowned womanizer, was a lover of Riefenstahl but in 1934 had an affair with Hettie, considerably his elder, when they were both on the Karakorum Expedition to the Himalayas. Considering it a breach of trust antithetical to the teamwork integral to climbing, Ertl admitted the transgression to the expedition's leader, that is, Hettie's husband. Dyhrenfurth, at least a head taller than Ertl, grabbed him by the shoulders and then spoke softly: "These things happen, my young friend!" [41] Ertl was speechless as Dyhrenfurth, explaining that he and Hettie were in an open marriage, shook his hand. The friendship between the two men endured, but Hettie was not anxious to see Ertl with his new paramour. So Gunter came alone at the last minute, unable to resist the temptation of being publicly acclaimed at an event barring Jews. He collected the medal.

When he was with the Dyrenfurths on the 1930 Expedition, my father was clueless about any shenanigans in their marriage. In any case, Hoerlin felt their medal was well-deserved: Gunter for his pioneering Himalayan mountaineering and Hettie for setting a women's world summit record. But my father's real delight in the tribute was that it flew in the faces of his nemesis Bauer and the Sports Minister, whose anti-Semitism was undisguised. It also felt like retribution for their ruthless efforts to destroy the *Alpenverein*. My father, known as a fearless liberal on the Verein's governing board, [42] continued to try and protect the club's autonomy. The constant intrigues and haggling, however, were wearing him down.

Hoerlin was also about to add "Physicist" to his resume. It had been a long haul to complete his doctoral degree; Regener was a fastidious advisor but finally the thesis was done: a definitive study of cosmic rays. His efforts has been continually cheered on by Kate. She even read, in an act of true love, a popularized explanation of quantum theory by the pre-eminent German physicist and 1932 Nobel Prize winner Werner Heisenberg. The Nazis had rejected quantum mechanics as "Jewish Physics" and were irritated by Heisenberg's unwavering embrace of the theory, earning him the designation as a "white Jew," although Heisenberg's background was solidly Lutheran. He did not endear himself further to the regime by being among seventy five established physicists, party members and non-members, who sent a petition in October 1936 to the Reich's Minister of Education warning of the declining state of German physics. [43] The petition was a rare instance of Germans speaking out against Hitler's totalitarian government. Among its signers was Regener, already under a cloud because of his Jewish wife. The contrarian act of signing the petition sealed Regener's removal from the Stuttgart faculty. On the other hand, Heisenberg was forgiven the offense and went on to lead the German war effort at building an atomic bomb.

Hoerlin's doctorate was timely; it was the last awarded to a student of Regener's before his dismissal. To celebrate, Kate had planned an August vacation with him and the children in Italy's Dolomite mountains. Although there had been many excursions around Munich with the young ones, the Dolomites were a particularly spectacular vacation spot for the newly emerging family. For Kate, it felt like a rebirth of a togetherness she had missed. Hoerlin was enthralled at watching her with the children and partaking in the day to day: "Everyone's joy at everything beautiful and good, your observations, your pointing out and teaching {to the children}, and still much more, how could I forget all of it." [44] My mother, recognizing that hiking in the Dolomites was hardly comparable to first ascents in the Himalayas, had been somewhat apologetic about this tamed down version, but my father was full of enthusiasm: "It's wonderful to know how exceptionally well one can hike <u>and</u> climb with all of you. It was definitely the best vacation I have ever experienced . . . the two weeks so full of beauty and the happiest love, that they still seem to me like a fairy-like dream." [45]

However the fairy tale soon ended, particularly for Kate. Soon after she returned to Munich, a "new anti-Jewish drive" had been implemented by the Nazis, accentuated by Hitler's virulent rhetoric and hectoring harangues. In the words of Saul Friedlander, ". . . a new atmosphere of murderous brutality was spreading." [46] In addition, for the first time, an <u>official</u> policy of total emigration for Jews, compulsory if necessary, was clearly articulated by the Reich. At a high level cabinet meeting on September 29, 1936 to discuss future anti-Semitic measures, a priority of "vigorous emigration" was adopted and became a firm guideline. [47] Implementation of the new objective started immediately, speeding toward the National Socialist goal of "cleansing."

The policy fell just short of "forced" emigration for all Jews, but the Nazis did their best to make the environment as humiliating and impoverishing as possible. Emigration expenses for Jews were significant, as Kate was painfully aware of based on her brother Fredi's experience. Fredi had sent her an itemized list of costs routinely levied against Jews: flight taxes on assets, requirements to change *Reichsmarks* to foreign currency with the concurrent devaluation, the price of entering a new country and other expenses needed to make one's way through the emigration bureaucracy.[48] Again Fredi asked Kate for money that she again provided. But Kate was tired of his continual requests and resentful about the debts Fredi had accrued to their mother in the past. When at last Fredi and his family set sail for America at the end of September, tensions between Kate and Fredi were high.

A few weeks prior to the emigation directive, Kate had gotten in contact with Wiedemann regarding her Jewish classification status and its implications. He had recommended scheduling meetings with relevant authorities in Berlin but no one replied to her inquiries, making Kate feel deflated, depressed and frightened. As she wrote to Hoerlin, "Beloved, this is the most awful state of affairs for me, I can hardly bear it . . . If I do not hear anything from Berlin at the end of this week, I will call again." Finally on October 19 and 20, 1936, Kate had a series of exhausting meetings with the Nazi hierarchy.

By then she had been classified officially as a *"Mischling ersten Grades"* (a half Jew of the first degree).[49] For the first time, she stood before the top brass of the Third Reich as a Jew. In all prior meetings she was deemed a Catholic, an accurate appellation as far as she was concerned. As she faced the impeccably uniformed functionaries, she was still brave outwardly; inwardly was another story. Wiedemann had recommended she leave Germany as soon as possible. Negotiating through the barriers to emigration was thorny enough but assuring that the stipends from Willi Schmid's wrongful death follow her and the children to wherever they settled was another matter.

She also sought to be released, without a financial penalty, from her Munich apartment lease, which did not expire for two years.

After a day of intense deliberations in Berlin, she could barely lay pen to paper in a letter to Hoerlin: "I can almost not write, my inner trembling extends so much to the trembling of my hand."[50] It was another two weeks before she got word from government officials and she typed the news to Hoerlin, something she seldom did: "Now I am writing you on the typewriter, because then it makes no difference that my hands are trembling. The content of the Berlin decision is in every way absolutely gratifying, astonishingly favorable; it permits me completely free choice with regard to where {to emigrate}, that is, it positions me in every respect with exceptional rights and special standing . . ." [51]

A year that began sunless showed rays of brightness. A year that started with fear and trembling now offered hope for the future. Hoerlin had written Kate, "I know that the dark door leads to light." [52] Although leaving her homeland was not easy, Kate had been feeling increasingly alienated: a country where she was not wanted, a government that had murdered her husband, a milieu spiraling toward destruction of values she cherished. Kate had compelling reasons to flee, but without a doubt she was being pushed out because of her classification as a Jew. As of September 1936, the urgency became palpable. After all the pressure, she felt a sense of relief although formidable tasks lay ahead: "Beloved, now I must save up all my strength for the children, for you and for me." [53] The goals of my father's 'birth of an idea' were set in motion: finding a place to live where they were free from tyranny and entitled to marry. Neither Kate nor Hoerlin had anticipated that they would leave Germany separately. The challenge now was how, where and when they could be joined.

Chapter 10

OUTWARD BOUND

After the pivotal meetings with the Nazis in Berlin, Kate was in search of a new country, a new city and a new home. Apprising the children was painful and the eldest, Duscha, age 12, was the first to know. "I had to break the news to Duttli today," she relayed to Hoerlin, "not the details but the big picture. Her eyes were wide with questions and worries as I told her important changes had become necessary in our lives and were imminent. The child had certainly sensed it for a long time and I found her unbelievably understanding and sweet."[1]

Over the past year, Hedi and Thomi had a surfeit of childhood ailments: flus and fevers for Hedi, a mastoiditis operation for Thomi. Duscha seemed to escape illness until Kate told her of impending developments; the sensitive child promptly came down with dysentery. Literally and figuratively, Duscha was having trouble 'stomaching' the news. Although they did not express it as vividly as Duscha, Kate's close friends were also upset as she told them of her plans to leave the country. The pressing reason for emigration, her classification as Jewish, was divulged only to a select few. In correspondence to friends outside of Germany, Kate described her homeland as where "... it's impossible for one to get by and not be harassed." [2]

The primary prospects for emigration were Switzerland and Austria, neighboring German-speaking countries in easy reach of her treasured social circles and lifetime memories. Kate wasted no time in exploring both. Each country had complexities in terms of its stance vis-a-vis Nazis and anti-Semitism. In Switzerland, the Nazis had gathered momentum by gains in recent Swiss elections. While discrimination against Jews was subtler than in Germany, it intensified with the assassination of the leader of the Swiss Nazi party, Gustloff, by a Jew. The 1936 murder reverberated throughout the orderly society and increased their prejudices. Anticipating the "Jewish peril" in 1933, the Swiss had imposed highly restrictive measures against emigration with the rationale that Jews, taking up coveted jobs and "alien to the Swiss way of life," would swamp the country. [3] Standard Swiss policy was that emigrants, and by this it essentially meant Jews, were allowed on a transitional basis with the assumption that they did not take up permanent residence and would move on to another country as quickly as possible.[4] There were no Nuremberg Laws as such, but those became the basis for Switzerland's determination as to who was or was not counted as a Jew. Switzerland proposed making identification more efficient by stamping passports of Jews with the red letter "J", a practice adopted by Germany in 1938. It was one of the first public brandings of Jews, preceding the wearing of a Jewish star.

Kate had immediately written to Swiss friends about her plight and was devastated by their response: "Shattering and non-understanding letters come from Switzerland: 'we do not look upon it with pure joy that you are coming to Switzerland.'" [5] Especially hurtful had been a letter from the family's friend, Marguerite Oehler, who had often hosted the Schmids and sheltered Duscha and Thomi on their beautiful estate after the death of their father. Marguerite was not supportive of Kate's move, causing Kate to lament to Hoerlin: "Can one be friends with someone who knows me so little? Or is it not so much Margrit as Switzerland, the other country in this strange world that cannot relate to my emotional needs and considers it unnecessary to leave. In any case, my resolve not to go to Switzerland is confirmed by this letter." [6]

Austria had its own set of issues. The country of Hitler's birth had a long history of anti-Semitism but it ". . . considered Jews redeemable if they converted to Catholicism." [7] In that regard, my mother would be less stigmatized. At the same time prejudice against Jews in Austria was obvious through numerous ferocious street incidents and raucous university demonstrations organized largely by the Austrian Nazi party, which led Chancellor Englebert Dollfuss to outlaw it in 1933. A year later he too became a victim of its violence. On July 25th, 1934, Dollfuss was assassinated by eight Austrian Nazis attempting a coup. A new government was installed, one more amenable to the Third Reich, its conservative members favoring German annexation. [8]

In July 1936 German and Austrian relations drew closer with the signing of an accord that eliminated a 1000 Mark (approximately $12,000 then) fee imposed early in the Nazi regime on Germans who traveled to Austria. The punitive measure, designed to cripple the Austrian tourist trade and largely successful in doing so, was a show of German economic domination.[9] Its removal indicated a "normalization" of German-Austrian bonds and was celebrated by both countries. On a personal level, Kate and Hoerlin were thrilled by the gesture of amity and the ensuing accessibility to the Tyrol, the heart of the Alps, a favorite hiking and skiing destination. Although they wondered about how the agreement would impact politically on the future, it still seemed that Austria had more welcoming arms for Kate than Switzerland's cold shoulder.

Two weeks after the German-Austrian accord, the *Alpenverein* held its 1936 annual meeting in Garmisch-Partenkirchen in a brand new hall built for the Winter Olympics.[10] Over the stage hung a huge Edelweiss, the *Alpenverein's* emblem, and left of the stage hung a large Nazi flag, the first time one was displayed at a Verein meeting. [11] Ten members of the Verein's Executive Committee were seated on the dais. One photo reveals my father on the far left, looking young among his cohorts—one of two members with a full head of hair. Projecting an air of casualness with hands crossed characteristically at his wrists, he masked his true state of mind. The meeting had all the trappings of a political gathering, a scenario that Hoerlin had fought hard to avoid.

Speeches extolled the re-born 'brotherhood of the rope' between Germany and Austria, underscoring that mountain huts would no longer be segregated by nation, trails and peaks no longer delineated by borders. Following the formal proceedings, about 600 attendees—led by the Executive Committee—boarded a special train to Innsbruck, where they were greeted by their Austrian brethren who cheered wildly as *Alpenverein* members marched through the streets of the Tyrolean capital to the blare of brass bands. [12] An unmistakable political message underscored this demonstration of unity: Nazi flags waved prominently amidst the welcoming crowds. A mountaineering version of an *Anschluss* 13 unfolded, preceding Germany's more ominous *Anschluss* of Austria almost two years later when Austria fell totally under the domain of German rule and Nazi precepts.

Flanked by a Nazi flag, the Executive Committee of the German-Austrian Alpine Club meets in 1936. Note Hoerlin seated on the dais, second from left. Reproduced with permission from the German Alpine Club.

Pockets of the Verein continued to resist nazification. The club had a history of standing for values of decency, truth and justice; it encompassed a broad spectrum of political leanings and—astonishing for the times—Jews were still members. [14] However, there were definite anti-Semitic factions, evident in many Austrian sections, surfacing in several German sections as well. Between this ugliness and the blatant politicizing of the 1936 meeting, my father considered resigning from the Executive Committee. My mother urged him to stay involved. While not always politically savvy, she was nonetheless a masterful strategist: "I plead with you not to give up your position in the *Alpenverein* in any case now—perhaps we will very soon discover that this aspect of your work will be worthwhile in relationship to our lives." [15] She was keenly aware of the prestige and high visibility that Board membership gave Hoerlin, also serving to remind people of his stellar accomplishments. When it came to leveraging influence in the Third Reich, this could be helpful.

Meanwhile, Kate was tapping all her connections, trying to assure her exiting from Germany went as smoothly as possible. In doing so, she enlisted two commanding personalities, both tied closely to the inner circles of the Third Reich. Internally, Hitler's adjutant Wiedemann steadfastly looked out for her interests. Externally, she relied on an economic advisor to the Fuehrer, an influential industrialist who sat on numerous national and international business boards. Paul Reusch headed one of the Ruhr's largest firms, *Gutehoffnungshuette* (GHH), a heavy industry company belonging to the Duesseldorf Industrialist Club, a business cabal that funded Hitler in 1932 and then again in the 1933 general election. [16] The Club, a group of conservative and anti-union tycoons, hoped Hitler would be the antidote to the chaos of the liberal Weimar Republic and put an end to Germany's devastating economic crisis. [17] Mistakenly thinking they could control Hitler, the industrialists soon discovered that while they had access to the Fuehrer, they could not sway him.

Reusch's span of influence extended well beyond control of GHH's 80,000 employees; he was close to the chair of its Board, Karl Haniel and his cousin Kurt, both members of the wealthy family conglomerate that also owned the *Muenchner Neueste Nachrichten* (MNN), Germany's largest circulation newspaper. While Hitler realized the paper would not endorse him in his 1932 presidential bid, he had depended on Reusch and the Haniels to pressure MNN's editorial staff to at least stay neutral.[18] But even the concerted efforts of these powerful industrialists failed to convince the MNN. A year later when Hitler was successfully elected as Chancellor in January 1933, he moved expeditiously to control the press. Remembering his prior rebuff, the Fuehrer made the MNN one of his first targets. Outspoken anti-Nazis and Jews were thrown out and treated ruthlessly; they were quickly replaced so that the newspaper would reflect the Party line.

This move had unanticipated repercussions on the Schmid family. Willi Schmid was a replacement hire for a Jew who had been fired and began work at the MNN in July 1933 as a music reviewer and critic. Although Willi had excellent credentials for the position, his hiring was undoubtedly aided by his friendship with the Haniels and Reusch. [19] Willi hesitated to take the job, but the scarcity of work and the need to support his family took precedent. For someone who avoided politics and was not a backer of Hitler's, he now found himself in the lion's lair of Nazi domination of the press. Even his job description reflected the stretch of Nazi ideology: Willi's responsibilities included *Musikpolitik*, that is, the political aspects of music.

Musikpolitik, a bizarre new word, was yet another example of the *Gleichschaltung*, the Nazi control of all aspects of German society. Musical organizations had been grouped under the Reich Music Chamber (*Reichsmusikkammer*) to promote "good" German music. The aim, according to the Chamber's Nazi President, was to ". . . construct a culture of {Aryan} blood and . . . protect the culture from Jewish infection." [20] Just as so-labeled Jewish physics and Jewish mountaineering were being eschewed, so was Jewish music. Composers like Felix Mendelssohn, Arnold Schonberg and Kurt Weill—among others—were not to be played and Jewish performers were expelled from the Music Chamber. [21]

In the year after joining the MNN staff, Willi Schmid attempted to ignore these political trends. His continuing friendship with Reusch and the Haniels also served as a protective shield, or so he thought. When Willi was killed, it shook Reusch on both a personal and political level. Did he unwittingly contribute to the tragedy by helping raise campaign funds for Hitler's ascension? Had Hitler not achieved power, the Night of the Long Knives would not have occurred. It is highly dubious that Kate ever made this link, but Reusch—with his considerable political acumen—probably did, perhaps in part motivating his extraordinary helpfulness to Kate. She called the 68 year old Reusch, "the splendid old man," and they shared a tradition of getting together during the Christmas holidays. [22] It is no wonder Kate enjoyed the company of a man who ". . . loved social life, cultivated conversations, a good wine and a heavy cigar." [23]

In a world of overlapping circles, Reusch was also a friend of Spengler's, who played the role of an apocalyptic prophet to Germany's corporate captains, his most ardent fans, meeting regularly with them in a salon-like setting. Spengler and Reusch often got together prior or post to such meetings and Kate prided herself on the fact that she often joined the two powerhouses in their stimulating discussions. Once when I asked her if she missed having a college education, she replied with a twinkle: "I had Spengler, Reusch, Bumke and Vossler. Who needed more?" Obviously a world famous philosopher/historian, an industrial Titan, an internationally known psychiatrist and the president of one of Germany's greatest universities provided edification enough for a bright and charismatic student. Twenty-five years later, she still regarded men as her primary source of education, declaring to a considerably younger female friend: "It's important to be around men . . . they <u>know</u> so much."[24] The remark made me, a feminist, cringe but was in keeping with her times.

Reusch and Spengler, both early supporters of Hitler, became similarly disillusioned by him, particularly by his radical racial hypotheses. Reusch like other industrialists, ". . . served with Jews in the war, rubbed elbows with them in professional life, found them loyal and cooperative in cartels and interest group, had first—or second-hand experience with intermarriage, and generally come to recognize the absurdity of group vilification." [25] Reusch disparaged anti-Semitism. However, he and his colleagues realized that appealing to the Nazis on moral grounds had little currency; they argued on a more practical basis against dismissing Jews from key boards and corporate positions, suggesting such moves would not be good for the German economy.[26]

As Nazi policies became more restrictive, Reusch proved to be a master of evasion and deflection.[27] He put those skills to good use in the case of my mother, ushering her expertly through bureaucratic mazes and barriers. She had first sought his advice in 1934 when she argued for a stipend for her and the children; in her subsequent confrontations with government officials, Reusch had been an ongoing resource, at times coordinating efforts with Wiedemann. In 1936, after watershed meetings in Berlin that portended her departure from Germany, Kate again turned to Reusch who connected her with bank directors and other critical persons to ensure she could leave with her assets intact.

Meanwhile Hoerlin was pursuing his central role in 'the birth of an idea,' the construct that would allow him and Kate to emigrate. The ticket for departure was my father attaining a position in another country. With Kate as his future wife, an academic appointment in Germany was impossible. As in the case of Regener, Aryans married to Jews were disqualified from university posts. Despite a newly minted and hard earned doctoral degree, my father knew his chances of receiving an academic appointment abroad were minimal; the market was flooded by emigrants who were more senior physicists, mostly Jews. Accordingly, the only viable option was industry.

While Regener was at first disappointed that his star pupil was not pursuing the academic route, he more than understood the political realities and gave him outstanding recommendations.

My father concentrated his job search on Germany's largest corporation, I.G. Farben, ranked as the 4th biggest industry in the world. Headed by Karl Bosch, the 1931 Nobel Prize winner in chemistry, Farben at that point was esteemed as a progressive force in pre-war Germany. [28] In 1932, the Nazis had waged a nasty fight against Farben, considering it to be under the control of "money mighty Jews." [29] Unlike other major industries, Farben managed—as harassment grew—to retain Jews on their supervisory board as well as transfer a significant number of Jewish managers to subsidiaries in other countries. But its status under the Nazis mirrors that of other organizations: Farben's independence gradually eroded. By 1939 it was a key player in German rearmament, fully embroiled in the State machinery. [30] I.G. Farben, which initially had protected Jews, was guilty of using Jews as slave labor during the war. However, in 1936 the Nazis had yet taken it over it and its extensive portfolio of over 50 overseas subsidiaries was conducive to Hoerlin's intent to seek a job abroad.

One of its subsidiaries, Agfa films, seemed particularly suitable for my father. [31] Founded in 1873, Agfa had become the 2nd largest film manufacturing and production facility in the world. Its state-of-the-art film factory at Wolfen, an industrial site near Dessau in northern Germany, signified major competition for Kodak, both firms focusing on color film photography for popular use as well as cinematography. Hoerlin's involvement with photographic science and technology, pursued during his 1929 studies in Berlin, had been expanded by his experiences with high altitude photography in the Himalayas and enhanced by his doctoral research work. Furthermore, Agfa had always been Jewish-owned and operated and perhaps would be more facilitative towards helping an employee, involved with a Jewish woman, find a position in a satellite company in a country where anti-Semitism did not reign. When Hoerlin was offered a job by Agfa at their Wolfen plant, he took it.

Throughout these successive decisions, Hoerlin and Kate's letters continued to brim with passion. He loved untangling the curls of her thick black hair, she loved running her fingers through his straight fine blond hair;

he spoke of the lightness in her step, she spoke of the touch of his gentle hands; he restored her, she enriched him. Their ardor fused with a mutual resolve, cast in iron, to start a new life together. They had been unyielding in their support of one other in their respective struggles: Kate dealing with her personal loss and battles with Hitler's regime and, Hoerlin striving toward his doctorate and fighting against nazification of mountaineering. These were distinct, and not necessarily comparable challenges, but both required tremendous strength and energy. But now, shifting their focus, individual pursuits were supplanted by a combined goal. As Hoerlin commented, "Together we have come a considerable distance. I believe we have made headway, not gone in circles; what could be more wonderful to wish for than that this path goes on for us both without end. "[32] The path forward led to a life together and negotiating it would require ingenuity and, as acknowledged by Kate, a strong dose of perseverance: "I want my sights to be firmly fixed on our goals and not be distracted by anything." [33]

Since the spring of 1935, they referred to each other as husband and wife but hopes of marriage had been dashed by the passage of the Nuremberg Laws in September. In her typically independent manner, Kate rejected honoring such absurd laws and created her own: "I stand totally under the law of love for the four of you." My father answered, "Beloved, you could not write me anything more beautiful than this sentence. I am indescribably happy about it." [34] Kate had warned Hoerlin repeatedly that marrying her meant fundamental changes in his life: the evident one of being a father to the three children, the more subtle one of reconciling his world of relative quietude and solitude to her emotional needs and intensely social persona, and—the most blatant one—leaving Germany. It required leaving his widowed mother, physics colleagues and mountain climbing buddies. The familiar would be traded for the unknown. Hoerlin made abundantly clear to Kate his willingness to shed more conventional routes, both in his personal and professional proclivities. He had already explored other countries and other continents—admittedly from the perspective of their highest peaks—but he was open to new adventures.

Nonetheless, departing from one's homeland can never be an easy task, although the specter of Hitler made it considerably less wrenching. Hoerlin knew that living freely with Kate was synonymous with fleeing the Third Reich. Pointedly, Kate had written him about the Duke of Windsor abdicating the British throne because of his love for an American divorcee: "That made me pensive and preoccupied me very much—admittedly not only because of the romantic and chivalrous overtones, but also because of the unbending laws, the reality, that stands behind this event." [35] My mother made the association although my father was certainly neither a King nor fervently pro-Hitler like the Duke. She and Hoerlin were also in a situation where laws, in their case the Nuremberg laws, and certain realities, in their case the advent of National Socialism, dictated their future.

The hardest part for Kate was saying goodbye to friends and musical connections. And although she was leaning toward moving to Salzburg, the city of Mozart (her favorite composer), she would be leaving a city that was at the center of classical music. With three major orchestras and numerous chamber groups, Munich was where new composers premiered their works and where the three B's, Bach, Beethoven and Brahms, were daily fare. Almost everybody who was anybody in the world of musical performance came and concerts were routinely sold out. Some of the greatest cellists, pianists and quartets, Pablo Casals, Rudolf Serkin, the Budapest String Quartet played there often. All of them were friends of Kate's. However, that life was disappearing from Munich: Casals refused to play in a fascist country and Serkin and the Budapest Quarter had emigrated to America.

While many musicians fled as a matter of conscience or because of persecution, others stayed, seeking an accommodation that would allow them to continue their art. Germany's most visible musician and cultural icon, the conductor Wilhelm Furtwaengler of the Berlin Philharmonic refused to become a Nazi, much to the embarrassment of the Party, and never gave the Hitler salute. His allegiance was to classical greats such as Beethoven as well as contemporary composers such as Hindemith, labeled as degenerate by the Nazis. In the beginning years of National Socialism, he viewed the political situation as transitory and was convinced that music, as an inspiration for moral good, was a compelling counterforce. This naïve belief, as time went by, became increasingly untenable to maintain.

Furtwaengler too was a friend of my mother's. When she dined with the fifty year old craggily handsome, albeit balding, conductor in 1935, he told her he was considering leaving Germany to take the helm of the New York Philharmonic. She had written my father about their late evening: "Yesterday evening with Furtwaengler was very lovely, full of connections." Falling into the recurring stereotype of musicians not being particularly smart, although creative, as if the two traits were mutually exclusive, Kate added: "He is so intelligent that one can hardly consider it possible that in spite of this he is such a good musician." [36]

A few days after Kate and Furtwaengler's dinner, the maestro sent his chauffeur to bring my mother along with Duscha to spend the afternoon with him and his mistress, Frau Hutchinson and their 13 year old child, Iva. A legendary philanderer, the conductor had at least 5 illegitimate children [37]; by 1931, his first marriage had dissolved but his ongoing relationship with Hutchinson continued, although that too—worn down by his long absences—was now coming to an end. While the two young girls played in the garden, Kate found herself a witness to the break-up as she relayed to Hoerlin: "I had difficulty staying with the conversation, particularly since it revolved around very personal things about these two people . . . many difficulties have ensued and the relationship is over. For that reason, he is departing. I felt awkward about {being part of} this intense intimacy and was relieved when the conversation turned toward politics . . ." [38] My mother's underlining of "for that reason" reflected her incredulity that Furtwaengler may be departing Germany because of a failed romance. In any case the Nazis aborted the New York Philharmonic prospect by portraying the conductor as dedicated party member. [39] Furtwaengler remained in his beloved homeland throughout the war, at times putting himself under enormous personal risk in continuing confrontations with the fascist regime, and saving the lives of many Jewish musicians.

As entangled as her emotions about leaving Germany were, Kate's predominant response was one of relief to no longer be under the yoke of oppression. In answer to Hoerlin's concerns of whether she was happy, she replied: "Should I say, that I am happy? That is such a weak word for my liberation, you dear man." [40] Things were in full motion. Kate and the children were definitely moving to Austria. Reusch had helped secure the transfer of my mother's assets, Wiedemann assured the continuation of the stipends for her and the children. Reusch and Wiedemann had worked together to make sure she could get out of her lease without a penalty. My mother marveled at the speed of the emigration preparations: "Everything proceeds blow by blow—almost too quickly! Today the official certification from the Reich's Chancellery already arrived, which I asked Wiedemann for. It was as expected: when I referred to these documents at the rental office, I was immediately released from my rental agreement until October 1938 and my termination accepted for March 1. So that also was settled." [41]

With thorny decisions made and logistical hurdles resolved, Kate concentrated on the children and the advent of Christmas. "It must be festive," she intoned to Hoerlin. Life carried on and Kate was never a by-stander: she put up the crèche, bought a wreath and tree, and carefully selected presents. Hoerlin would come for the holidays and they would be family again. He would also be helping his mother move from Schwaebisch Hall, now that the store and house had finally been sold. The prospect of Maria Hoerlin being alone was softened with her plan to move back to her extended family in Ludwigsburg, known for its magnificent Baroque palace, near Stuttgart. In her unselfish way, she never made her son feel guilty about his inevitable departure from Germany. On the contrary, she encouraged her son's romance with Kate, in spite of the complications and implications of my mother's background. "Mutter" Hoerlin had never seen Hermannle in love before and was happy for him.

Christmas was followed by planning a farewell party for Kate, a celebration of both the past and the future. The formula was failsafe: there should be live music, dear friends and good food. Members of Willi Schmid's former Viol Quintet would play, along with a renowned harpsichordist. [42] Kate made a guest list of thirty dear friends.[43] Mouthwatering aromas floated through the Munich apartment. Kate, an outstanding chef herself, oversaw the cooking, making sure everything was properly flavored and prepared: the veal goulash heavy with paprika; boiled potatoes; green beans with almonds; and flourless walnut cake—a nod to her mother's Passover dessert. Maia, the relatively new domestic helper who would follow the Schmids to Salzburg, was nervous with excitement but Anna, the cook, had things under control. On February 20, 1937, amidst neatly piled moving boxes, good conversation and wine flowed. The gala was exactly as Kate hoped. With Hoerlin at her side, she said her goodbyes.

The two of them had witnessed how Nazism had collided with not only their lives, but the lives of those around them. Its effect on culture, science, society and even recreation and sports was unrelenting. Everyone was touched: some friends seduced by Hitler—at least for awhile, others vehemently opposed him, and still others tried in vain to dismiss him. Throughout the turmoil, Kate and Hoerlin retained their steadfast optimism and enduring love. Their eyes fixed on the future, a future described by Kate as "... Once there will be a time when it will be so calm that we can hear the wind and gaze at the clouds and stars, and when I will impart nothing new to you, only the much treasured old." [44]

Chapter 11

TOGETHER BUT APART

Kate and Hoerlin, in their quest to be together, had to live further apart. She was moving south, he to the north and yet they were traveling to the same ultimate destination. The logistics of seeing one another would be considerable. To get from Dessau to Salzburg meant a train trip of altogether 12 hours travel time, with time in between for two changeovers. Kate had tried to comfort Hoerlin, "I am not leaving you, I am coming to you." [1] But as the reality hovered closer, she wrote: "The separation from you seems to me, very often and always more often, to be unbearable. But the circumstances around us are guilty of this rift. I see you always before me . . ." [2]

Moving for Kate did not go smoothly. Hedi was diagnosed with severe rheumatic fever a few days before departure. Tremors, high fever, inflamed joints and a badly swollen tongue descended on her with a vengeance. The four year old was hospitalized, under medical orders to follow a strict regime of complete bed rest and quiet. Doctors recommended keeping her there until she recovered, strongly advising against any traveling for the gravely ill child, although Salzburg was only 142 kilometers (about 86 miles) from Munich, a distance covered in two and ½ hours by automobile and even less by train. It is hard to assess whether mother or child was more traumatized by the separation. For Hedi to first lose her father and then have her mother and siblings seemingly disappear, must have been agonizing.

On March 1, 1937, Kate set out from Munich to Salzburg in her new, spiffy Steyr car during a fierce snowstorm. In the tiny villages she and the two older children passed through, cars were still a rarity and a woman driver almost unheard of, especially one driving in hazardous conditions. As the car slid up and down icy roads, more than one local farmer bestowed blessings on the passengers, praying for their safety. Ritualistic signs of the Cross must have been effective because by the time the stressed travelers reached Salzburg the weather had cleared. Freshly fallen snow and bright sunshine made the romantic town, with one of Europe's largest medieval castles overlooking its Baroque spires, sparkle magically.

The children were further enchanted upon entering their lovely new apartment in *Schloss Freisaal,* a castle-like villa surrounded by gardens and a moat. Kate, who always distilled joy from the small pleasures of life, celebrated the comparatively country-like setting where she could hang her laundry outside: "... now {the wash} will smell like air and wind and sun, as you have wished for years for me," she exulted to Hoerlin. "You will certainly shake your head at what I consider important things to tell you," she continued, "but they make me so happy . . . the mountains are so close one can touch them, the air warm and soft—there is no city here, no walls . . ."[3] Maybe at last she had found sanctuary from fear and trembling, a haven of quietude and beauty.

Schloss (castle) Freisaal in Salzburg,
where the Schmids lived after leaving Germany.

The scene in Salzburg could not have contrasted more than from Dessau in north Germany, 20 kilometers (12 miles) from the Agfa plant where

Hoerlin reported for work. Instead of elegant steeples and snow-covered Alps on the horizon, he looked out on spewing factory chimneys and a harsh industrial wasteland. The stench of a nearby sugar-refining factory permeated the small room he rented. His aversion to the area was shared by Kate after she traveled there: "It is a good thing I visited Dessau to understand more why you cannot breathe there for long," she stated, and confirming their impression, added: "Wiedemann is familiar with it and is of the same opinion: Dessau is the worst and most dreadful place in Germany." [4] Its distinction as the birthplace of Moses Mendelssohn (1729) and of the Bauhaus style (1925) was not enough to ingratiate the city to Kate, Wiedemann or the young physicist. Hoerlin's surroundings had always been important to him and, other than when on mountain climbing ventures, he had lived in places overlooking gardens and trees with views of hills in the distance. He missed the gently rolling landscape of the Swabian hills around Schwaebisch Hall and Stuttgart. The highest elevation around Dessau seemed to be the Scherbelberg, a 110 meters high (360 feet) former rubbish dump. Although cities in other similarly flat landscapes boasted a branch of the *Alpenverein*, Dessau was one of the few locations devoid of one, eliminating any prospect for companionship with other climbers or hikers.

The move coincided with the end of Pallas' serious involvement with German mountaineering. The venerable Verein was in shambles, no longer able to withstand the assaults of National Socialism and finally succumbing to *Gleichschaltung's* wrecking ball. After years of trying to wield influence within the organization, Hoerlin resigned from its Executive Committee. And perhaps symbolic of the demise of German mountaineering, another expedition to Nanga Parbat ended in disaster. The 1937 expedition, again very political, was promoted by the unrelenting Paul Bauer, by now the czar of German mountaineering, and Fritz Bechtold. Finally, after all the battles with the *Alpenverein*, Bauer and Bechtold had crafted their own expedition, skirting the issue of Verein support by attaining funding through the Reich's Sports Minister. For somewhat confusing reasons, neither Bauer nor Bechtold were part of the expedition but they had carefully picked its members, choosing the like-minded Karl Wien to lead it. This time, for sure, Germany would reign victorious over a 8000er. Instead, the 1937 Expedition became an even greater calamity than the 1934 one, claiming the most lives ever lost—to this day—in the history of Himalayan mountaineering. [5] As they slept, sixteen men—seven German mountaineers and nine sherpas—were completely buried by a huge avalanche that hit Camp IV on June 15th. Among the casualties was Wien, who had stated to Bauer in 1935 that Hoerlin should "disappear." Now it was he who had disappeared under mounds of snow and ice.

Aghast and disbelieving about the fate of their friends, Bauer and Bechtold left Munich immediately on a rescue mission. Enlisting the help of English air forces based in Lahore, the two Germans organized digging through the 15 acre avalanche field, a laborious process that did not yield results until July 12th when shovels hit two tents under eight feet of the solid mass. [6] Five frozen bodies were recovered, their facial expressions showing no indications of impending doom; their wristwatches had stopped at 12:10 a.m. After this grim sight, the search desisted and—in accordance with Tibetan-Buddhist customs—the other climbers were left undisturbed in their final resting place.[7]

Erwin Schneider, justifiably embittered about being banned from the Himalayas by Bauer et al, was less than charitable about the tragedy in a letter to Hoerlin: "Those who are religiously inclined could interpret it as poetic justice." [8] Schneider, who knew the mountain well, could not imagine why Camp IV had been established in a direct line of high avalanche activity. "In any case," he said, "a record is accordingly broken, having mountain climbers wiped out 100% certainly never happened before." [9] At least the climbers had not died in the ghastly manner of 1934, when expedition members perished, one by one, over a period of eight or nine days. But the disasters were a haunting affirmation of my father's viewpoint that extreme mountaineering and the responsibilities of being a family man were not compatible. One of the 1937 deceased was the father of two young children; Hoerlin was soon to be the father of three.

In Dessau, Hoerlin was not diverted from his work by mountains or alpine politics. There was rarely respite from his job in order to socialize with friends or even see Kate, given that the trip between Dessau and Salzburg took the better part of a day. Uninterrupted, he toiled away, knowing full well that to be transferred by Agfa/I.G. Farben to another country, it was crucial for him to be a valued employee. In 1937 the major challenge for the 11,000 employees of Agfa was vying with America's Kodak in trying to dominate international film manufacturing and production. The strong competitive environment, with the concurrent exhilarating and draining pressures, ignited many research initiatives. [10]

When Kate visited Hoerlin in June, she found him exhausted by his job and depressed by the Dessau environs. Always a woman of action, Kate hurriedly set up a meeting with Wiedemann in Berlin, stopping to see him on her way back to Salzburg. Her hope was that the Adjutant could help Hoerlin transfer to another position, preferably out of the country. Trying to suppress her excitement, she reported to Hoerlin: "I just returned from the Reich Chancellery. Wiedemann made himself available immediately when I called . . . then I sat down with him . . . and as I showed him photos of Freisaal and one of me also . . . he asked if he was allowed to keep it, it was so lovely and dear, and he put it in his wallet and was very pleased. And then he asked about you. At last I told him your name and that I loved you and was committed to you, told him about I.G. Farben and that one cannot live in Dessau. And after he listened to me for a long time and in exact detail, he wants to speak with you this Saturday between 11 and 12 o'clock. I should come along since he wants to deliberate with us. I write you this calmly, but my heart shakes with joy about this man and that you will be meeting with him and perhaps a solution will be found." [11]

The scenario borders on the surreal. In the middle of 1937, my Jewish mother is meeting in the headquarters of the Third Reich with Hitler's top personal aide, who tucks Kate's photo in his wallet and offers to scheme with her and her future husband on how they could leave Germany. Without a doubt, Wiedemann—described as someone who ". . . missed no opportunity to pay court to a beautiful woman" [12]—was captivated by my mother's charms but she must have kindled in him a desire to redress the wrongs inflicted on her. At least in regard to "Frau Doktor"—as Kate was formally addressed by him—he seemed motivated by a basic sense of decency. In the arcane machinations of pre-war Germany, Wiedemann's deeds are among the most curious. A married father of three, he was having an affair with a divorced Jewish woman, Princess Stephanie von Hohenlohe. Hitler's trusted aide, in the top echelons of the Third Reich, was breaking the very laws—the Nuremberg Laws—imposed by the Fuehrer. The travesty had another bizarre twist: Hitler, although he knew of the princess' Jewish roots, played a critical role in awarding her the Honorary Cross of the German Red Cross in 1937, followed in 1938 by the Nazi party's Gold Medal of Honor. Apparently the definition of a dictator included the right to be inconsistent. The firewall erected by the Third Reich between Aryans and non-Aryans was sometimes more porous than it was thought to be.

The princess was based in England, working tirelessly to generate favor in the British press for Hitler's government. Wiedemann, on frequent visits to London, made no effort to disguise his relationship with her, causing Stephanie's maid to complain in her diary, "She always sleeps with Captain Wiedemann now . . ."[13] He was one in a string of her scandalous liaisons [14] leading British society to make a play on her last name, Hohenlohe, disparagingly calling her "that high and low woman." The Fuehrer's high profile adjutant risked the prospect of being further frowned upon by assisting Kate and Hoerlin. However, as Hitler's former superior during WWI and a recipient of expensive gifts—including a Mercedes—bestowed by the Fuehrer, Wiedemann had every reason to feel confident and secure. Nevertheless, he cautioned Kate and Hoerlin not to write each other sensitive information, especially regarding his involvement with them; their letters, sometimes opened by authorities, became even more coded.

Kate had set in motion a meeting between Wiedemann and Hoerlin but did not stay for it, wanting to return home as soon as possible. She was looking forward to a relaxing summer with the children after what had been a physically and emotionally taxing winter and spring. Hedi's illness had cast a long shadow over the Salzburg move. Kate's visits to her sick child had been sporadic, since the Munich doctors insisted that Hedi could become overly excited by her mother's presence, thereby hindering recovery. At last, after three months of hospitalization, Hedi was given permission to rejoin the family in Austria. Kate's anxieties about Hedi's state of health were finally relieved, replaced by everyone's jubilation about her recovery. Hedi was quickly brought back into the family fold and their new life in Salzburg. Her siblings enthusiastically introduced their little sister to the apartment in the grand villa, its enchanting garden filled with flowering fruit trees, and the surrounding moat where they sailed boats for her.

Duscha and Thomi had adjusted well to the move. Thomi's prior fears about school had previously prompted Kate to seek Bumke's professional opinion about the boy. The eminent psychiatrist allayed her concerns: ". . . after he observed {Thomi) for awhile, he told me everything was fine, as long as I had close contact with him, that was the most important thing."[15]

Now that Thomi was feeling more secure, he routinely rode his bike to school, where he was regarded as clever and highly verbal. He also loved the easy access to the outdoors, earning the admiration of his mother for his

**"The three Schmid children in Salzburg.
From left to right: Duscha, Thomi and Hedi.**

climbing skills: "Thomi is first rate on the mountain, better than Duscha." [16] Duscha, less intrigued by sports activities, relished walking with her mother across wildflower meadows, admiring and identifying the gifts of nature, or taking long swims in nearby lakes. Rounding out the family was Hedi, at last released from the confines of illness and institutionalization, an exuberant child, who proclaimed herself "I am the wild sow" (*"Ich bin die wild Sau"*). She was highly spirited, with no lingering effects from the rheumatic fever.

Kate had settled into a more pastoral and less hectic existence: "Every day is different and always surprising . . . Time proceeds so differently here than in the city, the passing of a day depends much more on weather conditions than the hours of a clock." [17] Hoerlin, happier visiting her in the embrace of

Salzburg's hills and mountains than in Munich's hectic streets, was overjoyed that the family had taken so well to their new home. On his visits, he often led them on skiing excursions, earning the feigned despair of my mother: "Oh you, you with three pairs of skis slung over your shoulder, what have you started with us??!" [18] He not only carried everyone's skis, but as an experienced skier offered pointers. Hoerlin also encouraged their hiking, very much engrained in the Salzburg ethos as well as his own. My mother, having climbed a nearby mountain one summer day with the children, acknowledged this tie to him by exclaiming: "We were so happy, were alone up there, all around us the beautiful, beautiful world—and we lay in the summer wind, smelled the thyme, and the summit carried us often to you."[19]

Shortly thereafter Kate told Hedi, Duscha and Thomi of her love for Hoerlin and their plans to marry. First she spoke with Duscha, her small confidante who had comforted her many a day and night after the loss of Willi. The sensitive and perceptive young girl understood that life could be blessed with more than one great love. All the children responded enthusiastically to the idea of "Uncle" Hoerlin becoming a permanent fixture in the family and Kate closed a letter to him conveying, "From the children, dearest greetings and their endless joy about you. They whoop with joy . . ."[20]

Kate's adjustment to Salzburg was enhanced by a steady stream of loyal friends visiting from Germany. Bumke, acting like a loving guardian, came frequently, as did Reusch, and the Garmisch-Partenkirchen relatives. Life was different, but the continuity held. The most disrupting factor was her separation from Hoerlin. They each spent untold time and energy plotting how they could see one another at any opportunity—not only in Salzburg and Dessau, but also in Berlin or Munich. No month passed without their meeting. In June 1937, on the eve of Willi Schmid's death, Kate wrote Hoerlin: "It has been three years since you, after June 30th, entered our house—death and birth lie so close to one another. And now after three years I will follow your love, wherever it calls." [21] Kate was committed and Hoerlin determined, but where to go was still an unsolved conundrum. As Hoerlin confessed, "Yesterday I sat for hours over a letter, and could not put pen to paper, because I did not see where our future goes, but I know that it will move forward."[22]

In the fall of 1937, Hoerlin began to make inquiries about transferring to another country to his immediate superior, Dr. Fritz Gajewski, director of *Agfa's* Wolfen factory since 1930. Gajewski's record of protecting Jewish scientists as well as those married to Jews had earned him the reputation of coddling a "friendly Jewish policy." [23] Jews were still under his employ and he had helped transfer others to IG Farben subsidiaries in the United Kingdom, the United States, India, South America, Egypt and Austria. Gajewski joined the Nazi party in 1933, but it seems to have been done more as ". . . a matter of practicality than conviction." [24] In private meetings in September and October, Hoerlin described his exact circumstances to the young Herr Direktor: his intent to marry someone of Jewish extraction, their desire to live outside of Germany, and his request for a transfer. "Gajewski asked me a lot," my father reported, "obviously trying to help, not only in regard to work but also on a personal and human level. He was friendlier and closer than the first time we met. They {i.e. *Agfa*} would most prefer to have me stay here, because they need me (on the one hand, this acknowledgement pleases me very much of course). In summary though it is difficult now to find something suitable, corresponding to my capabilities. He added however, that he would look around further."[25]

One of the things my father was loath to do throughout his life was to ask for special favors or treatment that was out of the ordinary. My mother was quite the opposite; she felt exceptional and considered it her due that people would respond to her accordingly. When my father met with Gajewski, he abandoned his usual reticence in asking for help, spurred by the urgency of finding a way to live with Kate. Although he made headway in the meeting with Gajewski, it was not enough to satisfy my mother. In typical fashion, she aspired for more immediate and concrete results. Kate quickly contacted Wiedemann again, asking him to write a letter of support for Hoerlin to Gajewski and coyly demurring to Wiedemann's communication skills, ". . . I certainly do not need to say what you write . . . that you know and can do 1000 times better than I . . ."[26]

The adjutant, who usually tended to Kate's entreaties promptly, took a few days before responding. He was actually near her home in Salzburg, a short train ride away in Obersalzberg, visiting Hitler's private mountainside retreat. Obersalzberg had become a holiday spot for several Nazi officials; Wiedemann, while vacationing there in August 1937, had visited Kate and her children at the *Freisaal* apartment when he came to attend a Salzburg Festival performance of "Don Giovanni." [27] This opera buffa of amorous conquests could have cast Wiedemann in the central role, given his reputation as a rake. Vocal talent, however, was not part of his resume. In any case, with Kate he continued to be on best behavior and for the first time was introduced to the family he played such a key role in protecting. Although still imposing while out of uniform, Wiedemann was regarded by the children as yet another amiable person who crossed the Freisaal doorway. They were more interested in what the tall visitor brought: a box of famous Mozart Kugeln, delicious balls of marzipan, nougat and chocolate. Long after the delicacies were devoured, Kate wrote Wiedemann: "The door to Freisaal is always open for you and I greet you with gratitude filled with trust." [28]

In October 1937, Wiedemann had again come to Obersalzberg but for reasons other than vacation. He, along with Princess Stephanie von Hohenlohe, had made arrangements for the Duke and Duchess of Windsor to travel through Germany on a trip funded by the Third Reich. [29] Stephanie had known Wally Simpson when she was a commoner; they lived in the same apartment building in London and shared an early approbation for Hitler. Now that Wally was married to the Duke, she and he were anxious to travel to Germany, where their romance had enthralled the population and they were treated regally, in stark contrast to the humiliations they experienced in England. The couple met the Fuehrer in Obersalzberg at his chalet-like residence, the *Berghof*, which he had purchased with proceeds from his 1925 signature book, "Mein Kampf." [30] Beautifully situated and lavishly decorated, it was featured in the British magazine, *House and Garden,31* and Hitler often entertained important figures and foreign dignitaries there. On October 22, Wiedemann had picked up the ducal pair at the nearby train station in Berchtesgaden and brought them to the *Berghof,* where the Fuehrer descended the villa's steps to warmly greet them. For lunch they consumed an array of vegetarian dishes preferred by their host, who disparaged the cruelty of slaughtering animals for meat consumption. As usual, Hitler's mistress Eva Braun was out of sight and not invited to join the guests. [32] This quasi-royal occasion delayed Wiedemann's subsequent letter to Gajewski.

Although Kate trusted Hoerlin completely, she sought reassurances from him that his "birth of an idea", the strategy to emigrate formulated two years ago, was still realistic. My father, who tolerated issues of time and process better than she, asked for her forbearance: "It is difficult, enormously difficult, for you to sit around the next months ostensibly idle. I beg you fervently to continue to love me and have faith in me." [33] Over the fall of 1937, he persisted in meeting with Gajewski but the liberal leaning director who had earlier placed Jews out of harm's way was now under Gestapo scrutiny. Increased pressures from the party and the state endangered his position and he felt the need to proceed carefully.[34] Now even Hoerlin's patience was being tested. Dessau grew even more desolate as the days grew shorter. He couldn't wait to be in Salzburg over Christmas vacation.

Meanwhile, Kate and the children were settling into life in Salzburg, which felt sheltered compared to Munich. But it was not "home," without Hoerlin there. Kate wrote him about this feeling: ". . . all of our happiness finds its home in you . . . so tranquil, so very blessed are the days for me, that I know for sure it cannot last this way, but it is a gift to me in order to summon up strength for the time when I need it." [35] Kate's evenings were often busy; she glided effortlessly into the heart of Salzburg's social life, which tended to overlap with the town's many musical offerings. Several times she was invited to recitals at the villa of Baron von Trapp, the head of the legendary Trapp Family Singers featured in "The Sound of Music." Soon, she befriended the family. Kate's view of the ex-nun, Maria, did not fit into the heavily fictionalized story line; she regarded Maria as somewhat of a clever opportunist, while the Baron was a "fine gentleman" whose anti-Nazi convictions resonated to Kate. Frequent invitations to their lovely estate were extended to Kate as well as the Schmid children, who played happily on the expansive grounds with the Trapp children.

In early December, Kate had an unexpected thrill. A letter had come from the great cellist, Pablo Casals, inviting her to come to Vienna, where he was performing on December 4 and 5th. Kate had met the world famous cellist when she was 22 and the friendship lasted throughout their lives. Born in Spain, Casals was a resolute opponent of fascism in all forms and changed his personal and professional life because of Franco's dictatorial regime. After the Spanish Civil War, he left Spain and lived in self-imposed exile in a small village in France—vowing never to play again in Spain until democracy was restored, a vow he kept. Kate admired the cellist's principled choices and regarded him as "one of the few men who never made a compromise." [36] Of course she was also in awe of his phenomenal playing. She described the concert to Hoerlin: ". . . heavenly. Furtwaengler sat next to me—he also felt it so, as a 'transfigured sound.' I was with Casals for several hours—he possesses a wonderful sensitivity and a deep tenderness that emanates from infinite goodness."[37]

By the time Hoerlin arrived in Salzburg for the holidays, he wondered whether Kate could be lured out of a picture perfect world. Christmas was a particularly appealing time in the old town: smells of delicious cooking and strains of music wafted from every house, church bells rang continuously, and people greeted each other with extra cheer. *Freisaal* was a beehive of activity, the children dancing from room to room with excitement. Maia, by now an indispensable part of the family, had been busy for weeks, helping Kate bake endless batches of Christmas cookies, preparing for Advent Sunday parties, and making the apartment glow with anticipation. Finally, when Christmas Eve came, Kate and Hoerlin lit the candles on the tree—yet unseen by Hedi, Duscha and Thomi—and rang a small bell to summon them. Appreciative gasps and observations that the tree was <u>much</u> more beautiful than previous years echoed around the tree, its balsam branches weighed down by hand-crafted ornaments and apples, allowing the candle flames to burn more safely.

The contrast of family life in Salzburg to Dessau, where Hoerlin led a plain and monastic life, was a distressing reminder to my father that he and Kate were still not living together, much less in the same country. And so far, there were no indications things could change soon. He felt discouraged and appeared, in the eyes of a friend of Kate's ". . . like he is bearing a great deal."[38] Kate worried about Hoerlin, who looked drawn and pale. He was working hard but any movement toward the future seemed to have frozen in place with the onset of winter. Hoerlin had made a promise to himself and given Kate his word that he would find a way to leave Germany. Was he failing both of them? He never wanted to cause her undue alarm, but wondered if he should tell her the plan he had so meticulously crafted was perhaps for naught.

Suddenly, with the ringing in of the new year, a glimmer of sunshine appeared. On January 8th, 1938, Hoerlin met with Wiedemann, who encouraged him to pursue a possibility in America. In follow up to their lengthy discussion, Hoerlin had written the adjutant a detailed letter first articulating the situation, then sharing his frustrations and finally thanking him for his advice: "I had not hoped for a quick solution but the minor progress since October has caused me considerable worry. Only one job comes up for consideration—at the film factory's sister firm in the U.S.A., Agfa Ansco in Binghampton (sic). However, Dr. Gajewski advised against it, because he believed that I would not be content to live in this culturally impoverished land. On the basis of our discussion yesterday I now want to more seriously look at Binghampton and take the necessary steps to do so immediately." [39] Wiedemann must have felt differently about the United States than Gajewski. Perhaps it would not be such a bad place after all. And what could be more "culturally impoverished" than Dessau?

Hoerlin, hugely relieved that he had not let Kate down with empty promises, dashed off a special delivery letter suggesting they meet in Munich as soon as possible. The Christmas holidays had been wonderful, but Kate and Hoerlin had had no private time together, to talk about their future, to find comfort in a long embrace. That changed in Munich: "Something happened last night," my mother wrote. "I can't even describe it, but I know that it is of utmost importance to our future. What an evening that was, full of you, of us and our life. I lay your hands on my eyes—what longs for you in me is boundless. And my will is there. You were so wonderful yesterday in the strength of your belief." [40] Meeting in Munich allowed them to take a deep breath and discuss the opportunity in the United States. Hoerlin was ready to explore it further and Kate was too. But not before they had exhausted all other options.

The next day Kate met with Paul Reusch. In the year that she had moved to Austria, she had seen Reusch several times, both in Salzburg and Munich. However, she had never discussed Hoerlin with him. Finally, she did: "Then I told him your name . . . and he said he had known about you for weeks and had received very good, very gratifying information from Stuttgart und IG Farben. He knew exactly about you—that's Reusch for you!!! And he gave us his blessing with deep and unconditional joy." [41] While Hoerlin was complimented by Reusch's comments, he also found it unsettling that he and Kate were so exposed. How Reusch knew so much was probably indicative of the extent of surveillance in the Third Reich. In any case, Reusch offered to consult with Wiedemann, whom he had collaborated with previously about Kate's stipend.

Perhaps it was a February thaw, but things finally seemed to be stirring. Everyone was springing into action, including Gajewski. Toward the end of February, *Agfa's* director opened up another prospect: a position in India. [42] Hoerlin again met with Wiedemann, whose advice he depended on as much as Kate did. There were pros and cons to both America and India. The amount of bureaucratic red tape to be negotiated for emigrating to either country was formidable. But hopes were riding high.

On the morning of March 12, 1938, life again changed radically for Kate and unavoidably for Hoerlin as well. The German army marched, unopposed, into Austria. Cheering crowds threw flowers in their path, swastika flags waved from balconies and Nazi salutes pierced the air. A few days later, Hitler himself was welcomed by the ringing of all church bells. For Kate, the difference between living in Germany and Austria was erased. The Nuremberg Laws crossed the border as quickly as the Nazi troops. Jews were now considered fair game, subjected to the same kind of degradations suffered in Germany. In a country that Kate had experienced as hospitable and friendly, she and the children were again under the menacing cloud of fascism.

Chapter 12

UNDER WINGS OF EAGLES

Over the days following the Anschluss, Jews were maligned and dehumanized. The depth of Austrian anti-Semitism stooped to new lows, literally and figuratively: on a Sabbath day in April 1938, Jews were forced by the Nazis to eat grass like livestock on the lawn of one of Vienna's amusement parks. [1] In this toxic environment, incidents against half Jews also increased. The fear and trembling that Kate suffered from in Germany now had an Austrian iteration. Although to all appearances, Kate and the children were observant Catholics, the threat loomed of being exposed as even part Jewish. Friends from Munich and the Schmids from Garmisch Partenkirchen converged at Freisaal, wanting to form a loving shield around the small family. As always, Bumke—a fatherly figure 22 years Kate's elder—was at her side. His presence was especially reassuring to her, given his standing as an eminent psychiatrist and although politically opposite, the brother of one of Hitler's highest appointees, the equivalent of a Chief Justice the Supreme Court. [2] In addition, Kate continued to be under the protective wings of Hitler's Adjutant Wiedemann and the powerful industrialist Reusch.

Six months before the Anschluss, Kate had written Hoerlin: "... I live for the future and I believe it is not too distant ..." [3] The Anschluss exerted even more pressure on them to emigrate ... and emigrate soon. Two serious options for a job abroad had at last surfaced. One was in India, a country that fascinated my father since he ventured there on the 1930 International Himalayan Expedition. My mother, gamely admitting she knew nothing about "this strange land and its people," nevertheless was open to it: "You must tell me all about it, you beloved man. I will listen to you and soon I'll understand—oh you, how old and new reaching consensus is {for us}." [4] The other option was in America.

As my mother and father looked further into going to India versus the United States, the choice became unambiguous. India was in a state of transition, with Gandhi's Civil Disobedience movement shaking up British rule. My father had witnessed the simmering unrest in the population when he traveled through the crown colony on his way to Kanchenjunga. By 1938, political turmoil was extensive and the country's stability uncertain; life in the Raj for German refugees could be rocky. In America, refugees seemed welcome. Kate had heard positive reports from European musicians who had gone on tour or immigrated there. [5] Kate's half-brother, Fredi, who settled with his family on Long Island in 1936, had found the country receptive. In addition, she had two dear friends from Germany living in the United States: Eva Reifenberg, married to the celebrated cellist Emanuel Feuermann and Trude Wenzel Pratt, married to a socially prominent New Yorker who championed liberal causes. The general reputation of the United States as a bastion of democracy had significant allure to both my parents. And equally relevant, American physics was gaining momentum as a major player on the international scene, an attractive development to Hoerlin particularly since he had been witnessing the demise of Germany's scientific eminence.

Hoerlin began to pursue vigorously the position with *Agfa*/Ansco that Gajewski, the head of *Agfa's* Wolfen plant, had mentioned previously to him. If Hoerlin had a contract with *Agfa*/Ansco, his entry to America would almost be guaranteed in spite of quotas and the press of refugees. On the other hand, if Kate, whose only visible means of support was a government stipend, attempted to emigrate on her own with the children, the chances of success were between slim and none. One issue was whether Germany would allow her leave; the other was whether America would let her come. In either case, Kate needed—and wished—to be Mrs. Herman Hoerlin. A trifecta of interrelated goals was on the agenda: a job abroad, marriage and emigration.

Ongoing efforts to achieve all three goals were accelerated by the Anschluss. In early March both Kate and Hoerlin had each written to Wiedemann, declaring their intent to marry and formally asking for special dispensation from the stranglehold of the Nuremberg Laws. [6] Following protocol, Wiedemann referred the query to the deputy health minister, Dr. Kurt Blome, who was the arbiter on such questions. [7] My father subsequently wrote Blome asking that an exception be made to the Nuremberg Laws.[8] With bureaucratic efficiency, the medical expert informed my father promptly that it was necessary to also make the request to the German Consul in Salzburg since Kate had lived in Austria for a year.[9] This March 24, 1938 letter refers to my mother as a *Mischling;* in other correspondence from my mother to the Consulate, she describes herself as "not of Aryan descent."[10] The motivation for emigration was not hidden. The Consulate, referencing the support of Wiedemann for the exception, replied immediately in the positive. [11] My father wrote both Blome and Wiedemann of this development, thanking them for their ongoing assistance.[12] In a letter a few days later, Blome informed Hoerlin that he was proceeding with the next steps within the Interior Ministry.[13] It is noteworthy that in his extensive correspondence with the Third Reich bureaucracy, my father always concluded his letters with the salutation, "With German greetings" and never with the "Heil Hitler" sign-off that prevailed during those times. Even when the stakes were high, he did not want to bow to distasteful practices.

Wiedemann tipped off Kate and Hoerlin early on that Dr. Blome was predisposed to approve their request: "I have spoken with the responsible expert, Dr. Blome, who will submit a dispensation for your case. This answer can still not be regarded as a definitive decision, but is certainly more favorable than I anticipated." [14] There were reasons to be surprised. Blome's vetoes of similar requests were notorious. As the in-house genealogical expert, the exacting doctor advised the Interior Ministry, the ultimate decision-making body responsible for the Nazi's legislative rulings on German Jewry.[15] In 1938 Blome's files bulged with thousands of petitions asking authorization for mixed marriages. After petitioners were subjected to weeks and weeks of degrading inquiries into every aspect of their lives, Blome almost inevitably gave a "flat out no." [16] When Blome gave my parents a preliminary nod, they were elated. However, their elation was mixed with a healthy dose of caution in view of the odds and Kate's prior prolonged crusade to get a governmental stipend for the children after her husband's murder. The wheels of Germany bureaucracy could turn efficiently under some circumstances, but grudgingly in others. Or they could be inexplicably reversed.

A nagging concern was Kate's classification according to the Nuremberg dictates. Jews who claimed part-Aryan parentage were scrutinized carefully by authorities for incidents of misrepresentation. Being a *Mischling* instead of a full Jew made things somewhat easier in the Nazi state and sometimes the claim of mixed blood was suspect. To tend to this thorny point, my father had written Wiedemann on March 20, asking if it was necessary to procure certification of my mother's descent that "... lay in the Sippenamt of the Schiffsbauerdamm."[17] Apparently, the Schiffsbauerdamm files with their definitive genealogical tracking contained information about Kate being the illegitimate daughter of von Alvensleben. Kate had decided the previous year (1937) not to invoke this lineage and Hoerlin agreed, noting: "It feels right to me, that you do not pursue further the route over the Schiffbauerdamm, not only right, but also kind."[18] Whether Kate did not want to sully the reputation of her mother or whether things were too painful regarding her status as an illegitimate child, is an open question. When I was a teenager and my mother told me of the von Alvensleben affair, I thought it wildly romantic. But living with the reality of it in an age of more rigid moral codes may have been quite another story.

As conflicted as Kate may have been about the circumstances of her birth and as principled as my father was about not cowing to the Nazis, they obviously reconsidered in 1938 the usefulness of such records. According to a Holocaust expert, there were essentially three ways to be "upgraded": (1) via a special exemption granted by Hitler; (2) via an administrative procedure involving the Reichssippenamt, the office administering racial policy within the Ministry of Interior that could issue an *Abstammungsbescheid* (court verdict) certifying racial status, and (3) via a court decision based on a law enacted in spring 1938 that allowed the state prosecutor to open a case for the clarification of a person's ancestry. [19] Whether or not any of these routes was ever pursued is unknown to me. [20] But whatever the reason, Kate had been declared a *Mischling ersten Grades* (a mixed Jew of the first degree) [21] by the Nazis. With their obsessive approach to classification, they did not do so lightly or without strong evidence.

While the possibility for permission to marry was looking favorable, prospects for a job transfer were faltering due to Third Reich bureaucratic barriers. It seemed like Kate and Hoerlin were riding a seesaw of high and low hopes. Although Gajewski at *Agfa* was entirely sympathetic to Hoerlin's situation and continued to valiantly circumvent the strictures of National Socialism, he was under heavy scrutiny by the Nazis.[22] Things had come to a standstill. Again, the hand of Wiedemann was helpful. He wrote Gawjewski urging him to find a position for Hoerlin abroad. This explicit approval for Hoerlin's transfer from high up, specifically from the Reichs Chancellery, gave Gajewski the leverage he needed to move things forward.

Wiedemann's efforts did not stop there. Knowing full well that a woman can be a powerful influence on her husband, the adjutant also wrote Lilly von Schnitzler, the wife of a member of I.G. Farben's Executive Board: "I myself regard the only possibility for a solution is that Herr Dr. Hoerlin leaves quickly to go abroad. If you can in any way assist Dr. Hoerlin and accordingly Frau Dr. Schmid, I would be very indebted to you, very esteemed dear lady."[23] Known for her elite salons and unwavering backing of Expressionist painter Max Beckmann (labeled a degenerate artist by the Nazis), Frau von Schnitzler was a leader in Germany's cultural circles. Familiar with Willi Schmid's case, she would no doubt be an advocate for his widow. Wiedemann, leaving no stone unturned, also contacted von Schnitzler directly.

Hoerlin's expertise and work ethic put him in high standing as a prime candidate for a transfer but the interventions of Wiedemann in the foreground and Reusch in the background provided a major boost. By the end of March 1938, the path had cleared for Hoerlin's employment at *Agfa/ Ansco* in Binghamton. The first people he profusely thanked were Gajewski and Wiedemann. Wiedemann in turn thanked Gajewski for his trouble, adding somewhat misleadingly, ". . . during a chance visit from Frau Dr. Schmid I discovered, in what a compassionate way you undertook the case of Dr. Hoerlin." [24] The gratitude was not disingenuous, but the image of my mother fortuitously dropping in on Hitler's adjutant was. She arranged her visits to Wiedemann with advance notice and with definite purposes. The two of them were well matched as superior tacticians.

Once Hoerlin landed a job, a major piece of my parents' strategy had been accomplished, but it was not neatly synchronized with marriage and emigration. Hoerlin needed to take the *Agfa*/Ansco position *post haste*, while it was still open and before the window of bureaucratic opportunity closed. That meant leaving Germany without Kate and the children. It was a high-risk move, given the unfinished agenda, but it seemed there were no other options. Again, Kate and Hoerlin's abiding faith in a future together framed their decisions. Bolstered by Wiedemann's convictions that administrative wheels were turning slowly but surely in positive directions, Kate decided her time might best be spent visiting America and getting a sense of a new country in preparation to moving. Leaving the children in the capable hands of Maia, Kate decided to accompany Hoerlin on his voyage. Her plans were almost derailed by yet another snag, getting a temporary visa. After Kate was initially refused one, Wiedemann wrote a letter on her behalf, chiding the American Consul in Berlin: "Mrs. Kate Schmid is planning a short trip to the U.S.A. Is it not possible for you to issue a visa? Considering there are no negative concerns either from our vantage—and as far I can judge, from that of the United States, I ask you for this courtesy."[25] Judged not to be a menace, Kate promptly acquired her visa.

On April 7, Hoerlin and Kate set sail on the *SS Europa,* one of the fastest ocean liners of the period, taking only five days to reach New York City from the German port of Bremen. Traveling first class, my parents took full advantage of this glamorous mode of transport. The luxurious liner was Kate's introduction to travel on the open seas and although Hoerlin had ventured across oceans before to Asia and South America respectively, the *Europa* was a far cry from the lumbering and rudimentary ships that carried members of mountain climbing expeditions. Resembling a pre-marital honeymoon, the voyage sequestered my parents from the persistent tensions of the past months, allowing them a romantic interlude. Kate, who had a natural affinity for elegance, was in her element: dressing beautifully for every occasion, circulating among the elite, and radiant with the bliss of love. She easily engaged in banter with the other passengers while Hoerlin, quieter and more reserved, sought more serious exchanges. At long and sumptuous dinners, Kate sat erect without touching the back of a chair and held court, with Hoerlin beaming at her side. When the live orchestra started playing, my father—almost a head taller than she—proudly guided his beloved around the dance floor with the only step he knew: the waltz.

When they reached Binghamton, spring had arrived and the unassuming town looked its very best, nestled between two rivers and surrounded by gentle hills. People were friendly, neighborhoods pleasant and everyday life was devoid of the oppression perpetrated by a totalitarian society. Kate and Hoerlin did not worry about <u>what</u> they were saying and to <u>whom.</u> They gratefully breathed the air of a democratic and free country. Kate approved of the small town. In addition to the convivial milieu in general, Hoerlin found the work environment to his liking. Although they contemplated getting married in United States, Kate and Hoerlin knew such a marriage, flying in the face of the Nuremberg Laws, was not recognized by the Third Reich. Therefore, a key requirement for Kate's emigration from Germany and immigration to America, that is, her status as Mrs. Hermann Hoerlin, would not be fulfilled. The only option was to marry in the Third Reich.

The timing could not have been more propitious regarding Hoerlin's employment. In Germany, members of I.G. Farben's central committee, the group that oversaw *Agfa* as well as all other companies in the conglomerate, met on April 25, 1938, with Dr. Bosch. Bosch, by then retired as the company's director, had been retained as a senior advisor and chaired an extremely sensitive gathering at his home in Heidelberg. The private setting was indicative of how volatile their topic was. After heated discussions that included Gajewski, it was reluctantly agreed to dismiss all non-Aryan scientists as well as those married to Jews. A month later Jewish members of the Farben Board "resigned." [26] The proud and independent giant of industry had finally stooped to become complicit with the Nazis.[27] The company culture was radically altered.

Within the I.G. Farben conglomerate, *Agfa* had always been known as a Jewish firm. [28] When it was subsumed under the I.G. Farben banner in 1925, it did not lose its Jewish identity; once the Nazis were in power, it—consistent with Farben's own conventions—did its best to protect Jewish employees. [29] However, when Farben's central committee made the decision to dismiss all Jews under the conglomerate's employ, *Agfa* had to follow suit. Its sister firm in America, *Agfa*/Ansco, was another matter. Jews, non-Jews, refugees and Americans worked side by side at the state-of-the-art plant, its sophisticated equipment having been constructed in Wolfen workshops. An air of cutting edge innovation permeated the young company; in 1938, the year that "You Can't Take It with You" won an Oscar for best production, *Agfa*/Ansco won an Oscar for outstanding advances in motion picture film technology.

Hoerlin had landed well, in all respects except one: Kate and the children had not moved with him. It was excruciating for him and Kate to part again, especially because of all the unknowns ahead. They both shared tremendous optimism, but were they being naïve in their plans to have Hoerlin return to Germany in a few months, marry Kate and come as a family to America? Would Wiedemann's assurances be stymied? Would something fall through? Would war be declared? But there seemed to be no better alternatives than what they were doing. Kate, stopping in New York City for several days before she returned to Germany, wrote Hoerlin immediately: ". . . it seems to me that the most wonderful thing in this new country is my ever growing love . . . this land gives me such a deep joy in that I will be your wife and live for you . . . I believe we may have faith that our life is blessed . . . We now will certainly go on our way." [30] By return mail, Hoerlin reported that after a few days of work, ". . . I feel more at home in Binghamton that I ever did in Dessau. It will be good and wonderful for us five here."[31] To Kate, Binghamton was looking particularly attractive in comparison to the hustle and bustle of New York: "The good Lord has the best of intentions, when he leads us to this small town and to our quiet good life there." [32] Meanwhile, as she pithily summarized, she was ". . . learning, learning, learning." [33]

Kate utilized the time in New York to contact some musician friends and visit with Fredi and his family, who lived in Queens. As previously, the family was struggling; bureaucratic barriers stymied Fredi's efforts to set up a private medical practice. Although relations between Kate and Fredi's wife were cool, Fredi continued to rely on Kate, asking her to purchase and arrange to send him x-ray apparatus and other medical equipment once she returned to Germany. She agreed, but his dependency was tiresome.

While in New York, Kate also followed up on an important recommendation made before she left Germany. Kate's devoted admirer, Reusch, had contacted one of his dearest and oldest friends, Max Moritz Warburg, about Kate. Reusch and Warburg had known each other since the early 1920's, exemplifying the cordial relations between Aryans and Jews within the German economic community during the Weimar years.[34] With the rise of Hitler and the relentless marginalization and malignment of his Jewish friend, Reusch had unfalteringly stood by him. Max, who headed M.M. Warburg, one of the world's largest banking dynasties, was convinced the bad times would pass and that his wealth and prestige would spare him from ruin. Thinking of himself as a German first and a Jew second, Warburg slowly came to the painful realization that was not the opinion of the Third Reich. Nonetheless, Max had stayed in Germany, reluctant to sever emotional ties to his homeland and duty-bound to help fellow Jews, wishing to emigrate, with financial advice and support. [35]

Reusch correctly surmised Max could be of valuable assistance to Kate, among other things connecting her to the American branch of the Warburg empire. In a communication from Reusch to Max, he extolled Kate with such warmth that Warburg immediately wrote his sister-in-law, Nina Loeb Warburg, in New York entrusting Kate to her care. [36] Simultaneously Warburg informed Kate he was at her disposal and urged her to let him know how he could be of further assistance and smooth her way in America. [37]. Warburg's gentlemanly generosity was legendary, but his feelings of indebtedness toward his loyal and fearless ally Reusch indubitably added special motivation.

On April 27, Kate was chauffeured out of New York City for an hour up the Hudson River, a world away from the city's skyscrapers and concrete landscape. Kate was enchanted by the beautiful scenery, so proximate to the big city, and the Warburg country estate, where she and Nina strolled slowly amongst blossoming "German Apple" and "Japanese Quince" trees. [38] In hindsight, this peaceful scene was a bitterly ironic when one thinks of the war soon to come. But in 1938 there was still peace in the world and the two chic, lively women took to each other immediately. Nina was formidable, her commanding personality accentuated by a cane she wielded due to a limp caused by a childhood mishap. Widowed for six years, she had been happily married to Max's brother, Paul Moritz Warburg.[39] An early advocate of establishing the U.S. Federal Reserve system, Paul had been deeply enmeshed in the Washington scene, a connection carried on by his son James who was a financial advisor to President Roosevelt. Nina still missed her husband terribly, confiding to my mother that since Paul's death, "You are the first person with whom I can come here peacefully and almost with joy."[40] Nina, age 68, provided exactly what her brother-in-law Max had hoped for: a strong support to Kate, like an American mother to her. It was a relationship sometimes viewed with a certain amount of jealousy by Nina's daughter, Bettina Warburg, a psychiatrist only a year younger than Kate. However, the Warburg and Schmid/Hoerlin bond was strongly forged amidst flowering fruit trees.

When Kate disembarked from her return voyage on May 8, 1938 in Hamburg, she first tended to Fredi's long list of needs for medical equipment and then, on May 10, responsive to Nina Warburg's advice and Reusch's recommendations, went to meet Max Warburg: "I went to dinner at his beautiful, venerable house and had my first encounter with this exceptional person. On Wednesday, I met with him again, we spoke through everything in detail. It is all very complicated, he will summon me again to Hamburg, when the time comes." [41] Kate and Warburg discussed transferring her German and Austrian assets into American dollars; to facilitate this, Warburg instructed his staff to contact the Reichsbank. [42]

It was amazing that Warburg met with Kate at all. It was a tumultuous period: his hold on W. W. Warburg was slipping, he had been dropped from the Board of I.G. Farben (and a number of other corporate boards), and was being debased by the Nazis in any number of ways. The atmosphere was terrifying. Yet this proud and dignified seventy-one year old found time to be with my mother, showing her the opulent family estate, Koesterberg, which sat high on a hill overlooking the Elbe River. The bucolic setting with acres of ancient trees and formal gardens was more grandiose than its American counterpart up the Hudson; it included an open-air theatre, a self-sustaining farm, numerous servants and seventeen full time gardeners. [43] Its insular, other worldly, aura may have contributed to Max's proclivities toward optimism and denial, a lethal mix under a fascist state. These two traits were sorely tested in late May, when the Warburg's German domain crumbled. On May 30, 1938, the firm of M.M. Warburg was forcibly Aryanized and Max, trying to project some dignity, graciously surrendered control to "non-Jewish hands." [44] In August, the family began shutting down Koesterberg and by the end of the month, Max Warburg and his family set sail for New York. [45]

Kate made it back to Salzburg by May 13, her birthday, in time to celebrate with the children and field their many inquiries: "Yesterday evening I needed to tell them about everything until 11 p.m., they listened to me breathlessly, asked dear and thoughtful questions, ready for that which is new, for that which we have prepared them." [46] Kate's carefully couched letter is an indication of how often her correspondence was exposed to a censor's eye. Kate was feeling under increasing surveillance and the children too needed to be careful, talking of their mother's visit abroad as an exciting distraction rather than a future destination. The three children had been exposed to a sprinkling of Americana: Duscha had read "Tom Sawyer" and "Huckleberry Finn," Thomi had spent countless hours playing cowboys and Indians, and they had all seen Walt Disney's enchanting "Mickey Mouse" movie. To them, this was America.

Hoerlin's elderly mother had not availed herself of these cultural gems and was more hesitant about a country that she thought had so little history or gravitas. Over the past months, Hoerlin had gently kept her apprised of emerging developments but now the reality was setting in that her son and his family would be living on another continent. After Kate had first met "Mother" Hoerlin in November 1935, she appreciated and shared Hoerlin's deep love and respect for her. They had asked Mother whether she would join them in coming to America, but she considered herself—at 63—too old and frail to travel. If she were ten years younger, she claimed, she would go along. [47] She was fond of Kate and, having lost her only daughter to tuberculosis three years earlier, bravely exclaimed: "My heart is full of joy that I again have a beloved daughter." [48] However, Mother Hoerlin had never met Kate's children, a situation remedied by Kate with visits in late May and early June. The newly anointed grandmother delighted in Duscha and Thomi, but particularly in "little Hedi" to whom she gave the favorite doll and necklace of her deceased daughter.

As Wiedemann had predicted, Hoerlin and Kate's application to marry was threading its way through the approval maze. Copious correspondence among internal ministries in Berlin and external missives between German and Austria authorities finally inched to an end. On June 20, 1938, the long-awaited permission was granted by the high-ranking official Bernhard Loesener in cumbersome German legalese:

> With the consent of the Fuehrer's deputy, I hereby grant permission of the application—based on section 3 of the first decree of the law covering the protection of German blood and German honor dated 14.11.1935—of the Jewish *Mischling* of the 1. degree Kaete Schmid nee Tietz, of Munich, presently residing in Salzburg, to marry the German blooded German citizen Dr. Ing Hermann Hoerlin of Dessau, presently residing in Binghampton, N.Y., USA. I respectfully request that the applicant as well as the responsible local registry be immediately informed. [49]

Loesener had drafted the Nuremberg Laws in 1935, claiming they were intended to ease relations between the German and Jewish peoples. He argued that the Jewish people, intent on preserving the purity of their blood, would surely welcome such laws. [50] By 1938 the laws had spawned nothing but widespread hatred and oppression. Loesener, as the interior ministry's expert on the law, continued to interpret and make judgments on their applicability. Though he had received the recommendation of the medical consultant Dr. Blome about the Tiezt/Schmid and Hoerlin application for an exemption, it was Loesener who signed off on the request.

**Kate Tietz Schmid, a Mischling, and Hermann Hoerlin,
an Aryan, on their wedding day in 1938 Berlin.**

On July 12, 1938, the *Mischling* Kate Tietz Schmid was married to the Aryan Hermann Julius Wilhelm Hoerlin in a brief civil ceremony in Berlin. "We, the engaged couple, swear that we are Germans of the same type of blood" was on the official Intent to Marry printed form. This wording was crossed out and underneath it, in firm handwriting, my mother penned: "I, the fiancée, am a *Mischling* of the first degree."[51] There had been no public notice of their intent to marry, a procedure usually pre-dating marriage by a month. Nor was there an announcement of their marriage, once it had taken place, published anywhere. "Every official in the Third Reich," as Dr. Jana Leichsenring—a historical researcher—commented, ". . . at first glance of the marriage notification would know that things were not in order . . . posting a notice about the marriage would be dangerous for those who issued it. It would appear as though he legitimized it . . ."[52] The only aspect of the marriage following ordinary European customs occurred a few days later when Kate and Hoerlin were wed again in a religious service among friends at the small chapel in Garmisch-Partenkirchen. Afterwards, amidst white roses, the newlyweds celebrated with the Schmid relatives who had proclaimed Hoerlin to be "one of us." [53]

Permission for a full-blown Aryan to wed a Jew of any ilk was basically unheard of by 1938. How could this astonishing feat have been permitted? Several theories come to mind. 1) Since it was assured Kate and Hoerlin were leaving the country, the marriage would not—if it produced a child—taint the purity of German blood and accordingly not threaten National Socialism's goal of a nation devoid of Jews and *Mischlinge*; 2) My mother was extremely well connected to pivotal figures in Germany, including those in uppermost echelons of German government and industry; the sign-off on the permission letter for marriage evoked the consent of the Fuehrer himself; 3) My father was not easy for the Nazis to brush off: a reputable scientist and high profile mountain climber who had held a world record and starred in a popular film about it; and 4) The presence of my mother was a continuing source of discomfort to the Nazis for two very different reasons: one, their embarrassment regarding the murder of Willi Schmid and having his outspoken widow remind them of their "mistake" and another, known to only a few Nazis, Kate's blood relationship to several von Alvenslebens serving under Hitler, particularly the high ranking S.S. Colonel Ludolf Hermann ("Bubi") von Alvensleben. In either case, having Kate depart was desirable. Most probably it was a confluence of these factors that enabled Kate and Hoerlin to marry and leave Germany. But most of all, my parents need to be fully credited for their incredible persistence and extraordinary strategizing. While my father originally crafted the plan, my mother played a central part in its execution. They were a formidable partnership in courage. Would Hoerlin have left Germany had it not been for her? Perhaps. Could Kate have left Germany were it not for him? Most probably not.

Kate, Hoerlin, Duscha, Thomi, Hedi and the faithful Maia sailed from Germany on the SS Columbus on August 9th, a month earlier than originally planned. To stay longer was becoming more dangerous every day. Fittingly, the name of their ocean liner was the same as the explorer who discovered America. The combined Schmid/Hoerlin family were about to discover a new continent too, and begin a new life. Leaving Germany for America, they traded one national symbol for another, both sporting eagles. For years, Germany had used the large bird as its national emblem but when Hitler came to power, he made his own adaptations. The Third Reich eagle sat rigid and menacing, with its claws tightly grasping a Nazi swastika. Yet my parents had miraculously found protection under its feathers. America's emblem is also an eagle, but a bald eagle, the only species of eagle unique to North America. Adopted as the national image in 1782, the eagle carried in its beak a scroll inscribed with the motto "E Pluribus Unum." When my parents immigrated to America in 1938, a bald eagle welcomed them, soaring in the air over them with wings outspread, the quintessence of flight and freedom.

The newly-weds, Kate and Hoerlin, with Duscha on the SS Columbus sailing from Germany to America.

Landing in New York on August 17, 1938.

PART II

AMERICA

Chapter 13

THE ONLY <u>REAL</u> AMERICAN

It wasn't that easy being born. I was told my mother, then age 40, almost bled to death giving birth to me. She said that Hoerlin had been so traumatized by her hemorrhaging that he declared, "Never again." I wasn't certain whether that meant I would not have a little sister or brother in the future or whether it indicated my parents would never engage in activities that might lead to such an outcome. The latter interpretation is dubious, given that they always spoke of me as their "love child." By that my mother meant a child born out of great passion, although the typical American implication is that I was illegitimate. I was more than legitimate and the passion leading to my birth followed it as well. For years, I amused people by saying I was conceived in Germany but born in the U.S.A. But when I finally did the math, it would have entailed an eleven-month pregnancy. Not very likely. My parents were ecstatic about my birth and my older sisters and brother spoiled me hopelessly, interspersing their attentiveness with heavy doses of teasing. Taking my father's biological cues, I was a blond with greenish-gray eyes, looking quintessentially Germanic. But I prided myself as having been born in this country. As I once crossly reminded the rest of my family, "I am the only <u>real</u> American." It was terribly embarrassing if my mother or father spoke in German to me in public. I pretended to have no understanding. Even in the early years, I knew "we" (that is, me and other Americans) were at war against "them" (that is, my parents' country of origin). A sacred time in our house was listening to Edward R. Murrow broadcasts about the war. Not a peep came out of me. I remember viscerally experiencing the horrors of the bombings and death, underscored by the pained expressions of my mother's and father's faces. Their homeland was being obliterated and people close to them threatened by, or succumbing to, death: my father's mother and relatives, my mother's and Schmid relatives, old climbing *companions fighting on the front and friends throughout Germany. This memory is probably responsible for my visceral aversion toward violence to this day. However, throughout these broadcasts, throughout the war, it was crystal clear to me which side my parents were on. When the German army invaded Russia in May of 1941, my father was elated. "That's definitely the end of it," he predicted. As often, he was right, although it took too many more years to prove him so.*

On August 17, 1938 the SS Columbus docked in New York City and the newlyweds, Kate and Hoerlin, disembarked with their three children. Duscha, almost 14, Thomi age 11, and Hedi age 6, were whisked through customs with the help of the ever-cheerful Maia. Sorting through the piles of official papers, the customs officer may have noticed a document describing my mother as *"Mosaisch."* Jewish, from the tribe of Moses. When one says *Mosaisch*, it sounds so soft and lovely: you can hear the *"s's,"* soothing like a lullaby. Moses, the river baby, floating among the reeds, soon to be scooped up, saved, protected, nurtured. My mother too had been carried to a safe shore. The harsh red letter **"J,"** required for all German Jewish *(Jude)* immigrants less than two months later, was not stamped on her passport. [1]

The children naturally felt overwhelmed by Manhattan's giant skyscrapers and the bustling pace of a metropolis. Hedi was mesmerized by the sight of curly, black-headed, little children (the population of Negroes in Munich was non-existent), Duscha shyly attempted to practice her English and Thomi appeared to be simply stunned, barely able to open his mouth. The family was relieved to arrive in Binghamton, where Hoerlin had found a small, comfortable house. It took awhile until their collective worldly possessions, sent via a freight boat, caught up with them. It was the second ocean voyage for the precious vicuna blanket that my father had so carefully brought from the Andes and lovingly bestowed on my mother. For other items, it was their first time outside of German territory. The "Biedermeier" and the "Meissen", as my mother referred to them—making them sound more like stowaways than graceful furniture and fine porcelain—also arrived safely on American shores. Before leaving Germany, Kate had burned many of her letters and documents (probably including the letter from von Alvensleben), wishing not to be burdened by them for either practical or personal reasons. In contrast, my father kept all of his documents and letters, among which were the 400 love letters written to him by Kate. There were no household items in his inventory: only numerous mountain maps, a few tents from Himalayan and Andes expeditions, his ice axe, and—representing the latest in German ingenuity—a folding kayak.[2]

Kate and Hoerlin's first year in the United States was spent with my father plunging into his position as head of *Agfa*/Ansco's physics laboratory, my mother adjusting to new customs and routines, and the three children negotiating the local public schools with their limited English. Shortly after their arrival in Binghamton, my parents declared their intention of becoming U.S. citizens, not having a sliver of doubt on the matter.[3] They relished the atmosphere of freedom and opportunity that had replaced the fear and oppression of the past several years. Meanwhile, any remnant of civilized life in Germany was disintegrating rapidly. Prior to my parents' departure in August, anti-Semitic riots were commonplace and in the fall, on November 9-10, *Kristallnacht* or 'The Night of Broken Glass' hit cities all over Germany. Led by the S.S., Gestapo and the Hitler Youth, it had all the markings of "an officially sponsored pogrom."[4] In a rampage of violence and vandalism, over 200 synagogues were destroyed, 7,500 Jewish stores wrecked, thousands of Jews arrested, approximately 30,000 Jewish men sent to concentration camps, and some 90 Jews killed.[5] Several more victims died because of abuse in the camps, and still others due to a number of suicides after *Kristallnacht*.[6]

Widely reported in the American press as well as newspapers worldwide, *Kristallnacht* consolidated anti-German sentiments bubbling in the United States. American reporters had heretofore viewed anti-Semitic brutalities in Germany with a mixture of skepticism and confusion, feeling they were "beyond the pale of believability"[7] in such a civilized country. Although *Kristallnacht* rattled these perceptions, there were still Americans who retained "persistent incredulity."[8] An article in a popular American magazine reported: ". . . there are those . . . who shrug complacent shoulders and who say, 'Things can't be as bad as we hear.'"[9]

Kate and Hoerlin knew things were bad and on a daily basis counted their blessings. Just prior to *Kristallnacht*, the Third Reich took an uncompromising position on "the Jewish question," putting an irrevocable end to exemption requests from anti-Semitic dictates. As the German State Secretary wrote to the Interior Minister, "The Fuehrer is of the opinion that exemptions from the special regulations valid for the Jews have to be rejected without any exception."[10] Since my parents definitely had been handled as an "exception," they could not help but shudder about how this, if enacted earlier, would have squelched their marriage and subsequent emigration. When a new wave of anti-Semitic measures were enacted after *Kristallnacht,* there was no question that rules viewed as transitory by many were a permanent fixture of the Nazi state. In rapid succession, a series of decrees were passed in the fall of 1938 forcing Jews to sell all businesses, houses, and valuables (November 12), expelling all Jewish children from German public schools (November 15), removing Jews from the general welfare system (November 19), and prohibiting Jews from owning automobiles or having a driver's license (December 3). [11] Although such restrictions had been formerly adopted by some localities, they were now instituted on a national level; Jews were forbidden to enter parks, forests, recreational and cultural venues (December 6). [12] Life for anyone identified as a Jew had become intolerable.

My parents felt a mixture of relief that they were in America and grief for those left behind. Yet they needed to press forward, rather than become mired down, as they reconstructed their lives. New life of another kind emerged on June 1, 1939 when I was born. My parents were thrilled—a healthy pregnancy was not guaranteed for my 40-year-old-mother. The first <u>real</u> American in the family was named Eva Maria Bettina; with the collateral of being named after three saints (Bettina is a derivative of Elizabeth), I was definitely going to be brought up as Catholic. In a garden ceremony, I was christened by the same German priest who had been Willi Schmid's close friend and had overseen the baptisms of my siblings and served as the family's continuing spiritual guide. When the Schmids had come to Salzburg in 1937, Pater Thomas (Father Thomas) was already there, his muffled anti-Nazi sentiments having somehow reached the ears of the Munich archdiocese, who reassigned him to what seemed like a more tolerant diocese in Salzburg. After the Anschluss, another move was in store for Pater Thomas. Somewhat miraculously, the omnipresent priest happened to be on an extended stay in the United States.

The family gathering to celebrate my arrival included my godmother, Maia, along with my godfather, Hannes Schneider and namesake, Bettina Warburg. My parents had intended to have Bettina be my godmother but she graciously declined saying, "In my tribe, we don't do that sort of thing, but don't worry, I will keep an eye on her." Hannes Schneider, no relation to my father's climbing partner Erwin Schneider, was ten years older than Hoerlin: they had met in the early days of ski touring in the Dolomites and the friendship had continued as Hannes began to devote himself fully to perfecting the novel sport of downhill skiing.[13] Over the years, he developed and refined what was called the Arlberg method, turning skiing into a technique that could be uniformly taught; in 1921, he established one of the first ski schools in the world, the Hannes Schneider Ski School in St. Anton, Austria. European royalty, millionaires, movie stars and American society women all flocked to the school, making skiing fashionable for the elite. A series of ski films, starring Hannes—and on one occasion co-starring Leni Riefenstahl—assured him the crown of "The Father of Modern Skiing." [14] Having become a famous Austrian, Hannes—to the dismay of government officials—was an infamous anti-Nazi. Because of the mutual animosity between him and the Nazis, including Hannes' incarceration for several months in 1939, he left his burgeoning ski empire and came to North Conway, New Hampshire, to head its ski school, much to the delight of townspeople.[15] His international reputation had preceded him. In a much-publicized trip to Japan in 1930, he had been invited by the government to teach skiing there. Now Americans too would benefit from his expertise.

Hoerlin and Kate were beginning to create a new tapestry of friendships, weaving new strands with old: Europeans they knew or had not known in the old country, who—like them—had fled totalitarian regimes. Among them were many world-class musicians such as members of the Budapest Quartet, the pianist Rudolf Serkin and the cellist Emanuel Feuermann. It was not surprising that artists and musicians, mostly Jewish and mainly from Germany and Russia, were flocking to the United States. To quote Feuermann, an international star: "America is the last frontier for artists. Here, the idea that a musician or composer would be barred because of his racial background would be as ridiculous as it would be for me to destroy my Stradivarius cello because it was made by an Italian." [16] Feuermann was married to Eva Reifenberg, an attractive young woman from Cologne, who had stayed with the Schmids during a 1933 Munich sojourn. The story told in my family related that Eva, a privileged daughter of wealth who was clueless about domestic routines, was shipped off to Kate to learn to cook. Although Eva never mastered the culinary arts, she nonetheless attracted the affection of one of the greatest cellists of all time. [17] Now that the Feuermanns were living in the United States and had a daughter, Monica, the same age as me, additional ties were formed.

As for new friends, my mother had an uncanny ability to sniff out extraordinary people and find them even in a small town in America. She dove headlong into the task of generating a busy social life, a task at which she had excelled in Salzburg. But the flirtatiousness she exuded in Munich and Salzburg did not travel well to upstate New York. It did not sit well with wives of Binghamton society. Kate was adept at calibrating the depth of charm an audience would bear. Sensitive to how she was perceived, she made the needed adjustments and reinvented herself.

Although generally positive, my family's reception in Binghamton was not without setbacks. America was not always the sanctuary for refugees that the Statue of Liberty promised. Opposition to liberalizing immigration laws was strong, not even wavering for those who had been persecuted. [18] The cry of "100% American" echoed across job lines and was raised against emigrants in general, but certainly against Jews. The *Binghamton Press* was among those newspapers that warned readers of a plot to populate the United States with Jews.[19] Once the United States and Germany were at war, hostilities multiplied. Anti-German sentiments frequently did not distinguish between those immigrants who were avidly anti-Hitler and others who were still pro-German. The youngest of my older siblings, Hedi, nine years old in 1941, remembers that no one would walk with her to school; her peers walked on the other side of the street. My older siblings by that time were in progressive boarding schools, [20] more protected from the prejudices that characterized many communities.

My parents, who were trying their best to assimilate, were often in situations that undermined their resolve. In 1939, the von Trapps—their friends from Salzburg days—pulled up in front of our house in their blue touring bus boldly inscribed "The Trapp Family Choir."[21] They had fled Austria after it became clear that the anti-Nazi Count had defiantly refused to fly a swastika flag from his estate and declined an invitation to sing at Hitler's birthday. On a concert tour in the United States with a show in Binghamton on their schedule, the Trapp family entourage emerged from the large bus to the amazement of curious neighbors. The ten children were all impeccably clothed, the girls in traditional Austrian dirndls and the boys in lederhosen. The Trapps had not yet attained the fame resulting from the release of "The Sound of Music," but they were definitely a popular draw. In 1939, it was a mixed blessing to be descended upon by such an overtly Germanic assemblage especially if one is attempting to culturally blend into the American melting pot.

**The Trapp Family singers in a celebratory mood,
holding up Kate when they visited us in 1939.**

In spite of some local incidents of bigotry, life proceeded relatively smoothly and happily for the Schmid/Hoerlin family. Quickly adopting the American trend toward mobility, we moved from a middle class to an upper middle class neighborhood. The spacious white shingled and green shuttered house on a tree-lined street gracefully sat on land that allowed for a large garden. It was a pictogram for the all-American dream.

My older sister Duscha took me for walks around the neighborhood, particularly on fancier streets a few blocks away. Admiring the architecture (at least some of it), we would make up stories of the lives within agreeing that being rich did not mean being happy. The subtext was that <u>we</u> were happy as a family, although not wealthy. My early memories of family life attest to that happiness, particularly when Duscha and Thomi came home

Our home in Binghamton, New York.

for vacations from their respective boarding schools. That is when the children took over the house. After a particularly delicious dinner prepared by my mother, we would be on clean-up duty. It is one of my fondest memories: doing the dishes with four of us singing. Thomi, who would become a member of the Harvard Glee Club, had a particularly fine voice. Both my choral and clean-up contributions were minimal, but to me we sounded better than the von Trapps at their best.

The author, Bettina, with her mother Kate: 1942.

As a child I was protected from what was happening in the outside world. Germany's 1939 invasion of Poland, which sparked the start of World War II and led to the Allies' declaration of war, was indeed a distant drum. And when the United States finally entered the war on December 8, 1941, I was still too young to understand its meaning. Kate and Hoerlin were of course fully supportive of America joining with the Allies. However, they were not prepared for the ramifications. In the early months of 1941, the U.S. government seized the *Agfa*/Ansco film facility, the largest asset taken over by the government in World War II. [22] Although the firm had been sold in 1939 to an American company, General Aniline, its prior history as a subsidiary of I.G Farben fed rumors that there was still a Nazi virus in *Agfa*/ Ansco's atmosphere. [23] Sadly, there was truth in the rumors that a certain number of pro-Nazis were employed there, although *Agfa* had been founded and managed by Jews and they had transferred several Jews to Binghamton.[24] When my mother met with the head of Ansco/*Agfa* during her first visit to the United States in April 1938, he—himself a Jew—warned her not to speak about Willi Schmid's murder by the Nazis, fearing that would arouse suspicion and negativity toward Hoerlin's employment.[25]

Under the Trading with the Enemy Act, the U.S. Treasury Department was placed in charge of the film firm and approximately fifty German-born executives and key workers were summarily fired in the early months of 1941. Other employees were suspended, awaiting the results of an investigation conducted by Treasury into the backgrounds of employees. My father, who was among the latter group, was stunned. Although he recognized the reasons for an investigation, he was distraught to see that pro-Nazis were promoted to positions previously filled by anti-Nazis, many of whom were Jews. There seemed to be no distinction between people like Hoerlin, strong opponents of Hitler, and those who had cheered German victories since the war began.

Along with his suspension at Ansco, Hoerlin got two other pieces of bad news. In letters from the First National Bank in Binghamton [26] and the Federal Reserve Bank of New York,[27] he was notified that his respective accounts were frozen. This included all securities, safe deposit boxes, and property within their custody, effectively rendering the Hoerlins to be residents without assets. Furthermore, the stipends from the German government to the Schmid children resulting from the wrongful death of their father had ceased. [28] Hoerlin and Kate decided to appeal for help to two friends, both formidable women, Bettina Warburg and Trude Pratt.

To meet Bettina, a psychiatrist by training, was intimidating in spite of her petite stature. She was brilliant, feisty and rebellious. Much to the consternation of her domineering mother and doting father, Bettina was defiantly independent and chose to pursue a career in psychoanalysis.[29] A person without frills, Bettina displayed a clinically cool exterior that hid an inner warmth and playfulness. She did not fall under the spell of enchantment that my mother so successfully (most of the time) cast over others; she gravitated much more toward my father, relating well to his more direct and unembellished demeanor. Her ties to our family had been assured by the introduction of my mother to her mother Nina, the sister-in-law of Max Warburg. Bettina revered her Uncle Max and she and he had worked together establishing a fund in Germany to quietly assist refugees. [30] Bettina viewed the Hoerlin/Schmids as an extension of such tutelage.

Trude Wenzel Pratt was Bettina Warburg's opposite on several counts, although they shared a rebellious streak. An impudent young girl, Trude had been thrown out of the convent school she attended in Germany. She never looked back. Tall, blond, and beautiful, Trude was at ease socially and intermingled with élan among the wealthy and powerful. Trude combined warmth, good intuitions and political sophistication. She had known my mother since student days, when she came for a short time to study in Munich. She and Kate had immediately taken to one another, but it was not until reconnecting in the United States that their close friendship evolved. Trude had come to the United States on a one-year teaching fellowship and became a citizen in 1932 upon marrying the debonair New York philanthropist Eliot Pratt. When Kate and Hoerlin emigrated in 1938, Trude was among the first to welcome them. Politically active and fervently anti-Nazi, she was then acting as director of the International Student Society. That position had previously been held by Joseph (Joe) P. Lash. [31] Through Joe, a protégée of Eleanor Roosevelt's, Trude had been introduced to the President's wife and became a frequent guest at the White House, an informal advisor on Germany. When Trude and Joe found themselves falling in love, "Mrs. E"—as she was called by them—played a major role in encouraging their courtship.[32] As Trude agonized about leaving Eliot and a marriage with three children, my mother acted as her trusted confidant.[33] And now, with Hoerlin's suspension, Trude found herself in a position to help Kate and Hoerlin.

Hoerlin had written[34] almost identical letters to Trude and Bettina telling them of his problem, the Treasury Department investigation of enemy aliens at *Agfa*/Ansco, and lamenting the appointments of Nazi sympathizers to key positions at the firm. In regard to the latter, he reported, "The new man transferred to the position of director of research suffers from each Russian victory or British-American bombing . . . I'm afraid that the {Treasury Department} investigation will get almost nowhere. It is difficult to prove that somebody is a Nazi as long as he has not *done* something." My father looked for guidance from each of his female sages, asking their opinion as to whether to leave the firm. He concluded his letters saying, "I feel I should quietly look for another job—in a 100% American outfit."

By return mail, Trude immediately advised him *not* to resign, ". . . as that might be taken as a sign that you fear investigation and would rather go before you are asked to leave. I am writing to Mrs. Roosevelt about your case—she is a specially close friend of Secretary of Treasury Morgenthau." [35] Similarly, Bettina urged Hoerlin to stick things out and on his behalf wrote an acquaintance of hers, Otto Brodnitz, an influential consultant to the intelligence arm of the Treasury Department.[36] In a subsequent letter to Brodnitz, Hoerlin thanked him for taking an interest in his case, noting that although he had cooperated with investigators, he had not yet been cleared.[37] As events unfolded, it became evident that two issues muddied the waters: 1) Kate and Hoerlin's relationship to Fritz Wiedemann and 2) Hoerlin's connections with the German Alpine Club's 1939 Expedition to the Andes.

Wiedemann, who arguably was the key mover and shaker in allowing Kate and Hoerlin to marry and emigrate to the United States, had found himself in an increasingly untenable position vis-a-vis the Nazi regime. He had suspected his days in Hitler's inner sanctum were numbered since *Kristallnacht*. According to Goebbel's diary, ". . . {Wiedemann} did not perform well and lost his nerve completely" during that event. [38] The Propaganda Minister had pushed for the Fuehrer to get rid of his personal aide. It is not far-fetched to surmise that Wiedemann was horrified by this display of sanctioned barbarism, often viewed by historians as the beginning point of the Holocaust. But the coup de grace was when Hitler was informed about Wiedemann's affair with the "Jewish Princess," Stephanie von Hohenlohe. The Fuehrer summarily dismissed his old World War I company commander and appointed him as German Consul-General in San Francisco. The post was welcomed by Wiedemann who left Germany in March 1939 with his wife and children. Nine months later, his mistress—the persevering Princess Stephanie—joined him. American government authorities almost immediately placed both the Princess and Wiedemann under suspicion as Nazi spies.

The other association that sullied my father's repute was almost comical, since it was so misinterpreted. It falls into the category of "no good deed goes unpunished." In the spring of 1939, the *Alpenverein* funded its 3ʳᵈ expedition to Peru; my father had been on the first one in 1932, there had been another one in 1936 and now a third one that focused on the southern section of the Andes' extensive Cordillera Blanca range. Composed primarily of researchers who combined climbing interests with geographic, cultural and archeological studies, the group included several old friends of Hoerlin's—or of "Pallas"—as he continued to be known by them. Since their major trip documentation was to be photographic—photos and movie camera footage—and since color film was being used along with black and white, the expedition members were in constant contact with Hoerlin. They asked for his input on exposures, film types and cameras and most importantly, requested that he facilitate having large shipments of film processed at Binghamton's *Agfa/*Ansco plant. At that point there was no technical capacity in Peru to develop color film, nor, as it turned out, for black and white film.[39] At the same time, Hoerlin was getting feedback from the six expedition members on how the *Agfa/*Ansco film was faring under alternatively tropical and high altitude conditions, at the mercy of humidity, dust, dirt, snow and ice.

Over thirty letters, mainly single spaced and several pages long, dated from March 1939 to January 1941, were sent to my father on the letterhead of the *Anden-Kundfahrt des Deutschen Alpenverein* (Andes Research Trip of the German Alpine Club). [40] When I pulled them from my father's files, it was amazing to read the depth of technical details about films and filming, but also the human story behind the expedition. The group made six first ascents of Cordillera Blanca peaks over 6000 meters high, but was devastated on August 29, 1939 by the deaths of three members killed by a falling ice cornice. A week later World War II broke out in Europe, just as the expedition party was preparing to return home. It was impossible to find a boat back to Germany; furthermore, most shipping lines would not accept German currency, the *Reichsmark*. They were stuck.

The small group hoped that the war would be short-lived but as the days and battles dragged forth, they realized it would not be. Their feelings were clear: "We still certainly hope for a speedy, perhaps a surprisingly speedy, end to this crazy game. Perhaps there will be time to bring several of our leaders somehow—that is with force—to their senses without this unnecessary sacrifice."[41] However, the war only expanded; nobody or nothing stopped Hitler. It was not until November 1940 that the remaining expedition members could make their way back to Germany, booking themselves on a Japanese ship to Yokohama; from there, they made their way across Asia, arriving in Berlin at the end of January 1941.

It is hard to fathom that three young German climber-scientists in Peru, who were anti-war and disparaged Hitler, would be objects of suspicion to the U.S. Treasury Department, but that is exactly what happened. What triggered misgivings about them and their link with Hoerlin were the many letters exchanged, the film Hoerlin regularly sent them, and the hundreds of photographs and extensive camera footage they sent back for processing in the United States. At first, their photographic bounty passed through U.S. Customs easily, but as the war became more menacing to Americans, there were longer and longer delays. The far-fetched suspicion was that the films were for some kind of espionage or reconnaissance work in which Hoerlin somehow played a role. By the time the expedition returned to Germany, the issue had been put to rest.

After Hoerlin's letters to Trude and Bettina and their impressive ability to pull the right strings, my father was reinstated in April 1942 at *Agfa/Ansco*. The Treasury investigators, undoubtedly influenced by words from on high, cleared him, saying he had a clean record. Hoerlin's dealings with the Peruvian expedition had been fully explained and his relationship to Wiedemann, while still problematic, was put on temporary hold. As Brodnitz articulated to Bettina, ". . . I understand the Hoerlins' feelings of gratitude for the decency Wiedemann showed to them . . . however, the Hoerlins must understand that we are interested in Wiedemann as an official of the Nazi government. **It goes without saying that there can be no better proof of loyalty to their country than to assist us in this broader aspect.**" [42] The dialogue had shifted from distrust to proving one was trustworthy. The term, "enemy alien", a designation Hoerlin shared with foreigners from the Axis powers who had not gained U.S. citizenship, grated on him. But loyalty was a volatile issue in regard to enemy aliens and for Hoerlin to confront it he needed to take up the gauntlet bluntly thrown down by Brodnitz.

In 1942 and 1943 Hoerlin provided the American government with assorted cartographic information that purportedly helped with the Allied war effort. In official correspondence, Hoerlin was described as ". . . a mountain climber of some renown . . . in a position to assist with the geographical and topographical details of locations in question. I am sure that he would appreciate an opportunity to be of service to you if given the opportunity." [43] Hoerlin indeed wanted to be of assistance to his adopted country; the "locations in questions" were detailed on his treasured climbing and hiking maps, which he had carefully packed when he emigrated. Now they were put to use by Army Intelligence. Hoerlin sent maps of the Italian and Austrian borders [44] and the area around the Berchtesgarden mountains, highlighting dams and power stations near the site of Hitler's vacation retreat, information collected for reconnaissance and/or bombing missions. [45] Although Hoerlin most certainly suffered from occasional pangs of guilt, knowing that this knowledge could put friends or family in harm's way, he had no hesitations about wanting an end to Hitler. In fact, he was praised by Treasury Department officials during the *Agfa*/Ansco investigations for his cooperation: ". . . at a time when Hoerlin, among others, was the subject of an intensive investigation, every contact with Hoerlin was a pleasant one . . . he answered all questions put to him frankly." [46]

With his impeccable grasp of cartography, Hoerlin was also able to draw and pinpoint locations of I.G. Farben's vast array of manufacturing plants that were totally dedicated to the war effort. [47] He included key railway connections in his renderings. In addition, Hoerlin was asked to provide information about raw materials used by I.G. Farben's film plant in Wolfen, where he had been previously employed. [48] Highly flammable chemicals used for film production could also be used for explosives.[49] Obviously, the Americans were gathering intelligence information to assess German weapon-making capacity.

Having been reinstated at *Agfa*/Ansco by Treasury officials in April, my father was in for another shock in August 1942, when he was informed that the Office of the Secretary of the Navy requested his removal from the film—manufacturing department at the firm.[50] The prospect of an 'enemy alien' sabotaging photographic materials used by the Navy or Army, was the basis for this action. The president of *Agfa*/Ansco, needing to comply with the Navy's directive, met with Hoerlin to tell him he was being transferred to another department. Headed by a man who Hoerlin knew to be a Nazi, my father refused the transfer. He had not come across the Atlantic Ocean, fleeing from National Socialism, only to work for an Americanized version of the same. The company's president—to his credit—subsequently filed an appeal to the War Department on behalf of Hoerlin.[51] This time things moved quickly. On September 30, Hoerlin was reassigned to his prior position. The fine hand of Mrs. Roosevelt had again been brought to bear; a note from the official-in-charge to Mrs. Roosevelt stated: "In view of your interest in Dr. Hermann W. Hoerlin . . . I know you will be pleased to learn that approval has recently been obtained from the War and Navy Departments for his reinstatement."[52] A copy of the note had been enclosed in a letter to Hoerlin from Trude, in which she cautioned him, ". . . {this} must be kept completely between you and me. I know that Mrs. Roosevelt has done a great deal to help you, but it would be very much better if her interest was not mentioned . . ." [53] Like so much of what happened in my parents' lives, this was never mentioned to me.

With the war continuing to rage in Europe, my parents proceeded with life in Binghamton. Food and gasoline rationing affected the Hoerlin/ Schmids in ways similar to the general population. However as enemy aliens, the Hoerlins had to deal with additional stresses: societal stigmatization and governmental actions targeting them. In 1942, German nationals were ordered to remove short-wave bands from radios and 'surrender' cameras to local authorities. Homes were regularly inspected for violations. My father's extensive photographic equipment, used for both personal and professional reasons, was carefully stored at *Agfa*/Ansco.[54]

But at least the specific misgivings about my father's trustworthiness had been allayed. It helped that Wiedemann had been ordered in July 1941 to leave the United States by President Roosevelt. [55] He returned to Germany briefly before being posted as Consul-General to the Chinese seaport of Tientsin, an appointment that had overtones of banishment. His wife and children were not permitted to leave Germany and travel with him; by then his relationship with Princess Stephanie was over. Wiedemann went alone. The other issue, my father's relationship to the 1939 Peru Expedition, had also been resolved and the films reunited with their rightful owners in 1942. [56] By 1943, the government bureaucracies that had interfered with my father's employment at *Agfa*/Ansco had been appeased and by 1944

Hoerlin's banking assets were unfrozen. On July 28, 1944 another big step was taken. Hoerlin's status from 'enemy alien' was changed to U.S. citizen. Kate's citizenship had preceded his by two months.

There was a two-fold celebration. First, one in Binghamton, surrounded by friends and neighbors who had been supportive of the family. On the day after the United States had declared war on Germany, Kate and Hoerlin answered their doorbell: standing outside was a neighborhood family, formally dressed, who had come to assure them: "We are your friends." Others quickly rallied to their side. She and Hoerlin had decided to thank their loyal compatriots in a typically American way: a cocktail party. That evening my parents moved the living room furniture to the side and rolled up the rug. The cocktail party, adding a European touch, would have dancing. After glasses had been raised high and often and the revelry had come to an end, Kate and Hoerlin—exhausted and exhilarated—headed for bed but not before my mother commented, as she would so often, ". . . only in America . . ." It was as though a magnanimous wand had been waved over their heads, anointing them—even in a time of war—from foe to ally.

The second part of the celebration was in New York City, where the new citizens were similarly toasted. It was a smaller and more intimate gathering. My father recalled years later to me how he was struck by the three women who dominated the party: Trude, Bettina and Kate, whom he fondly dubbed the three Valkyries. Trude was the only one that captured the mythological women's physical attributes but each of them, all German-born, [57] exemplified in her own way a fierce will and ingenuity. Like the pagan heroines before them, they rode the earth with female fearlessness. Less than a year later, this decidedly mortal group gathered again to celebrate for another reason, a much more far-reaching one. Germany surrendered unconditionally to the United States on May 7, 1945. The war was finally over.

Chapter 14

METAMORPHOSIS

The day after my kindergarten classmates taunted me in the school—yard, pointing and laughing, "Little German girl, little German girl," I had my mother cut my hair. No more braids. They advertised my 'otherness.' Even with the war over, I was acutely aware of and uncomfortable with my family's "German-ness." There were so many ways we could be told apart. We had not adopted the car culture of America, continuing instead the sacred European custom of Sunday afternoon walks. After we children were carted off to church with the devout Maia in the morning, we were expected to join "the parents" in hikes in the surrounding hills. Devoid of the maze of country paths common in Europe, at least the excursions offered "frische Luft"(fresh air), a prerequisite to a healthy existence in any German lexicon. This ritual, among others, distinguished me from my American peers as it seemed everything else did. The furnishings of our home were emphatically European, the smells of red cabbage and sausages equally distinctive and the sounds of heavily accented English—or worse yet—of spoken German were pervasive. The kitchen was a staging area for filling parcels, limited to weighing five pounds, to be sent to survivors in a devastated Germany. Tea, coffee, sugar, vitamins and medicines were lined up, assembly-like fashion, waiting to be packed. While I would hold the flaps of boxes down, my father—applying skills learned from working in his parents' china store—methodically sealed them. The older I got, the more the war came into my understanding . . . still vaguely so, but enough to know that terrible things had happened, things my parents didn't want to talk about. There was the world of Binghamton, the real world to me, and another world, unknown to me, somewhat mysterious and foreboding.

Metamorphosis is defined in biological terms as a profound change in form from one stage to the next in the life history of an organism. World War II transformed the world, changed Germany radically and forever impacted lives both inside and outside of the country. My parents saw how it affected those who had survived in Germany, many suffering from the anguish of ambivalence, still loving a homeland that had not always been under the boot of a draconian dictator. Although there continued to be protestations of innocence about the Holocaust, and worse yet, denials of its existence, the full extent of this atrocity was unfolding in excruciating detail. Did a shred of decency remain in a country that formerly represented the apex of civility and culture? My parents also experienced America's response to the war. A brush of collective guilt painted all Germans. As emigrants who had been given U.S. citizenship, Kate and Hoerlin were trying to assimilate and reshape their lives, striving for acceptance and integration. Did this mean disassociating themselves from Germany? And on another level, I was trying to find my own identity, trying to escape from being a *"little German girl,"* to being 100% American. In Kafka's famous rendition of The Metamorphosis, Gregor Samsa woke up one morning from unsettling dreams and asked, "What has happened to me?" After the nightmare of WW II, Kate and Hoerlin had to sort out what had happened in Germany and what was happening to them. I, in turn, focused on what was happening to me.

It was more than a month after the war ended that my father found out his mother had survived. On June 15, 1945, a one-line letter arrived: "Your mother has asked me to convey to you that she is still alive and in reasonable health."[1] The notice from a kind American serviceman brought enormous relief to our whole family. Prior to the war, Maria Hoerlin had moved from Schwaebisch Hall to a pretty suburb on the outskirts of Stuttgart, not far from where she had grown up. Stuttgart, a central rail transportation hub and industrial center, turned out to be a strategic air offensive target of the Allies, repeatedly attacked from 1940 to 1945. Altogether 142,000 bombs were dropped and 4,590 lives were lost.[2] A raid on October 8, 1943 that left 101 people dead had spared Mother Hoerlin, but barely. Parts of her home were destroyed by fire, but enough of it was left to allow two bombed-out neighbors to move in with her. Other neighbors had been killed.

Mail between Germany and the United States had been erratic at best during the war and the last time my father heard from his mother had been in January 1945. It was not until eight months later that a letter of hers came through: "I can calmly say that I regard it as a special blessing, that I have been spared . . . the quiet in the night, now that we are no longer frightened by air alarms, is a welcome reprieve; one could not have stood the air raids much longer in the last months of the war."[3] Living among the ruins, the seventy-one-year-old woman—anemic and in shock—begged her son to send iron supplements and food. In spite of widespread famine and deprivation, it was not until December 1945 that food relief shipments to Germany were allowed by the Allies. [4] Even then, packages—as with letters—seldom made it through the chaos of post-war Europe. In mid-January 1947 Mother Hoerlin underwent another setback: she was ordered to vacate her home—even thought she still shared it with two others—to make room for U.S. occupation forces and their families. Having read rumors of such displacements, Hoerlin had dispatched a raft of letters to the U.S. military in Germany, asking that his frail mother be allowed to stay put. He also made the point that she had always been anti-Nazi, but this did not sway the occupation forces. Maria Hoerlin was moved to a church-run old lady's home in March 1947. Although it was terribly disorienting for her, at least she was being cared for regularly.

Overseas travel to war-torn Europe from the United States was complicated, but finally in 1948 my parents made the voyage. It happened that two of their children had preceded them. In 1945 Thomi's education at Harvard had been interrupted by the draft. By the time he finished boot camp, Germany had surrendered but his unit was nonetheless shipped overseas. Shortly before sailing, his unit marched by a nearby German prisoner of war camp and Thomi overheard one prisoner say to another in German, "Look at how sloppily they march." Thomi, without missing a step, shot back in impeccably accented Bavarian-German, "Yes, that's why we won the war." [5] Stationed subsequently with the U.S. Signal Corps in Salzburg, the same town he had moved from nine years earlier, Thomi had an enviable Army experience, keeping the peace in one of the world's prettiest spots and surely charming many a Fraeulein with his wit and suave good looks. With the benefit of GI bill funding for his college education, he returned to the States in 1947.

Duscha too had an assignment that serendipitously circled back to her childhood. Having graduated from Smith College in 1946, she had taken a position as a translator in the Army's Civilian Censorship Division located in the town of her birth: Munich. Most of her colleagues in the Division were former refugees like her and one of them, who had fled Germany to England, became her husband. When Kate and Hoerlin journeyed to Europe it was to see the newlyweds as well as friends and relatives, especially Hoerlin's mother.

It had been ten years since Kate had disembarked from a trans-Atlantic voyage bringing her back to Germany, that time returning from her introduction to America. Then too she had landed in Bremen, near Hamburg. In May 1938 she had gone to see Max Warburg on his magical estate, Koesterberg. Max had fled Germany a few weeks afterwards and died in America in 1946. Delirious on his deathbed, he talked about the coachman readying the horses to take him back to Koesterberg. [6] He would have been heartbroken to see it now. Occupied by German officers during the war, Koesterberg was transformed into a military outpost with barracks erected on its lawns, Wehrmacht cars had parked in the stately gardens and antiaircraft guns and radar topping its buildings.[7] Allied bombs wrought further devastation on the property, which once had been a shining example of Jewish wealth and success combined with German aesthetic sensitivities. In the post-war era, Koesterberg underwent another iteration: it was an orphanage for children from Theresienstadt and other concentration camps.

Although forewarned, Kate and Hoerlin were not prepared for the extent of the destruction in their homeland. The grim realities of bombing and battles hit them hard: the landscape was physically and emotionally scarred, leaving behind mounds of rubble and hordes of displaced and dispirited persons. Attempts were made to continue the rituals of everyday life, but against a background of devastation.

A religious procession in the midst of Munich's ruins in 1948.

Mother Hoerlin in Stuttgart had correctly written her son that he would not recognize the town he had lived in for so many years: 60% of its buildings were damaged or obliterated. Her son barely recognized her, much less the environs. Mother Hoerlin was a shrunken version of her former self, thin and drawn. She had not seen her beloved "Hermannle" for a decade, but did not complain. She found consolation in dozens of photographs my father brought her, showing the good life he lived in America. The photos of me, her only grandchild, brought tears to her eyes.

Hoerlin meets with his mother Maria in post-war Germany.

While in Stuttgart, Hoerlin also saw his doctoral thesis advisor, Erich Regener. Regener had been ousted from his chairmanship of the Physics Department at Stuttgart Technical University by the Nazis in 1937 for refusing to divorce his Jewish wife, but was reinstated in August 1945. In the interim, underscoring the capricious twists of war, Regener had been recruited by a young Wernher von Braun, the rocketeer whiz, to design instrumentation for rocket flight research. The technology was originally intended to measure the temperature, pressure and density of the upper atmosphere but regrettably, by the end of the war, it was applied to the construction of long-range missiles. Hoerlin found his old professor in a crumbling, bomb-scarred building amidst heaps of debris on the University's grounds. Classes had been convened again; as a precondition to admission, students were required to help with rebuilding the campus. But rebuilding German physics took more than hauling away physical wreckage, the intellectual ruins needed restoring as well. Regener became one of the strongest post-war advocates for restructuring physics toward its former glory, the time before the exodus of Jewish scientists and the rejection of "Jewish physics."

As systematically as the National Socialists had gone about nazifying all facets of German society, the Allies set themselves to the task of denazifying them. "Denazification" became a rallying cry. The objective was removing active Nazis from influential positions, especially government bureaucracies, and reeducating them toward democratic ideals. In the U.S. Zone alone, 13.5 million Germans filled out a 131 point questionnaire about his or her political activities during the Third Reich and were categorized according to degrees of complicity with the Nazis: major offender, offender, lesser offender, a follower or exonerated.[8] The process, its guidelines loose, was inconsistent and arcane. [9]

Three men who played a role in my parents' flight from Germany are examples of its complex workings. The most bizarre case was that of Fritz Wiedemann, who had been so central to my parents' odyssey when he was Hitler's Adjutant. He had not resided in the Third Reich throughout the war, appointed first as German Consul to San Francisco and then to Tientsin, China. His tenure in San Francisco combined elements of party boy, espionage, and deft instincts. A year after his arrival in the United States, the dapper officer was featured in a five page spread in LIFE magazine with numerous photos of him and his family and a narrative that commented on his courteous and affable ways, his readiness to laugh easily. Reporters at the bar of San Francisco's Press Club had concluded the new consul was "... no Machiavelli, a forceful man of strong character but incapable of subtle intrigue ..." [10] As Germany became more and more aggressive, Wiedemann became increasingly ostracized because of growing distrust about his clandestine actions. Wiedemann assiduously avoided commenting on the Fuehrer and according to a report of the head of British intelligence in the United States, he was a genuine and serious opponent of Hitler.[11] He was still suspect, however, mainly because of his affair with Princess Stephanie, who was notoriously pro-Hitler. Finally, when Wiedemann leaked information to American and British intelligence on Hitler's plans to invade Russia, he was taken seriously.

Expelled from America by President Roosevelt in 1941, Wiedemann stopped briefly in the United States en route from China to Germany in 1945 and was described as follows: "Newsmen who remembered Wiedemann as the tall, black-haired fashion plate scarcely recognized the baggy suited, graying and unshaven man who deplaned in California." [12] He was quickly whisked away to Nuremberg where under prolonged interrogations, he declared Hitler as "... crazy, stark crazy ..."[13] His testimony was used in the prosecution of Nazi war criminals. [14] In November 1948, a denazification court classified him as a "follower" and fined him $600. The court president proclaimed: ". . . Wiedemann was an opponent to Nazism despite holding high offices. Evidence showed that in San Francisco Wiedemann committed high treason against the Nazi regime . . ."[15] It was not until May 1948 [16] that he was declared "denazified" and released from detention, returning to the dairy farm he had been reluctant to leave when Hitler first called him into service. [17]

Kate's friend, Oswald Bumke, was also placed in the denazification program. The eminent psychiatrist had been initially declared by the occupying forces as "politically innocent," but that changed in the fall of 1945 when a Swiss newspaper article accused him of close cooperation with the Nazis. He was promptly dismissed from his position as head of Germany's most prestigious psychiatric hospital, the University of Munich's *Nerven-Klinik*. In 1934, he had changed the name of the hospital from Clinic for Psychiatry to Clinic for Nervous Disorders hoping to mitigate stigmatization. [18] Early on, Bumke had spoken out brazenly in public, warning about the dangers of National Socialism's sterilization programs. His critics nonetheless faulted him for staying in ". . . the first and foremost psychiatric chair in Germany" during the Nazi period and not speaking out more for the rights of persons with mental illness.[19] Although Bumke and his associates had sabotaged sterilization laws and not cooperated with Nazi directives to transfer patients to known death asylums, he was implicated by association. By 1947, the Allies deemed the accusations against Bumke groundless and he was reinstated to his professorship.

Also exonerated was Fritz Gajewski, Hoerlin's boss at I.G. Farben's subsidiary, the *Agfa* factory in Wolfen/Dessau. The I.G. Farben Trial, the sixth of 12 trials conducted at Nuremberg, accused 24 of Germany's top industrialists of genocide, slavery and crimes against humanity. Gajewski was among them, on the specific charge of denunciating the former head of the Filmfabrik, Dr. Gerhard Ollendorff, who was Jewish.[20] The case was a dramatic one, convoluted in that Gajewski had supported his colleague's plans to leave Germany in 1938, at the same time inexplicably informing the Gestapo of Ollendorff's agenda. After several months of imprisonment, Gajewski was able to secure Ollendorff's release and helped him immigrate to Brazil. At the Nuremberg trial, Ollendorff testified on Gajewski's behalf, highlighting his Jewish-friendly policies. Gajewski was acquitted on all charges.[21]

Kate and Hoerlin felt relieved that those people who had assisted them were absolved from Nazi injustices and crimes. The denazification proceedings had cast a wide net and although inconsistent and lengthy, had by and large successfully differentiated collective guilt from individual responsibility. Along with other "good" Germans, Kate's friend the Ruhr industrialist Paul Reusch, was distraught that after the war he was "thrown into the same pot as Nazis" by the occupying forces.[22] But over time justice did seem to prevail and the public airing served a crucial purpose. Denazification exposed the degree to which Nazism poisoned civilian life on an everyday basis and the Nuremberg Trials showed the depth and breadth of the government's genocide policies. My parents avoided talking about the Holocaust to any of us children. Like others touched by this horror, they felt it was too painful and shameful to discuss. And the magnitude of it was almost impossible to comprehend.

The atrocities had been broadcast in the United States by Edward R. Murrow, who reported after witnessing the liberation of Buchenwald in 1945: "I pray you to believe what I have said . . . I reported what I saw and heard, but only part of it. For most of it, I have no words. If I have offended you by this rather mild account . . . I'm not in the least sorry." [23] Approximately 6,400,000 people had been killed in extermination and concentration camps, among them 160,000 to 180,000 German Jews. [24] Kate's Jewish relatives had been among the victims. Her aunt, a sister of her mother's, had been interned with her physician husband at Theresienstadt, touted by the Nazis as a 'model' concentration camp. Although they survived, [25] it must have been especially cruel for a trained doctor to be in this mock ghetto, where over 30,000 deaths occurred, most of them due to starvation and typhus. With no medications or food available, there was no way to help. And Theresienstadt also served as a holding area for Jews on the way to Auschwitz, the largest of the camps, where over one million died.

Kate's treasured uncle Felix Hausdorff and his wife Lotte, though never imprisoned in a concentration camp, were nonetheless Holocaust fatalities. Hausdorff, a venerable mathematician dismissed from his professorship at the University of Bonn in 1935 because he was Jewish, found everyday life more and more restrictive with unceasing degradations. When told by the Gestapo in 1942 to report to an internment camp, he and his wife chose to commit suicide in their home instead. Leaving a note to a Jewish friend of theirs, they said, "What has been done against Jews in recent months arouses well-founded anxiety that we will no longer be allowed to experience a bearable situation. Forgive us, that we still cause you trouble beyond death."[26] It typified the kind of dignity, understatement and considerateness that Kate had observed on her many visits with them, from childhood on. As for Kate's other relatives, there was no trace of them.

Somber and saddened, Kate and Hoerlin returned to the United States. Reconciling a past life with the present can be a challenge, particularly when bridging different countries. But my parents were determined to rebuild and move forward, embracing the future. Their metamorphosis entailed adaptation and rebirth: they loved America and put their considerable energy into making it their permanent home. It is not as though they were blind to its shortcomings. Having seen the results of oppression and silence in one regime, they valued the tradition of protest in this country. "If you don't make yourself heard," my father once intoned, "then you have only yourself to blame when things go badly."

After the war ended in 1945, Hoerlin was distressed at the lack of American press coverage about reprisals in Poland resulting in the slaughter of thousands of ethnic Germans. [27] Would man's inhumanity to man never cease? And would the press again ignore—or bury—reports of genocide as they had about the Holocaust? He had written to his New York senators, the *New York Times* and the *PM Daily* and chided the recipients for not paying attention (again) to another disaster that was ". . . against every principle for which this war was fought . . ." and ended by saying, "I know that the German people cannot escape responsibility for the crimes committed during the war, but believe that the blind retributions and acts of vengeance in Poland are not the kind of justice on which a better world can be built." [28] It was the first of many letters of political protest my father wrote as a United States citizen.

Hoerlin and Kate were assimilating into life in Binghamton. As director of the physics laboratory at Ansco, [29] my father gave a number of local talks, mainly about cosmic rays, and was regularly asked by medical societies to speak about patient protection from too much radioactivity. [30] In addition, he was active in the American Physical Society; Hoerlin hosted the 1950 meeting of the New York section. As for my mother, she had joined the League of Women Voters and different music groups, attended a number of teas for well-known artists or authors, and gave talks to small cultural organizations about life in prewar Germany, music and musicians.

The only children at home were Hedi and myself. In 1945 Hedi was 13 years old and doing her utmost to fit into the American adolescence mold: listening to Tommy Dorsey records, belonging to a sorority and talking about cute boys. With Maia having left the family fold to marry a retired New York City policeman, Hedi was often responsible for tending to me. If she went to a football game, I went along. If I wanted to go the nearby stables to visit horses, she walked me to them. In retrospect, it is a wonder she didn't permanently resent me. As for me, I adored her even more than my buddy, "Peanuts," a sweet Shetland pony.

Peanuts and I had a straightforward deal: I would bring him carrots and sugar cubes and he would let me ride him. The pony was the faithful companion of a famous racehorse, Exterminator, winner of the 1918 Kentucky Derby and the 1922 Horse of the Year. [31] The large chestnut thoroughbred had long since retired to a life of grazing and was celebrated annually by his owners with a birthday cake of mashed oats and greens topped by upright carrots as candles. I hung around the stables so much that the stable manager, Mike, [32] taught me to ride little Peanuts. On special days, I had lunch with Mike and his wife, "Mrs. Terry," at their small house on the grounds. They behaved toward me as the child they never had and I could pretend I was <u>their</u> daughter. No one told me to take my elbows off the table or try to speak some German. In fact, there was not much talking at all. They quietly fussed over me and I quietly basked in their attention. <u>This</u> was the American way of life. Little did I realize how unusual their marriage was: a white man and a black woman in the 1940's. Slowly, this country would undergo a metamorphosis for them too.

Binghamton had all the attributes of contentment. As my mother would say, "What more do we want? ("Was wollen wir mehr?"). She made sure that the routines and rhythms of the everyday were punctuated by events that offered excitement and edification. When the world famous Budapest Quartet played in Binghamton, the Hoerlins hosted the post-concert party and Alexander Schneider stayed with them for several days; when the famous black actor and singer Paul Robeson gave a concert in Binghamton, the Hoerlins entertained him afterwards along with Uta Hagen, the Desdemona to his Othello in an electrifying Broadway performance; when the author Jan Struther came to talk about her book, <u>Mrs. Miniver,</u> on which the Academy Award winning film was based, she stayed with the Hoerlins, the first of several visits. Kate and Hoerlin had met Jan through Thomi, who attended a Quaker boarding school along with Jan's lovely daughter. Both mothers and children had become close: Jan had inscribed her book to Kate thus: "To dear Kate, who also gardens without gloves, feeling that if you dull one of the senses, you dull them all." They were soul mates. Kate thrived in circles of creativity and although Hoerlin's participation was more at the sidelines, he enjoyed his wife's sparkle and the camaraderie she generated. Together, they spun a cocoon of pleasure that attracted visitors . . . again and again.

Alternatively, my parents went to New York relatively often to see friends and attend concerts or plays. Usually on the agenda was seeing Trude, now married to Joe Lash and entrenched in political spheres of influence. Through Trude and Joe, Kate and Hoerlin were introduced to other activists, including Roger Baldwin, founder of the American Civil Liberties Union (ACLU). My parents had joined the ACLU in 1940 and my father had corresponded with Baldwin during the war. Now that they met, Hoerlin and Baldwin enjoying arguing: the freshly minted American citizen and the authoritarian Boston blue blood disagreed on pacifism (Baldwin was a committed pacificist), war-time union strikes (Hoerlin was against them) and the rights of members of the German American Bund [33] during the war (the reader can guess how Hoerlin and Baldwin diverged on this).

Because of Trude, my family also started spending summer vacations on Martha's Vineyard. In 1945, I contracted a severe case of whooping cough and my German refugee doctor prescribed a sure cure: "Take her to the ocean to breathe the fresh air (frische Luft)." Trude suggested coming to the Vineyard, frequented by her and Joe and many others whom Kate and Hoerlin had met in New York. We were invited to stay at Windy Gates, the beautiful Baldwin estate on cliffs overlooking the Atlantic. One thing Trude had neglected to tell my parents was that bathing suits were optional at their magnificent beach. In keeping with the freethinking and unconventional Baldwins, a motley cabal of naked reformers argued politics to the sound of crashing waves. Nudity was optional, political discourse was not. The next summer we rented our own house and, to the delight of everyone, my father brought his folding kayak, the Klepper from Germany, still a novelty in this country. Trude, years later, termed it "Martha's Vineyard's First Kayak," a designation that has not been challenged to this day.

**Summer on Martha's Vineyard and a time to tease
my father by messing up his hair.**

The Schmid/Hoerlin family in our backyard, ca. 1949. Seated from left to right: Duscha, Thomi, Hedi and Bettina; Kate and Hoerlin standing.

Summers on the Vineyard became a pattern, as did winter vacations to New Hampshire for skiing. When he first came there, the Austrian emigrant Hannes Schneider, had asked, "Where are the mountains?" North Conway's terrain did not compare favorably to that of the Alps, but Hannes proceeded to build a booming ski school. Furthermore, he performed his godfatherly tasks by outfitting me with skis every few years and putting me under his tutelage at his booming ski school. Learning stem turns under the watchful eyes of the father of modern skiing as well as my own father, I soon became a good little skier, a skill that stuck with me as a continuing source of pleasure.

My mother's efforts to inculcate me with culture were less successful than my father's to introduce me to the great outdoors. I took piano lessons, but couldn't get excited about music the way my mother was. However, I found one of her musical friends irresistible. Alexander Schneider, the endlessly ebullient, gregarious and remarkable violinist of the Budapest Quartet was a bushy haired Russian who could never bestow enough hugs and kisses on those surrounding him. When I was a twelve year old in 1951, he told me that if I had a <u>real</u> Jewish mother, she would be arranging my marriage to him. Merely some thirty years older than me, always falling in and out of love, he was outrageously flirtatious and joked with abandon.

When Abrasha, as my mother called him, began venturing into conducting, he went to France to study with Casals. To everyone's amazement, the passionate violinist convinced the acclaimed cellist to play in public again on the occasion of Bach's 200th birthday. The unparalleled sounds of Casals' cello had not been heard since he lived in voluntary exile in Prades to protest fascism in Franco's Spain. Abrasha knew Casals would not travel—certainly not to any country (such as the United States and England) that recognized a fascist regime and so, as he put it, "The mountains will come to Mohammed."[34] The Festival Pablo Casals was created in Perpignan.

Musicians and music aficionados alike flocked there, among them such famous performers as Myra Hess, Rudolf Serkin, Isaac Stern, Eugene Istomin and Mieczyslaw Horszowski as well as 100 youthful orchestra members, half American and half European. The 1950 festival was a triumph and Abrasha (or Sasha, as he was also named) and Casals jointly wrote to Kate, "You must come here next year—we both adore you." [35] It was a hard invitation to resist. Music had been the stream of continuity in her life that transcended place or time. So in 1951 Kate went to Perpigan with her friend since Munich days, Eva Feuermann, and quickly befriended there Abrasha's latest flame, Margaret Bourke-White, LIFE magazine's premiere photojournalist. The festival was a chamber music feast, where Casals played solos and in small ensembles or conducted the orchestra, singing along in rehearsals and urging orchestra members to "Attaquez, attaquez avec votre coeur" ("Attack, attack with your hearts").[36] The memories of that summer month sustained Kate in the more provincial milieu of Binghamton.

In 1952, it was my father and me who traveled to Europe, this time to Germany. My grandmother and I were finally going to meet. Seventy-eight years old and beset by health problems, Mother Hoerlin longed to see her only grandchild. Having managed until then to avoid associating with my German heritage, I had precious little curiosity about the country where both my parents were born and worst of all, I spoke hardly any German. Therefore, when my grandmother met me—her tall, polite and smiling granddaughter—I was basically mute. Maybe it was enough for her to gaze on me fondly, shifting her eyes only to admire her son, but how I wish I had told her how much I loved my father, the son she raised so well. The three of us Hoerlins made a pilgrimage to Schwaebisch Hall, slowly climbing the famous steps to the top, then visiting the old family home and store and admiring the wonderfully preserved town. After a few more days of doing my best to understand what she was saying, we parted—me bending down to give her a kiss and she whispering to me, "Sei brav, Kind, sei brav." Just to underscore how pathetic my German was, for years I thought "brav" meant brave. But "Sei brav, Kind, sei brav" translates as "Be good, my child, be good." Accordingly, for many of those adolescent years, I tried to be brave. Seldom was I good.

My father and I continued to travel afterwards—visiting the Garmisch cousins, Munich friends and his Austrian climbing partner, Erwin Schneider, who had no toes—a phenomenon I found morbidly fascinating. After heroic climbs in the Himalayas and Andes, the man known as "Seven-thousander Schneider" because of the numerous 7000 meter peaks he had conquered, had suffered severe frostbite on a climbing misadventure in the Swiss Alps in 1939. In one operation six toes were amputated, soon followed by another removing the remaining four. Erwin was fully awake for both procedures, refusing the assistance of any painkillers. [37] Doctors never thought he would walk again unaided,[38] but Schneider was tough and became an accomplished skier and gradually took up non-technical climbing. He wore specially made boots, and other than looking like he had strangely small feet, the plucky mountaineer walked briskly and well.

The two old friends reveled in each other's company; I was definitely an outsider but got a whiff of how exhilarating those pioneering days of climbing had been to them both. Nanga Parbat was part of their discourse. Planning was in the works for yet another German attempt, called the "Willy Merkl Memorial Expedition" in honor of the 1934 disaster that paradoxically brought Kate and Hoerlin together in the first place. Organized by a younger half brother of Merkl's,[39] first-rate climbers from Germany and Austria signed on to the effort. Hoerlin and Erwin wondered if this attempt would succeed. On July 3, 1953, Nanga was finally conquered. It had been the bane of German mountaineering over the years, claiming more lives than any other peak in the Himalayas. Thirty-one climbers had been killed on Nanga Parbat between 1895 and 1950, but in 1953 a lone climber stood on top. The Austrian wonder, Hermann Buhl, with Herculean stamina earned the added distinction of being the only single climber who made a first ascent of an 8000-meter peak. On the summit, he had planted a Pakistani flag with his ice ax. [40]

Imperceptibly except to me, the trip to Germany changed me. I had gotten to know the country that I had wanted to distance myself from, that had defined me as "other" in the eyes of my peers and that had enigmatic undertones for my parents. Parts of my father and mother, previously foreign, felt more familiar to me. I was no longer intent on shunning my German roots; they were part of my metamorphosis. I actually wanted to speak German. I was getting a more complete sense of my evolution, stitched together from various yarns. But there was one tangled ball of yarn yet to be unraveled.

Chapter 15

"OH, THAT WAS IN
THE PAST"

When I was 14, I discovered I was Jewish. At least I was according to traditional 2000 year-old Halakhic laws of matrilineal descent whereby one's Judaism is determined by one's mother. My grandmother was Jewish, therefore my mother was Jewish, therefore I was Jewish. I was a member of the tribe, even if a straggler. The revelation took place in New York City, where I was visiting my namesake, Bettina. In discussing the difficulties that members of her extended family, the Warburgs, encountered during the Nazi regime, she alluded to those faced by my mother because of her Jewish lineage. I was stunned, and more than a little excited to discover a family secret. My mother . . . **Jewish?** Bettina either knew very well or had no inkling about what a bombshell she dropped; to her all religion was passé and therefore not a big deal. When I came back home, it didn't take long for me to pop the question: "Mummy, what's this about your being Jewish?" She answered, "Oh, that was in the past."

My mother was legendary among her children for being able to cut off a conversation more effectively than a surgeon removing a tumor. Her skill was combined with the kind of grace, or perhaps a coup de grace, that often made you unaware of the cut. If you pressed on with questions, she quickly made it clear that you were being totally inappropriate. One sulked off guiltily for crossing an invisible line of demarcation. Try as I did to get beyond, "Oh, that was in the past," I was only successful in making her angry. My affront to her authority and privacy was painful to us both. Later that same day, I cornered my father. Brought up in the Lutheran faith, he never participated in any organized religion as an adult and had not shared in the family routine of attending Catholic mass. When asked *if he knew his wife and my mother was Jewish, he also brushed off the question. He said that coming to America for my parents was about looking forward and not backwards. The rest was indeed in the past.*

In all their official immigration and citizenship-related documents,[1] my parents stated they had left Germany because ". . . their political views differed strongly from those of present German Government," adding that "We are making this country our permanent home and are educating our four children as Americans." It was an explanation familiar to my siblings and me: my parents were *emigrants,* not *refugees.* Coming to America had been a choice, not a necessity. There was never any reference to Kate's Jewish background or how that heritage had forced them out of Nazi Germany.

Why did my mother turn her back so completely on Judaism? Why was it kept a secret, with my father as her willing accomplice? There can be several answers to that question, none of them complete, so all I can offer are speculations. At a time when foreigners were not particularly welcome in America, the nuance of coming to this country because of political principles, rather than because of religious persecution, was more palatable. Certainly it cast the decision in a more noble light and distinguished my parents from the hundreds upon thousands of people fleeing for their lives. It is not as though Kate and Hoerlin lied on the documents stating their reason for emigration: their political views did indeed ". . . differ strongly from those of the present German government." Once they adopted that statement as their primary one, perhaps it would have been awkward to add, "and, by the way, Kate is regarded as Jewish by Hitler."

Another factor was that my mother considered herself as Catholic after her 1921 marriage to Willi Schmid; she was truly assimilated. She found comfort in Willi's extended Catholic family, lived in the very Catholic air of Bavaria, brought her children up as Catholic, and celebrated the numerous Catholic holidays with alacrity. On the other hand, her bond to religion as such became less pronounced over time. When I turned thirteen, at the cusp of gingerly exploring adolescent independence but a year before I knew of my Jewish background, I announced to her that I felt alienated from Catholicism. Weekly confessionals were unappealing and immediate redemption (saying five Hail Mary's and ten Our Father's) seemed implausible to me. I decided that I was no longer going to mass. My mother responded that she too would then not be going, hardly the reaction of a committed Catholic. She unceremoniously terminated her ties to organized religion.

I have no doubt that anti-Semitism in Germany and Austria had been so ubiquitous and so upsetting that my mother was genuinely fearful of any connection to Judaism. She not only wanted to disassociate herself, but protect her children from the prejudices and dangers that seemed to accompany Judaism. Once in the relative safety of America, one might think that she could on some level acknowledge her roots. Regrettably, even the small town of Binghamton in upstate New York where Kate and Hoerlin settled was hardly devoid of religious discrimination. Overt anti-Semitism actually had risen in the States during the 1940s, peaking in 1944. [2] And then, precisely because of the horrors of the Holocaust and its impact on her relatives, Kate may have become even more invested in hiding her past.

As painful as it is, I must also address a strain of anti-Semitism on the part of my parents. Although largely unspoken, when my parents' religious prejudices surfaced—even if not toward family and friends—it was mortifying. One of my sisters was married to someone of Jewish descent; later on, I would also be. To use a contrite phrase, many of Kate and Hoerlin's best friends were Jewish. Certainly the majority of their musical friends were. And when my parents moved in 1953 to a mecca of science, a high percentage of the scientists there were Jewish. Especially in that setting, it seems my mother would feel safe at last in acknowledging her descent but that was not the case. She continued to practice a self-inflicted form of anti-Semitism.

The mecca of science referred to above was none other than the Los Alamos Scientific Laboratory in New Mexico, a remote site famous for its secret work on the development of atomic bomb during World War Two. Following the war, "the Atomic City" sought different kinds of skills, including analysis of nuclear testing at high altitude. My father's background in cosmic rays was particularly relevant; he was recommended for the job by the illustrious physicist and future Nobelist, Hans Bethe. Bethe, a professor at Cornell University—near Binghamton—and his wife Rose had become friends of Hoerlin and Kate, having much in common other than physics: they all had fled Nazi Germany, become enthusiastic Americans and delighted in mountain hiking. Coincidentally, Hoerlin had met Rose when she was a young girl, the attractive daughter of a physicist who was rector at Stuttgart Technical University when Hoerlin was a student there. [3]

The prospect of a move was hard for my mother—another big change, and one that would mean she was far from her three older children who had all settled in the East. My siblings were married; my brother had started a family and my two sisters were about to follow suit. But Hans and Rose convinced Kate she would take to the grand beauty of the Southwest. Basically it came down to the fact that my mother loved my father and wanted to see him happy. Before the family move, when he was away visiting Los Alamos, Kate wrote him: "We {Bettina and I} love and miss you no end—I told Bethe that it is ridiculous for a woman my age to be so in love—and he roared—and then looked at me, approving, understanding." [4]

The Hill, as Los Alamos is affectionately called, is perched on a high mesa, backed by the Jemez mountains and across the Rio Grande valley from the majestic Sangre de Cristo range. One of the earth's longest mountain chains, stretching from Colorado into New Mexico, the "Sangres" include ten peaks over 14,000 feet high, and more than twice that many over 13,000 feet. In the summer, one can take advantage of beautiful hiking trails skirting Alpine lakes and ascending to breathtaking views considerably above tree line. In the winter, there are numerous skiing opportunities, both downhill and cross—country. My father was thrilled. While in Binghamton, he wrote friends in Germany confessing to a "quiet homesickness" [5] for the mountains. Now that homesickness was assuaged.

My mother also loved the mountains but they were not as life-defining for her as for my father. For her, a home and a community were more germane. She had done a remarkable job of achieving both in Binghamton but was finding them difficult to replicate in Los Alamos. As glorious as the surrounding scenery was, the Hill was aesthetically wanting. A company town built by the U.S. government, its housing had more in common with the monotonous tract layouts of New Jersey's Levittown than with the inviting irregularities of adobe construction in the Southwest. [6] Los Alamos also contrasted sharply to Binghamton's tree-lined streets and varied architecture. Instead of owning a welcoming New England style three-story house with a large garden, we rented from the government a small one-story duplex with a chain link fence enclosing a postage stamp size backyard. The living room could not accommodate all the Biedermeier furniture and much of it was put in storage.

In 1953, the Hill was a quintessential gated community, one that required a government-issued pass to enter or exit through its guarded security gate adjacent to a tall watchtower that overlooked the surrounds. Like many closed communities, it conveyed a numbing sense of sterility: everything was well maintained, stores had to be pre-approved by a government agency, guests from the outside could visit only if they had been issued a pass in advance, there was no door-to-door soliciting by traveling salesmen, and 100% employment assured no poverty. No one was a stranger, the community was tight-knit and homogeneous. There were no museums, concert halls or recreational facilities. My mother was miserable at first. And so was I.

Moving from Binghamton had seemed to me the ruination of my young life. As a teen, I was totally enmeshed with peers and place and had no interest whatsoever in challenging my comfort levels. I was leaving the familiar for the great unknown and it was frightening. My parents made the long drive across the country to New Mexico with a sullen and unforgiving daughter. Things did not get much better when we arrived: routines like biking to the river were out of the question and there were no places for kids to indulge in typically annoying adolescent behaviors. It was definitely an adjustment, one I reminded my parents of with nagging persistence.

My new high school was different than my relaxed junior high school. Attended mainly by nerdy children of scientists, Los Alamos High had very competitive academic standards that reflected the expectations of the town's highly educated residents. As we sat in history or math classes, it was not uncommon to hear the detonation of explosives and experience the shock effects of small tests conducted at the nearby laboratory facilities. At a time when American elementary school children were diving under their desks in compliance with national air raid drills, we high schoolers were feeling our desks shake from the trial testing nearby. If someone had done particularly badly on a quiz, we'd joke with one another about radiation affecting our brains. But neither radiation nor testing were joking matters.

The cover of my 1954 Los Alamos High School Year Book is graced by a full-page fluorescent photograph of an atomic mushroom cloud. Hues of violet-purple burst forth with volcanic ferocity from the top of a column of smoke and dust. The shape, familiar at the time to any school child, heralded the advent of the atomic age. The image induces chills about the apocalyptic power of the atom and its horrifying aftermath: in Los Alamos it was also regarded as a source of pride.

My 1954 Los Alamos High School yearbook.

Beginning in 1942, a cadre of the world's brightest scientists, many of them refugees from totalitarian regimes in Europe, especially Nazi Germany, gathered there in top secrecy to harness the atom's energy and beat the Third Reich in the race to develop nuclear weapons. Going by the code name of the Manhattan Project, its strategic success engenders moral controversies that continue to this day. Was dropping atomic bombs on Hiroshima and Nagasaki, killing upwards of 200,000 Japanese civilians, justified because it won the war for the Allies and prevented innumerable casualties in the Allied forces? Or should it be condemned as a violation of human values? Was it a right or wrong decision? This was Los Alamos' perplexing legacy.

After the war, many of the scientists who had labored around the clock to build the bomb were aghast at what they birthed. They retreated back to their laboratories and universities, becoming outspoken opponents to the further development of nuclear weapons. But new tensions were now rising—not between the Allies and Axis countries—but between two world powers, the United States and the Soviet Union, now entering into a full-blown nuclear arms race. The rivalry, begun with American use of the A-bomb in 1945, was intensified by Soviet testing of atomic weapons in 1949, and furthered by the Americans developing an H-bomb in 1950. "Let us not be deceived," warned Presidential Advisor Bernard Baruch in 1947, "we are today in the midst of a cold war." The Cold War concept was novel: a war without physical engagement, a war of brinkmanship and deterrence. In its early iteration between 1945 and 1963, Russia and America vied for the superiority of their respective nuclear arsenals. They engaged in a military standoff enforced by mutually assured destruction (MAD), a strategy built on the premise that if either power used nuclear (or thermonuclear) weapons against each other, they would not only self-annihilate but also take most, if not all, of humanity with them.

It was during this volatile time that my father was recruited to the Los Alamos Scientific Laboratory (LASL) [7] to lead the Nuclear Weapons Effects Group, a section charged with studying atmospheric nuclear testing and improving physical measurements of detonations. After World War II, Los Alamos had described its role as continued weapons development along with basic nuclear research.[8] By the time my father arrived, much of physics research had become entwined with the military agenda of the country and he was excited to participate in influencing the nation's atomic energy policies. Hoerlin was pursuing uncharted territory that in the future would prove to be consequential. As my mother wrote to Mother Hoerlin in Germany: "For the time being, your son still buzzes around in world history. He is a bit too much occupied with everything that is new and worth knowing, concentrates totally on it . . ." [9] In one sentence, my mother managed to convey that Hoerlin was engaged in something weighty and pioneering, while couching it in a delicate complaint that he was working too hard. She also told his aged mother that her son had achieved what had been an original dream of hers for him, an academic affiliation. His job at Los Alamos entailed an appointment at the University of California.

Almost a year-to-the day after Hoerlin had accepted the Los Alamos position and well after receiving government security clearance, he was subjected to an interrogation typical of the Red Scare era. Stirred by Senator Joseph McCarthy of Wisconsin, a perverse nationwide hunt was on for Communists or Communist sympathizers. In 1953 McCarthy had become chair of the Senate Committee on Government Operations, giving him a platform to launch his attacks. Claiming there was extensive Russian infiltration and subversion throughout this country, the senator destroyed the lives of hundreds of Americans. In response to his directives, two agents of the U.S Atomic Energy Commission (AEC) grilled my father in 1954. [10]

In a series of questions designed to ferret out any suspicious Communist links, the officials focused on my father belonging to the American Civil Liberties Union, my parents' hosting the famed bass-baritone Paul Robeson in their home in 1945, and Kate's friendship with the esteemed author Jan Struther. Hoerlin answered the questions with his usual forthrightness and honesty. It was well known that Robeson often praised the Soviet Union, where he was greeted as a hero without encountering the racial prejudices that plagued him in America. My father explained that his connection to this tall, forceful civil rights advocate was based on Robeson's enormous vocal and theatrical talents, not his political beliefs or whether he was a card-carrying Communist. As for Struther, my father commented that while she was very liberal and had sympathy for the Russian people, he did not consider her a Communist. After all, Struther was the author of the book on which the 1942 Academy Award winning movie, "Mrs. Miniver," was based. The film that extolled the virtues of the U.S. entering World War II to help the Brits hardly seemed subversive. But Hoerlin's most ardent response was in regard to his ACLU membership: "...I joined because I came from a country where civil liberties were suppressed ... The ACLU has upheld and defended the constitutional rights of individual American citizens. I feel the organization should be supported." [11] As with the U.S. Treasury Department investigations at *Agfa*/Ansco in 1942, my father cleared this interrogation well, although he wondered if living the American dream of democracy entailed intensive governmental questioning every ten years or so.

Ever so slowly my mother and I adjusted to life on the Hill, often in the absence of my father. Along with many other Los Alamos scientists and technicians, Hoerlin's work pulled him away from home for long periods of time to bomb testing sites in Nevada and, later on, the Bikini Atoll in the Pacific. My mother, who valued female friends but thrived on the admiration of males, found herself in a predominantly woman's world and a somewhat monolithic one. Los Alamos, basically a one company town, had little diversity. For that one had to exit through the security gate, entering into the unique cultural mix of New Mexico. There were Native American pueblos, Hispanic mountain villages and Anglo artist colonies; there was Santa Fe and Taos and abandoned silver mining towns. Almost every weekend was spent outside the gate, rather than inside.

During the summer, the rather somber tone of Los Alamos was changed by the infusion of top-notch scientists, many of them alumni of the Manhattan Project and European. On a given Saturday or Sunday, my parents (bringing along their teenage daughter) would help organize hikes with scientists such as Bethe (born in Germany) and Enrico Fermi (born in Italy), or finding mushrooms with John von Neumann (born in Hungary), the latter the only non-Nobel winner of the three only because there is no Nobel Prize in mathematics. Afterwards, they would often invite them home. In a letter to English friends, my mother somewhat cavalierly commented, "I have Nobel Prize winners raiding my refrigerator." The summer crowd also did a good job of raiding liquor cabinets; a busy schedule of infamous cocktail parties rocked the Hill accompanied by lots of gossip and a few scandals. Everyone seemed to drink hard, play hard, and work hard.

It all was eye opening to me after the more conventional confines of Binghamton, not only because of my parents' new social circles and the cultural richness of life in New Mexico but because of the great outdoors. I was an avid skier with the ready accessibility of the Los Alamos and Santa Fe ski areas and the relative proximity of Aspen, [12] a decent mountaineer with climbing excursions in northern New Mexico's 13,000 foot peaks and southern Colorado's 14,000 foot peaks in the San Juan range (called "the Switzerland of America"), and a much improved horseback rider since artist friends of my parents had a stable of Arabian horses. With the exception of the latter, it was my father who led me in those directions. It became a special bond between us—his delight in my growing skills and my pleasure in pleasing him.

On the other hand, my relationship with my mother was becoming more complicated by the day. When I look back on it, some of the friction can be undoubtedly attributed to the usual teenager/parent tensions (especially daughter/mother ones) but unquestionably the adjustment to Los Alamos played a role. My mother had not yet fashioned her own domain. The austere setting did not lend itself to her dazzle and seductive femininity. I resented her intense dedication to trying to create, or creating, an aura of magnetic charm and knew the effort took a toll on her, often making her tired and irritable. To me, there was a disconnect between the public Kate, with her joie de vive, and the private Kate, struggling and discontent. It felt deceptive.

Which is not to say that I wasn't having my own challenges. I had attempted to fit into my high school, doing the best I could but generally unable to find a niche. I wrote for the Los Alamos high school newspaper, went out for junior cheerleader, won the New Mexico high school swimming competition in backstroke, and was invited to the prom by the heartthrob of my female peers, the quarterback of the football team. It still didn't do it. I hated high school. Fortuitously I had a like-minded friend and the two of us approached the principal about graduating a year early. He dismissed the idea, whereupon we enlisted the help of our respective parents and got permission. Graduating from Los Alamos High when I was 16, I enrolled at the University of Colorado in Boulder in the fall of 1956.

My departure for college overlapped with my mother finding her New Mexican bearings. In a coup that was described to me by one of her admirers as a "triumph," Kate managed to bring the famous Budapest String Quartet to perform in Los Alamos during the late fall of 1956. Since there was no concert hall, the group played in the high school auditorium. One person joked that the concert should make headlines: "Four Russians invade the Atomic City." The sold-out event kicked off a small chamber music series. Once the security gates to the town were opened in 1957, it became easier to invite outsiders, whether to give concerts or talks, and tap into a ready-made, highly educated audience. But this was a first.

The day after the Budapest concert, Kate and Hoerlin were invited along with the two brothers in the quartet, cellist Mischa and violinist Abrascha Schneider, to lunch at the home of the artist Georgia O'Keefe. O'Keefe had met Mischa in New York in the 1940's and Kate had known the quartet since Munich in the 1920's, but Kate and Georgia had not met one another. It marked the beginning of a long friendship between my parents and the reputedly asocial painter, launched by honoring Mischa's birthday with a surfeit of wine and spontaneous music making by Abrascha. Fortunately and understandably, world-class violinists never go anywhere without their instruments. The ethereal strains of Bach and more earthbound ones of "Happy Birthday to you, dear Mischa . . ." filled O'Keefe's rambling and sparsely furnished home, a renovated cow and pig sty, in the isolated farm village of Abiquiu. The setting was unlikely, but so was the assemblage: a pair of raucous Russians from one of the world's greatest string quartets, a statuesque woman who was arguably America's most iconic artist of her time, and two German refugees, one an earnest mountain climbing nuclear scientist and the other an indomitable personality who created her unique orbit of energy and excitement.

After that my parents were frequently invited by Georgia to her home. Most memorable were intimate Christmas Eve celebrations, sometimes eating dinner in Abiquiu, other times having a late lunch before driving to Taos. When I came home from college for winter breaks, I was invited along with my parents and six or so other guests. As the only non-adult, it sometimes felt tedious, especially since I experienced O'Keefe as intimidating and rather dour. Going to Taos Pueblo, however, was a remarkable event blending Native American, Hispanic and Anglo rituals and beliefs into a mystical experience unparalleled for me to this day. As the sun set over the ancient multi-storied pueblo and shed its glow on the nearby Sangre de Cristo mountains (exemplifying why the range was called Blood of Christ), huge bonfires were lit everywhere and an unforgettable procession of Indian dancers and musicians slowly made their way to the open doors of the pueblo's missionary church. The mingling of the dark frigid night, the smell of burning pinion wood, the sight of Native dancers performing in ancestral attire, and the sound of drumming combined with fiddles and flutes remains one of my most sensory memories.

Every time I came home from college, I was introduced to a new crop of my parents' friends and it became obvious that they were succeeding in doing what they excelled at: regrouping, engaging and conquering. The Southwest was beginning to feel more like home but their lives were constantly interrupted by my father's long stints at nuclear testing sites where hundreds of tests were being conducted. At the height of the Cold War, the United States engaged in a period of extensive activity aimed at advancing weapon technology, displaying a show of force and gathering data in order to detect secret nuclear testing. [13]

My father played a key role in detection efforts by conducting research to measure the physical effects of nuclear explosions in the atmosphere between 1955 and 1962. [14] He led research studies that questioned whether high altitude explosions burned a hole in the earth's ozone layer, identifying a new worry that could lead to climate change and harm living systems. The concerns, subsequently recorded by Hoerlin and his colleagues in a special Los Alamos report, are of historical interest as the first documentation of the possibility of human disruption of the ozone layer.[15] In subsequent years, this issue has become more and more prominent. In addition, his research on high altitude testing quantified how tests interfered with electronic systems, formed artificial radiation belts that damaged satellites, and disturbed the earth's magnetic field. Besides advancing knowledge in these areas, the information had a significant application. If one could identify how high-altitude tests altered the x-ray, gamma ray, neutron and light signals typical for nuclear explosions, that could pave the way toward an enforceable atmospheric nuclear test ban.

In April 1955, my mother and I drove to Las Vegas, Nevada to spend time with my father, who had been involved in testing there since February.[16] The atmosphere in the casino resort was carnival-like, a macabre parody of the serious intent of the testing effort. Gambling casinos sold "Atomic cocktails" and showgirls danced "The Bomb." At The Last Frontier Hotel, there was a crowning of "Miss Atomic Blast," who ". . . radiated loveliness instead of deadly atomic particles."[17] Bomb watching had boosted the local tourist and gambling industry. I too wanted to witness what had taken my father away so often; he somewhat reluctantly told my mother and me where to view a scheduled detonation, about an hour's drive from Las Vegas. Early on a beautiful spring morning, she and I drove there, parked the car at the side of the highway and watched a gigantic mushroom cloud appear on the landscape. The earth beneath us trembled and was followed by a large aftershock. It was awesome . . . and fearsome. Our trip back to town was made in contemplative silence.

"Anyone who has ever seen a nuclear explosion," my father would say, "has to be against war and work toward peace." The bombs tested in Nevada and the Pacific were sometimes 800 times more powerful than those dropped on Hiroshima and Nagasaki. As with most experiments, mistakes were made: mistakes in launchings, in calculating potency, and—most costly of all—mistakes in estimating the amount and effects of radioactive fallout. There was growing public concern about the harm on human lives and the environment. In college, I joined the young peace organization, SANE (The Committee for SANE Nuclear Policy), which sought to prevent the further deployment of nuclear weapons in space. It seemed like the perfect antidote to my adolescent years in Los Alamos when I was uncomfortable being associated with the terrors of the past (although we had moved there post-war) and the contaminations of the present. When I hesitantly told my father about joining SANE, I was relieved that he was sympathetic. Given that he and my mother were avid backers of Adlai Stevenson's bid for the Presidency in 1956 and supported his proposed nuclear weapons testing ban, it should not have come as a surprise.

The political will of both the national and international community was building pressure for an atmospheric testing moratorium and in 1958, the sonorous playing of the world's most celebrated cellist, Pablo Casals, added an eloquent voice to pleas for disarmament. A passionate crusader for peace, the 81-year-old former Spaniard performed at the United Nations General Assembly in New York, breaking his vow not to play in a country that recognized any fascist regime in order to honor the U.N's official founding exactly thirteen years earlier on October 24, 1945. The international language of music enveloped the great hall and afterwards Casals spoke out for ". . . bringing about fraternity and enlightened relationships between men the world over."[18]

My mother had seen the great Maestro a few months earlier at the Casals Music Festival in Puerto Rico, where she had traveled in part to fill the void of my father's prolonged absences from home. Music was always a balm for Kate and her relationship of over 35 years with Casals was a precious one. One evening, the cellist gently asked my mother, "Ma Cherie, why does your kind and good husband help make bombs?" To the man who years later won the U.N. Peace Medal, it was contradictory that Hoerlin could work for peace when employed by a branch of a huge war machine. "Ma Cherie" carefully explained that although not a pacifist, Hoerlin was convinced war could be averted by having deterrents in place and finding ways toward measurable, enforceable treaties. He, like others at Los Alamos, was an inherently moral scientist and, she assured Casals, "We are lucky to have him where he is." Where he was at the time was in Nevada, where in 1958 there was a burst of testing, a show of force that perversely contributed to a voluntary cessation of atmospheric testing by the United States, the Soviet Union and Great Britain. A nervous détente prevailed.

In the fall of 1961, amidst ongoing negotiations between the United States and the Soviet Union, the Soviets resumed nuclear testing, dropping the largest nuclear bomb in history, 4000 times more powerful than the Hiroshima bomb. It was a devastating blow for President Kennedy, who had campaigned in 1960 for a nuclear weapons testing ban as a critical step toward disarmament and who, once elected, pledged not to resume atmospheric testing. My parents had supported Kennedy, working doggedly to get out votes and raise funds for him in New Mexico. They were ecstatic about his victory and thrilled when he visited Los Alamos on December 7, 1962. Arriving by helicopter, he alighted as though it was ". . . a brief descent from the heavens," according to my mother's account. At age 63, her appreciation of handsome men had not wavered and she was enchanted when the President intoned in his unmistakable Boston accent, "There is no group of people in this country whose record over the last 20 years has been more pre-eminent in the service of their country than all of you here in this small community in New Mexico."[19] The next day he flew to the Nevada test site, where five months earlier his brother Robert was among the observers of the last atmospheric test conducted there. [20]

After the Russian bomb, Kennedy felt it politically essential to resume testing and ascertain further how explosions could be detected in outer space. From June to November 1962, a frenzy of 36 tests was carried out at the Pacific Proving grounds, 750 miles away from Honolulu. Almost 800 military, scientific and technical personnel were involved in operations based on Johnston Island, barely large enough for an air landing strip. Aircraft carried out the majority of tests, but four tests used Thor rockets outfitted with nuclear warheads. The first attempt to explode a high altitude nuclear device in the Johnston Island series failed spectacularly because of a malfunctioning tracking system.[21] Both the rocket and payload were deliberately destroyed. The failure made the front page of the *New York Times*, casting doubt on the safety and necessity of further testing. A second attempt failed as well. [22] A month later, another rocket ("Starfish") exploded 245 miles up in outer space. The explosion of the thermonuclear warhead, with a yield equivalent to 1.4 million tons of TNT, had strong and unexpected repercussions, knocking out two upper atmosphere satellites and damaging a third. [23] Worries increased about tampering with the space environment and the lives of Pacific islanders.

For almost five months in 1962, my father was out in the field at Johnston Island focusing on detection methodologies, gathering diagnostic readings and measuring interactions with the earth's magnetic field. [24] There were frustrating weather delays, technical postponements and more malfunctions. After a particularly bad run of weather, he made the following observation at a strategy meeting: "Tonight is better than yesterday under conditions worse than last evening." [25] I have been told the convoluted remark was greeted with good-natured teasing about the influence of the German language on a scientific mind.

It was his longest absence from Los Alamos, difficult for him and even more difficult for my mother. She knew he was working furiously around the clock while trying to keep intact the morale of his group of 25 scientists and technicians. My father was unrelentingly committed to getting things right and had little, if any, tolerance for sloppiness or laziness. His approach occasionally felt heavy handed to us at home as well as those in a work setting. But his associates seemed to grudgingly appreciate it. One of them wrote me a few years ago, "Herman was not always easy to work with or for, because he demanded much and pushed us hard. In retrospect that's what a mentor ought to do. I learned much from him and would not have had him change anything . . . I had great respect and love for him." [26]

Living quarters in Johnston Island's Quonset huts were minimalist, but this environment was not altogether foreign to my father. Like his mountain expeditions to the Himalayas and the Andes, there was a sense of high adventure, a goal to be met, the abandonment of usual comforts and a band of brothers closely bound by intent. In the Pacific, there were huts instead of tents, heat instead of cold, but similarly monotonous food, and definitely weather delays. Male camaraderie was hearty, although European mountaineers never teased Pallas about his German accent—that was left to American scientists on Johnston Island. Among his peers, my father's sly sense of humor thrived and he indulged in frequent hijinks, relieving everyday pressures. The situations also had in common an assumption of risk, although the risks encountered at Johnston Island were much more far-reaching than those on the world's highest peaks.

The paltry amount of information that my mother gleaned about the activities of her husband came mainly through the media. Rather than sit home and worry, my mother had made the rounds of visiting her children and while she was with Duscha and her family in Boston, she wrote: "I heard a short radio report that the high altitude shot has fizzled out. We should learn more details of what has happened in tomorrow's New York Times. All this is enough to make me think of, long for, love you more than I can express in words. As Duscha said, 'If patience and courage and perseverance are needed, there is no better man than Papa.'"[27]

As worldwide trepidations swelled about the effects of high altitude testing, the relationship between the military and scientists at the Pacific proving grounds was growing increasingly contentious due to conflicts between scheduling and safety. Radioactivity and chunks of debris had rained down on Johnston Island after some faulty calculations and aborted shots. At one point, the Los Alamos team informed the commander in charge that because of their safety concerns, the scientists would have to evacuate beforehand to Hawaii if the commander proceeded with a test. In the same breath, they promised to return afterwards and work with anyone who happened to be still alive. The career admiral quickly backed off, cognizant that those who knew most about the explosion were unwilling to witness it. [28] Another time, the tests were moved from one atoll to another because of eye burn risk to indigenous populations. [29] According to my father's colleague, Hoerlin played an instrumental role in getting them moved although, as usual, he did not take credit for doing so. As the colleague relayed, "... despite the costs, Hoerlin was very insistent and didn't give up until the decision was made to relocate ..." [30]

My mother, never a good sleeper, was worried about Hoerlin himself and the enormous responsibilities he shouldered. Her sleep was all the more disturbed in October 1962. The Cuban Missile Crisis brought the United

States and the Soviet Union to the brink of nuclear war. Until then, the behavior of the two enemies had been guided by fears of mutual destruction. After much deliberation and intense negotiations between President Kennedy and Premier Khrushchev, the crisis was averted. The Cold War had narrowly escaped becoming a nuclear war, giving new urgency to the ongoing efforts to arrive at an arms control agreement.

My father's return home from his Pacific sojourn in November 1962 was a time for taking stock. For years my parents had been talking about moving to Santa Fe and living in a more spacious house, more accommodating to their active social life and showcasing their beloved Biedermeier furniture. By Christmas they had bought a four-acre piece of land a mile outside of Santa Fe on which to build a home. They were enormously excited and when I came to spend the holidays, we slowly walked the property, extolling its spectacular views of mountains and mesas.

After a few months of relative quietude, on March 9, 1963 my father was summoned to Washington, D.C. to testify in hearings held by the Joint Congressional Committee on Atomic Energy regarding detection of nuclear explosions. In front of a bevy of high-powered politicians stood an unflappable German emigrant who meticulously fielded their questions one by one. In his testimony Hoerlin pointed out, in his understated way, "It is evident that the consequences of massive military operations in the upper atmosphere would be grave." By this, he meant that not only would satellites be damaged, as they were in the Starfish test, but radioactive fallout would prove seriously dangerous for humans and almost immediately fateful for an astronaut in orbit.[31]

Hoerlin attempted, in a less than subtle way, to dampen the military's enthusiasm for further testing. The event was covered by the ultra liberal muckraking journalist, I.F. Stone, who with his typical incisiveness wrote, "Fortunately there was an independent minded scientist from Los Alamos, Dr. Herman Hoerlin at the hearings on March 8, whose plain speaking annoyed the military." [32] Stone then described Hoerlin's assertions that efforts at secret testing in outer space would be "extremely difficult" and "a waste of scientific manpower." The hearings closed with a comment by one of the Congressmen to Hoerlin: "Doctor, I think if I was going to cheat and conduct a nuclear test, I would not put it in space with the testimony you have given here."[33]

On October 10, 1963 a Limited Test Ban Treaty was signed by the United States, the Soviet Union and Britain, in addition to many non-nuclear nations. Pledging to refrain from further nuclear testing in the atmosphere, in space or underwater, it marked the first arms control agreement of the Cold War and set a precedent for future treaties. Although hastened by the Cuban Missile Crisis, the 1963 treaty was undoubtedly made possible by verifiable detection measurements obtained through high altitude testing. The nation sighed in relief. Nowhere was the sigh more audible than on a mesa in New Mexico.

Chapter 16

HOME

The low-lying southwestern style house, contemporized by expansive glass sectionals, rests comfortably among hills of pinion trees and dry arroyos one mile north of Santa Fe. Its centerpiece is a large sunken living room embedded in a wide rectangular marble floor. In one direction, the floor opens toward the dining room and kitchen, in another toward the bedrooms. The other two sides of the rectangle, the longer ones, are defined by floor-to-ceiling glass windows and doors. To fully appreciate the design, one should stand in the large octagonal 'pit,' two feet below the rectangular marbled sides. Turn your head one way and you see the Sangre mountains, and the other way, the distant Jemez range. If you need more of a view, ascend two steps up, cross the marble floor, slide open a transparent door and step outside onto a generous stone patio, an outdoor extension of the living room space. The stonework, by local masons, is impeccable. "Only the Spanish know how to lay stone," my mother would assert. Although the patios are the same size, the one on the east side of the house, facing the Sangres, is preferable. The view is more spectacular, the sky bigger. That's where my father planted his rose garden, with fragrant and robust buds climbing up the house's façade and cascading over the patio walls. But if it's too hot, one can seek protection from the sun on the other patio, more shaded and more protected. There was always a choice.

I think it took my parents longer to site the house than to approve the architectural plans. I don't know exactly how many times they walked the land, imagining how to capture a view, avoid or embrace the sun, bring light into the house. They wanted it to be perfect for them. And when it was finished in 1964, it was. Kate, age sixty-five, and Hoerlin, age sixty-one, finally had built their dream house. The Biedermeier furniture never looked better, the Oriental rugs splendid and the contrast of antique and modern was striking. The pit could either be used for a cozy cocktail hour, a daily ritual of Kate and Hoerlin's, or for large parties, with the chairs and tables pushed aside or moved to other rooms. In winter, the eye-level fireplace in the pit often boasted a fire that glowed through an intricate handmade wrought iron screen. In the summer, the living room's glass doors were almost always open, inviting one to sit on the patio.

Hoerlin and Kate's dream house in Santa Fe.

The living room "pit," allowing a view of the mountains

My parents were elated to be in their new home, which Kate referred to as "Hoerlin's house." Of course, it was every inch as much hers as his, but it was her way of acknowledging that his hard work had made it possible. Their lives found well-deserved comfort in the rhythmic certainties of the everyday. My father continued to do research, described as "pioneering diagnostic techniques and physical measurements at Los Alamos," [1] until his retirement in 1982, when he became a consultant to the laboratory. He did not mind the 45 minute drive from Santa Fe, surely one of the most scenic commutes anywhere, passing through the tranquil Rio Grande river valley by Indian pueblos and sculpted mesas, the light playing off the land, bright in the morning and accentuating its contours toward evening. The long winding road that connected the Hill to the valley below had breathtaking views and my father joked that it took extraordinary discipline to keep his eyes on its many curves.

My mother fully engaged in the social, cultural and political life of Santa Fe, busy with friends and putting her extraordinary energy into good causes, often together with Hoerlin. In its infancy my mother supported the dream of a summer opera series—greeted with skepticism by many—and was one of its founders. The debut performances took place in 1957 and over time the Santa Fe Opera blossomed into a resounding success, attracting first class singers and an excellent orchestra. My parents were also key figures in helping establish in 1964 a Santa Fe campus for St. John's College in Annapolis with its unusual curriculum based on one hundred great books exemplifying classical traditions of Western civilization. For years, my mother taught the senior class on Goethe's "Faust." Her enthusiasm was infectious to students and her readings of Goethe mesmerizing. On her tongue, the German language was melodious and elegant.

Entertaining with aplomb was a high priority of my parents and their parties were legendary. "They were the only parties in Santa Fe," a friend once told me, "for which people dressed up." The gatherings drew from a wide spectrum: musicians, scholars, scientists, artists and whoever else was lively and fun, blending European sophistication with American jocularity. One of their friends, familiar with Munich's cosmopolitan scene, quipped it was "... Munich on the Rio Grande. "During some parties, my mother—whose beauty and flirtatiousness never abandoned her—would change dresses, in the summer complaining that she was too hot or in the winter too cold. It was a lame excuse for staging a grand entrance and receiving another round of compliments. Too much was never enough for her.

The other critical function the house served was accommodating visits from "the children" and the grandchildren. My sister Duscha was married with four children, my sister Hedi married with five children, and my brother Thomi and his wife had five children.[2] In 1966, I married a widower, a doctor, and became the instant mother of his two small children, Steven and Kristine. My parents adored them, becoming their "Oma" and "Opa," delighting in Steve's love of the outdoors and Kristine's early interest in science.[3] Four years later, I gave birth to Jason, followed in two years by another son Noah. We all visited the Santa Fe house, primarily in the summer, the respective families sometimes briefly overlapping. The various grandchildren loved jumping in the pit, playing in the surrounding arroyos, horseback riding and swimming, visiting Indian ruins or observing pueblo dances, and clambering around the ancient Anasazi cliff dwellings of Bandelier National Monument. But the grand finale of a visit was a family pilgrimage up a striking 12,372 foot mountain, Lake Peak, in the Sangres above the Santa Fe ski basin.

Lake Peak had figured prominently in weekend hikes and/or climbs since we arrived in Los Alamos. It was a favorite among mountain loving scientists: perfect for family picnics, mushroom hunts or serious hikes. The point of departure was the Santa Fe ski basin and if one went with my father, one could see his organizational mind at work. Early in the morning the car was parked in a spot, calculated with meticulous precision, to be out of the hot sun by the time the expedition returned. The formula, gauged by the slant of the sun and speed of the hikers, was upset only by changes of weather or, occasionally, a faulty assessment of someone's fitness. It was a wonderful hike through aspen trees and ponderosa pines, meadows with wild flowers, ending with a final traverse across an exposed, craggy ridge before reaching the summit. On top, the views extended to the west across the Rio Grande valley toward the Jemez above Los Alamos, to the east across the vast expanse of the Pecos wilderness, to the north toward the higher mountains of the Sangre range approaching Colorado, and to the south across the plains to Albuquerque and the Sandia mountains. It was spectacular and one never tired of it, a huge reward for relatively little effort compared to other climbing ventures.

The Hoerlins would almost invariably make an annual trek to Lake Peak with the Bethes, who spent most of their summers in Los Alamos. The couples' friendship had a long history and became even closer after Hans had recruited Hoerlin to Los Alamos in 1953 and later invited him to be a visiting professor at Cornell University during 1959-60. They all looked forward to being together, when the men could talk physics, Rose and Kate about everything else but physics, and all of them would enjoy hiking. Hans, who was described by *The New York Times Magazine*, as "America's outstanding and influential advocate of nuclear disarmament" and my father had many things in common, including their political leanings. But they also shared a methodical approach to life and a deeply ingrained sense of integrity. At Hans' memorial service in 2005, I spoke with Rose and commented on his great integrity. She answered, "There was no one who had more integrity than your father. Hoerlin's integrity shone. It was a star that was even brighter than Han's." They were perhaps not as closely matched in other realms. When Hans won the 1967 Nobel Prize (fittingly for his work on the properties of brilliant stars), my mother was heard to say, "Hans may be a better physicist, but Hoerlin is a better mountaineer." Neither man would have disputed that, if they had been in earshot.

As my mother began to opt for shorter hikes, perhaps stopping along the trail and enjoying the scenery, my father continued to climb Lake Peak for many years, establishing another ritual. He introduced his grandchildren to climbing, demonstrating for them the famous "Hoerlin step", a steady, slow and uninterrupted pace that guaranteed, he posited, conquest of Lake Peak. For the last leg of the rocky ridge, he roped up his young followers who—often with trembling legs—made their way across an edge that dropped precipitously off on both sides, one to a mountain lake far below. It was high adventure, the stuff of memories for each of the grandchildren. By the time his youngest grandchildren Noah (age eight) and Jason (age ten) were able to handle the challenge, he was no longer capable of making the climb. So it was up to me to lead them up the mountain, after Opa had lovingly packed a knapsack, complete with a climbing rope, and longingly looked at us depart. According to grandmother Oma, on that day Opa spent an inordinate amount of time on the house's patio, from where Lake Peak was barely visible, looking toward it with binoculars. There is no way he could have seen us, but it was reassuring to him just to look and know we were there. When we came home late that afternoon, he joyfully shared in our triumph. His only three direct descendents had made it to the top. It was as though we had equaled his world record-breaking Himalayan ascent of Jongsong.

Looking toward Lake Peak from the patio of the Santa Fe house.

For years my parents took pleasure in rich lives, grateful for their Santa Fe nest, visiting children and grandchildren, enjoying trips abroad. A 1965 journey to Mexico was particularly notable since my father summited Popocatepetl, an active volcano and Mexico's second highest peak at over 17,800 feet. [4] He had long dreamed of climbing the magnificent mountain with its snow-capped cone encircling a huge, smoke-spewing crater. Although Hoerlin was still making some serious climbs in his 60's, including the classic alpine rock route up the east face of Long's Peak in Colorado, [5] he was beginning to slow down. It had become clear that another dream, a return to the Himalayas, would never be realized, although he had been invited several times—notably in 1949 by the British mountaineer Frank Smythe [6]—and on various mapping excursions in the 50's and 60's by his loyal climbing companion Erwin Schneider. Somehow it was never the right moment, due to constraints of work and/or finances. My mother never discouraged him from the dream, but knowing him, I would guess he considered it too indulgent.

In 1971, when he and my mother made what was—for all purposes—their farewell swing through Europe, Pallas met Erwin in Austria and the two of them revisited climbs they pioneered in the early days of their friendship. Since then, their lives had diverged considerably,[7] but they remained touchingly close, their silences saying more than their conversations. Everywhere my parents went on that trip, described by my mother in a journalistic chronicle as "Herbstfahrt" (Fall Journey), they were feted by dear friends. It was a trip through time and memories, visiting the grave of Willi Schmid in Munich and seeing the Garmisch relatives, my father's high school comrades in Schwabisch Hall, his climbing companions in Stuttgart and the (adult) children of Hannes Schneider [8] in Austria.

My father never lost his German accent and his pronunciation of English was sometimes amusing. "V's" were especially tricky for him to enunciate and most often sounded like "w's". As he aged, he periodically confessed to me, "Growing old is <u>very</u> hard." The <u>very</u> sounded more like wary, serendipitously a more accurate description of his state of mind: he was wary of how Kate and he would finish out their days together. And if one indulges in word derivations, he was also weary. He and Kate were not going gently into the sunset; on the contrary, they were doing their best to resist the sun's fading rays. It took a toll on them, which my father articulated with trademark understatement, as "... sometimes we are not patient enough with one another." [9]

Their path had taken some tragic and difficult turns. In 1979, my brother Thomi had been the only one of the four children to come to Santa Fe for my mother's 80th birthday on May 13th. The rest of us, all living in the east, were planning to make amends over the summer, but Thomi was in relative proximity and drove down from Utah.[10] On the drive back, my much beloved brother died in a one-car accident, trying to avoid hitting a deer. I don't think my mother ever got over it; my father quietly said, "I have lost my best friend." It was a blow that took the wind out of them, literally so with my father. He was beginning to suffer from the effects of a hardening of his lungs, making breathing labored and hiking impossible. There was cruel irony in the theory that his lung disease may have been associated with the weeks he had spent at high altitudes in the Himalayas and Andes. My mother's health was fragile also, although she had survived a bout of cancer. And worrying about the "three girls" never stopped, and became even more of a strain. Duscha had been divorced for a number of years. Much to their disapproval, I was also divorced. In terms of marriages, they were able to breath easily only with Hedi's happy union.

The 7000 foot altitude of Santa Fe was making it unmanageable to live there with my father's lung disease. Also, my mother missed terribly the children back east. In the summer of 1983, Kate and Hoerlin moved to a retirement community in the Boston area, where both Hedi and Duscha were living. It was unimaginably painful for my father to leave "his" mountains, and for both of them to leave friends and the home they had so dotingly built. Duscha and I had come to Santa Fe to help with the final packing, all of us trying to be brave and positive. As we weeded through their possessions, it seemed like none of them were free of sentimental value, whether a pocked saucepan or a frayed climbing rope. The moving van was full as it left for their small independent living unit near Boston and we headed toward the airport in Albuquerque. In one of those small coincidences that make life so unpredictable, we were driven by the son of my father's PhD advisor from Stuttgart. [11] By now a middle-aged man living in Albuquerque, the son had never forgotten how Hoerlin shielded his family from Nazi thugs; he and my father had stayed in contact over the years. My father did not utter a word during that long drive. I held his hand as he gazed at the moving landscape and at one point asked him, "How are you doing?" He responded, "My heart is crying."

A few weeks after they moved, children and grandchildren celebrated my father's 80th birthday in the garden of Hedi's house in Boston. I had called my father, asking him if I could bring someone with me from Philadelphia to participate in the festivities. Hesitantly, he asked, "Is this someone special?" I answered, "Well, he's a physicist." The two physicists met and liked each other immediately. Four months later, on November 6, 1983, my father died of a heart attack. His memorial service was held at the chapel of Boston's Mount Auburn Cemetery, known for its dignified history and superb arboretum. Hans Bethe gave a stirring eulogy, talking about Hoerlin's three great loves: mountains, science and family. The head of the Los Alamos Lab [12] had flown in to add his comments, emphasizing that ". . . because most of his research was classified, Hoerlin's technical excellence was not well-known." Members of the family and friends also spoke, on a more personal level, to round out the picture of this extraordinary man. The ceremony, ending with an unforgettable Bach sonata for viola, [13] would have pleased my father through and through.

Shortly after Hoerlin's death, I was going through some of the things on his desk with my mother and we found a copy of <u>Who's Who in Physics</u> with a marker to the page that lists Gino Segre. My father had clearly checked out my future husband. I knew he approved. And by meeting Gino, he got an inkling of why I was in love. As one of my oldest and dearest friends who had observed my bumpy romantic vicissitudes proclaimed: "You're forty-three years old and you finally got it <u>right</u>. "My mother thought so too and added Gino to the long list of men she charmed. At one point, Gino somewhat incredulously asked, "Is your mother really *flirting* with me?" At age 83 she was still incorrigible, particularly with a tall, good-looking Italian-born academic. But in the two years after Hoerlin's death and before her own, my mother often questioned why she should go on living. "It makes no sense," she once told me, "to be without Papa." Thirty years earlier, she had written Hoerlin: "The moral of the story is that I experience everything with you, through you, but nothing without you." [14] In the interim, my mother became ever more reliant on my father and when he died, she grieved his death each day. Nevertheless, when I told her Gino and I were getting married, she rose to the occasion. She willed her way to the wedding in April 1985, weakened but not diminished by age and a yet undiagnosed recurrence of her cancer. Gino had insisted on a grand celebration and that we had: our friends, my children, his children, my sisters, his brother and . . . my mother. She and I had picked out an elegant cream—colored suit for her to wear. She looked stunning—her hair white, her brown eyes full of warmth, her posture erect as she stepped lightly into the circle of our love. Hoerlin would have been proud of her, looking adoringly toward her as he took her hand. A month and a half later they were rejoined.

Theirs had been a remarkable odyssey from Germany, to the United States, and to Los Alamos during significant times: the golden age of mountaineering, the horrors of Hitler, the unfolding of the Cold War and finally a time of relative, but still nervous, peace. Their lives had been touched and transformed by these developments, shaping their personal choices and existence. Pallas had explored the Andes and Himalayas at a time when few Europeans tread in those mountain regions, much less conquered their highest peaks. My mother and father, together, had managed to flee

Hoerlin and Kate in their 70's.

Nazi Germany in spite of all the obstacles, foremost among them, my mother's Jewish roots. They had come to a country seeking respite from terror, only to be embroiled in the midst of another terror: the threat of a nuclear apocalypse. When the non-proliferation treaties were at last enacted, their lives could flow more securely, uninterrupted by events on the world stage.

Many years before, about to begin life afresh, Kate had written Hoerlin, "I know of no other person in the world, who can accompany me as well as you." [15] She meant, of course, that they would proceed hand in hand, approaching challenges with the kind of courage my father commended to future generations on that sunny afternoon of his 80th birthday. He had been her protector to the end, even making sure she was on safe turf, ensconced in family, before he died. With scientific objectivity, Hoerlin had calculated that his days were numbered; the move east was motivated more by concerns for Kate than his own health. Thoughtfulness and selflessness were consistent throughout his life. Once when my parents had visited me in Philadelphia and I was helping them unpack in their hotel room, I came across a climbing rope. I asked my 78 year-old-father about its purpose and he answered, "In case of fire, I can rescue Mummy." The image of the two of them rappelling down from the 18th floor of a burning building stayed with me.

My parents' ashes lie in a grassy spot near flowering fruit trees overlooking a pond in Mt. Auburn Cemetery. But not all of my father's ashes are there. With my mother's blessings, Gino and I took a portion to New Mexico the summer after he died. We climbed the "family" mountain Lake Peak, made special by countless ascents, and gently tossed his ashes to the winds. Just as we finished, a brilliant blue bird—its plumage colored with hues of light and cobalt blue—flew onto a nearby scrub bush. Sightings of mountain bluebirds, who prosper at high elevations, are not uncommon, but I had never seen one perched on a mountaintop.

The familial rite of climbing Lake Peak continues to this day. Years ago, the only dog I ever had—the incomparable Kaya—scampered to the top. One of my sons proposed to his now-wife there. Six granddaughters of Kate and Hoerlin, living all over the United States, met in Santa Fe in 2007 and made the climb. And whenever Gino and I visit the Southwest, we put Lake Peak on our agenda. We have not caught sight of a bluebird on the summit again, but I am certain he's there.

ACKNOWLEDGEMENTS

This book was birthed by many midwives. Over the years, as I told my children and friends segments of my parents' saga, a frequent response was "You <u>must</u> write about them!" The chorus of encouragement came to a crescendo in the Fall of 2005, when I went with my husband on a one month fellowship to the Bogliasco Foundation's Liguria Study Center on the Italian Riviera. The other participants, in their cheerful way, bordered on being obnoxiously insistent that I begin the process.

When I subsequently found my mother's tightly bundled love letters in a dusty suitcase, it was as though I was being summoned to tell the story of how my parents met and fell in love in pre-war Germany. Nonetheless, I approached the task hesitantly, first trying to discover how exactly they could have married in 1938 in Germany, given my mother's Jewish background and my father's Aryan one. In my correspondence with German bureaucracies, I was lucky enough to be referred to a historical scholar who, on my behalf, uncovered key official documents in Berlin and other localities. So first let me thank Dr. Jana Leichsenrung,[1] who generously and doggedly conducted research and shared with me the fascination about what had transpired.

By the time I actually started <u>writing</u>, another amazing connection occurred. Out of the blue, an email arrived from Nicholas Mailaender, an authority on the history of German mountaineering[2] and an outstanding climber himself. In his email Nicho wondered whether I was related to the mountaineer Hermann Hoerlin, who in his research had stood out as a fervent anti-Nazi in the 1930's. Our subsequent communications were both a source of tremendous knowledge to me and, as importantly, an inspiration to keep on writing. When I finally met Nicho on a trip to Germany, it felt like reconnecting with a long lost Swabian cousin. He is special indeed.

My sister Duscha Weisskopf has been an invaluable resource for this book, knowing the personal context and spending precious time with me in sorting out the complexity of details. And my other sister Hedi Randall has also been enormously supportive, with her enthusiasm and commentary. Both my sisters (technically half-sisters, but whole to me) contributed important stories and viewpoints, going carefully through the manuscript. An extra set of eyes was also lent by my son Noah's father-in-law, Hans Meyers, a retired German banker whose eagle-like ability to find mistakes was formidable and much appreciated.

So many people encouraged me along the way that I hesitate to list them for fear of leaving someone out. But I'll risk expressing my gratitude to a few (with apologies to others): Kathryn Davis a.k.a. The Book Doctor, Buzz Bissinger, Evelyn Eskin, Jean and Michael Levin, Ronald Goldfarb, Lucie Prinz, Shelly Yanoff, Liz Werthan, Gerda Paumgarten, Jerry Singerman and Liliana Weissberg. Some read the entire manuscript, others a few chapters, still others referred me to experts in the field, and many expressed the kind of excitement that sustained me over time.

I also wish to thank my children—Noah, Jason, Kristine and Steve Yaffe—for their wholehearted encouragement and my daughter-in-laws, Suzanne and Kathrine, for their much-welcomed thoughts. And finally, major thanks and love go to my husband, Gino Segre, who saw me through many a day and has tolerated my obsession with this story with his usual grace and humor. Often he offered critical perspectives but always gave me loving support. Luckily, we are never at a loss regarding things to talk about, but I am forever grateful to him for letting this book dominate our discourse over the past few years.

---

[1]   Dr. Jana Leichsenrung was the editor of "Frauen und Widerstand (Lit Verlag: 2003) and has taught at the Berlin Technical University and the Westfaelische Wilhelms Universitaet/Muenster. She currently is a historical specialist at the German Parliament (Referentin: Geschichte, Zeitgeschichte und Politik, Deutsche Bundestag).

[2]   Nicholas Mailaender is the author of "Im Zeichen des Edelweiss: Die Geschichte Muenchens als Bergsteigerstadt" (AS Verlag: 2006) and several other mountaineering books and articles. He has a number of notable climbs to his credit.

Notes

Chapter 1 Notes (Pages 3-14)

3   Noah (born May 28, 1972); Jason (June 25, 1970); Kristine (July 4, 1962); and Steven (July 6, 1959). All of them have their father's surname, Yaffe.

4   Maria Hirrle was 10 years younger than her husband Adolf. She came from Ludwigsburg, outside of Stuttgart, approximately 30 miles from Schwaebisch Hall.

5   Introduction to "Winterfahrten im Mont-Blanc-Gebiet" von Hermann Hoerlin, Sonderabdruck aus *Die Alpen*, Jahrg. IX, Heft 1, 1933

6   The Academic Ski Club of Stuttgart, the Academic Alpine Club of Stuttgart, the Academic Alpine Club of Berlin, the German Austrian Alpine Club/Swabian section, and the Sonderbund.

7   Letter from Hoerlin to Kate, December 24, 1935

8   *Akademishcher Alpen-Verein Berlin Jahresbericht 1926-1927*, p. 23-24. These included the 2nd winter ascent of the Taeschhorn in the Wallis range (Switzerland) and the first ascent of the Lyskamm north wall.

9   ibid, "Winterfahrten."

10   There have been changes, however, such as new roads, trams, cog railroads and shrinking glaciers.

11   ibid, "Winterfahrten."

12   The others were Peter Hardegg and Max Fischer; they had met as students and my father was particularly close to Hardegg, who had introduced him to alpine climbing.

13   ibid, Jubilaeumsclubbericht.

14   Peter Hardegg was killed on a climb in the eastern Alps.

15   *Rundbriefe des Sonderbundes*, ibid. p. 25. "Was wir in unseren kuehnsten Traeumen kaum gehofft hatte, ist Wirklichkeit geworden."

16   Frank S. Smythe, *The Kanchenjunga Adventure* (London: Victor Gollancz Ltd, 1930), p 58.

17   *Rundbriefe des Sonderbundes,* Februar 1971, p 25.

18   Alexandra Richie, *Faust's Metropolis: A History of Berlin* (New York: Carrol & Graff, 1988), p. 325.

19   Frank S. Smythe, *Climbs and Ski Runs* (London: A&C Black Limited,1929), p. 176

20   Smythe's book on Kanchenjunga launched a prolific writing career. He continued to climb and stayed in touch with my father, seeking his recommendations regarding film use (exposure levels, color film, etc) when he participated in subsequent Himalayan climbs, including the 1933 British attempt on Mt. Everest.

Chapter 2 Notes (Pages 15-27)

1   Gandhi's non-violent Dandi March, 400 kilometers (247 miles) long, began on March 12 and ended on April 6 in Dandi, where Gandhi and his thousands of followers, in an act of civil disobedience, broke the law by making their own salt from seawater.

2   The Earl of Halifax was subsequently appointed Britain's Foreign Minister from 1938 to 1940 and later during WWII served as England's Ambassador to the United States.

3   Mountain measurements vary slightly according to different surveys and years, partly due to inaccuracies but also to the fact that mountains can grow. New technologies such as the Global Positioning System (GPS) used by the National Geographic Society and the Boston Museum of Science in 1999 measured Everest at 8850 meters (29,035 feet).

4   Mallory had made the attempt with his British co-patriot, Irvine. In 1999, a NOVA expedition to investigate their disappearance found Mallory's body at 27,000 feet.

5   F.S. Smythe, *The Kangchenjunga Adventure* (London:Victor Gollancz Ltd 1930), p.55

6   Gunter Oskar Dyhrenfurth, *Himalaya: Unsere Expedition 1930* (Berlin: Verlag Scherl, 1931), p. 30.

7   This tactic was especially galling since my career has been in public health, having served as Deputy and then Acting Commissioner of Public Health of Philadelphia.

[8] In 1764, Catherine the Great who wanted to introduce modern hygiene to Russia, had herself inoculated against smallpox to assuage public fears against vaccinations.

[9] 1930 was around the beginning of European appreciation of sherpas, an ethnic group living in the high altitudes of Tibet and Nepal and known for their toughness and guiding capabilities.

[10] Smythe, ibid., p 99.

[11] The English climber/explorer Freshfield circumnavigated Kanchejunga in 1899 and recommended a northwest route up the mountain. The unsuccessful 1929 German expedition approached from the east and attempted to ascend the mountain's north ridge.

[12] Originally a silver coin, by 1930 the rupee had been converted to paper currency due to the shortage of silver after WWI. To underscore British rule of India, the rupee prominently displayed a portrait of George the Fifth. Porters on Himalayan expeditions typically earned between one and two rupees a day (approximately 40 to 80 cents).

[13] Dr. Helmuth Richter chapter in Dyhrenfurth, ibid., p. 154.

[14] Jonathan Neale, *Tigers in the Snow: how one fateful Climb made the Sherpas Mountaineering Legends* (New York: St. Martin's Press, 2002). Chettan was the most experienced of the porters, having been on three Everest expeditions and on Bauer's 1929 Kanchenjunga attempt.

[15] The peaks were Ramtang (7105 meters; 21,981 feet) and Nepal (7153 meters; 23,470 feet).

[16] *Memsahb im Himalaja,* ibid., p. 49.

[17] This may be disputed. The controversial American Fanny Bullock Workman had made a number of ascents, including Pinnacle Peak (22,735 feet) in 1906, in the Karakorum, sometimes regarded as a different range than the Himalayas.

[18] *Memsahb im Himalaja,* ibid., p. 61. "Pudern konnte ich mich allerdings nicht; denn ich war einfach Schwarz geworden, - so dunklen Puder gibt es sicher gar nicht."

[19] Hettie Dyhrenfurth, *Memsahb im Himalaya* (Leipzig: Deutsche Buchwerkstaetten G.M.B.H., 1931), p. 5.

[20] Letter from Bauer to Reichssportfuehrer von Tschammer und Osten, December 10, 1934, as quoted Peter Mierau, "Die Deutsche Himalaja Stiftung von 1936 bis 1998," (Munich: Bergverlag Rother, DAV 1999). Bauer also attacked Schneider for not planting the German flag, conveniently not recognizing that Schneider was Austrian.

21 Hermann Hoerlin, "Geschichte des Sonderbundes 1859-1959/Technischen Hochschule Stuttgart" *Sonderbund* (1960), p. 63.

22 *Memshab im Himalaja*, ibid., p. 52.

23 Smythe, ibid., p. 246.

24 Schneider account in Dyhrenfurth, ibid., p. 131. "Pass auf, Pallas, gleich werde ich fliegen!"

25 Nickel, ibid., p. 108.

Chapter 3 Notes (Pages 29-43)

1 Reinhold Messner, *The Big Walls* (Oxford University Press: 1978), p. 22. "In the Alps, there is no other wall which, in terms of height and savage grandeur, represents such a danger area as the Monte Rosa East face."

2 "Hall und Umgebung: Zum Thron der Goetter," <u>Stuttgart Tagblatt</u>, April 2, 1931.

3 Also prominent were Walther Bothe and Werner Kolhoerster who in 1929 first postulated that ultra-radiation may be of a corpuscular nature. Along with Max Born, Bothe received the 1954 Nobel Prize in Physics.

4 The experiments were conduced by Victor Hess at the University of Vienna.

5 Robert Millikan was awarded the 1923 Nobel Prize in Physics for his earlier measurement of the electron's charge.

6 Hoerlin lecture on *Cosmic Rays*, March 11, 1952 at Sigma Xi meeting (note: Sigma Xi is an honorary scientific research society)

7 Bruno Rossi, Italy's foremost cosmic ray physicist and later professor at MIT wrote this in *Cosmic Rays*: McGraw Hill, 1964

8 Ernest Rutherford, "Discussion on Ultra-Penetrating Rays," *Proceedings of the Royal Society of London A 132:133. 1931.* Rutherford, originally from New Zealand, was awarded the 1908 Nobel Prize in Chemistry.

9 The Stuttgart group used unmanned devices, electroscopes for deep water readings and high atmosphere measurements. The latter were made via balloons; for his Master Degree, Hoerlin designed lightweight ionization chambers for the balloons.

10 Borchers had been on the 1928 German-Russian expedition to the Pamirs, along with Erwin Schneider, that conquered Pik Lenin (7134 meters; 23, 406 feet), the highest mountain climbed before Jonsong broke the record in 1930. In 1931 the Jongsong record had already been broken by none other than

Hoerlin's friend Frank Smythe, who summited Kamet, the first mountain over 7500 meters to be climbed. It took another six years to break that record.

[11] The *Alpenverein* sponsored three separate expeditions to South America in the 1930's (1932, 1936 and 1939) and is widely credited with bringing attention to its mountains to the outside world.

[12] Borchers et al, "Die Forschungsreise des D.U. Oe.A.D in die Cordillera Blanca (Peru)" in *Zeitschrift des Deutschen und Oesterreichischen Alpenverein* (Innsbruck: 1933).

[13] Philipp Borchers, *Die Weisse Kordillere* (Berlin: Verlag Scherl, 1935), p. 27.

[14] Daniel J. Kevles, *The Physicists* (New York: Knopf, 1971), p. 231. Compton won the 1927 Nobel Prize in Physics.

[15] The Kaaba is a cube-shaped building in Mecca, Saudi Arabia, built within a mosque. Muslims from around the world, no matter where they are, face toward the Kaaba to pray.

[16] Borchers, ibid., p. 28. "Der einzige der von Anfang an wirklich intensiv arbeitete—war Hoerlin."

[17] Letter from Erwin Schneider to Pallas (Hoerlin), March 9, 1968. "Ich habe fest im Auge, bald einmal nach Suedamerika zu reisen und . . . dabei GOTTES EIGENES LAND (his emphasis) mit zu beruehren."

[18] Humboldt did not reach Chimorazo's peak, but climbed to 5878 meters (19,286 feet).

[19] *"Ueber einen Versuch den Gipfel des Chimborazo zu ersteigen"* von Alexander von Humboldt. Otto Hendel: 1894. Note: this is a booklet of an original article that appeared in a larger collection of Humboldt's in 1804.

[20] In a 1934 article, "Deutsche Bergsteiger im Ausland" ("German Climbers Abroad") written for the German and Austrian Alpine Club, Hoerlin used Humboldt as an outstanding example of alpine climbing in foreign lands.

[21] A bloody rebellion led by the American Popular Revolutionary Alliance (APRA), a populist group made up primarily of poor peasants against the armed forces erupted in July 1932 and was ongoing for the next decade.

[22] Borchers, ibid., p. 83. "Den Rat befolgten wir gern . . . ."

[23] The peaks over 6000 meters, in order of the climbs, included Huascaran, Tshopi-Kalki Artison Raju, Huandoy, and Hualcan. Among my father's many photos of the region's magnificent mountains, one of Alpamayo (5947 meters) is a favorite.

[24] To settle the controversy, Bullock commissioned a well-respected French team of geographic surveyors to travel to Peru. Based on their calculation, the Academy of Science declared in 1911 that Bullock was the world record holder.

25 In 1909, Peck planted a "votes for women" flag on the summit of Peru's Mt. Coropuna. She took up mountain climbing relatively late in life at age 44 and one year later (1895) became the 3rd woman to climb the Matterhorn.

26 Borchers, Hoerlin, Bernard, Hein plus the Tyrolean, Schneider were the summit team.

27 Borchers, ibid., p.96. This too must have been held against my father, who had hoisted the Swabian flag in the Himalayas, much to the disapproval of the Nazis as described in Chapter 2.

28 Borchers, ibid., p.78. Some of the villagers had served as porters to Peck. Their accounts independently corroborated with those of Peck's Swiss guides who reported that she had not reached the top.

29 One of the mountains was Huandoy (6,395 meters; 21,103 feet).

30 See Hans Kinzl and Erwin Schneider, *Cordillera Blanca Peru* (Innsbruck: Universitatsverlag Wagner, 1950).

31 Hoerlin account in Borchers, ibid., p. 165. "Der intelligente Mann . . . ueberraschte mich mit Kenntnissen ueber unser Sonnensystem, . . . der anderen Planeten . . . und auch politische Gespraeche . . . "

32 This has a nice echo. In Greek mythology, Nestor was a hero of the Trojan War who was considered a wise adviser. Between Nestor and Pallas, things were in good hands!

33 Hoerlin account in Borchers, ibid., p. 178. "Da sass ich zufrieden und gluecklich vor dem Zelt und freute mich der Schoenheit dieser Hochgebirgslandschaft und der weiten Welt. Stundenlang konnte ich so sitzen . . ."

34 Hoerlin's account in Borchers. ibid., p. 180.

35 Letter from Liesel Hoerlin to Hermann Hoerlin, September 2, 1932. "Mutter guckte das Photo an und sagte: Ist das mei Bua? Nein, er ist es nicht. Oder doch? Nein, nein der ist es nicht."

36 Schneider and Borchers climbed Aconcagua in Argentina, the highest peak in the Americas.

37 Kevles, ibid., p. 180

Chapter 4 Notes (Pages 45-57)

1 John Ricker, *Yuraq Janka: Guide to the Peruvian Andes* (American Alpine Club: 1977), p.7.

2   The fire, allegedly set by a Dutch Communist, was treated by Hitler as irrefutable evidence that Communists were planning to overthrow the government.

3   William L. Shirer, *The Rise and Fall of the Third Reich: A History of Nazi Germany* (New York: Simon and Schuster, 1960), p. 198

4   Saul Friedlander, *Nazi Germany and the Jews, volume I: The Years of Persecution, 1933-39* (New York: HarperCollins, 1997), p. 68. According to Friedlander, 23,000 Jews left in 1934, 21,000 in 1935, 25,000 in 1936, and 23,000 in 1937 (p 62).

5   Friedlander, ibid. p. 5.

6   Peter Fritzsche, *Life and Death in the Third Reich* (Cambridge: Harvard University Press, 2008), p. 87.

7   Friedlander, ibid., p. 50.

8   Schwaebisch Hall Standesamt and Evangelische Stadtpfarramt, respectively signed and sealed, May 29, 1933.

9   Ewald's wife had an uncle was an influential Rabbi. In 1939, their daughter Rose married the physicist Hans Bethe, winner of the 1967 Nobel Prize. In the United States, Bethe was one of my father's best friends.

10 As quoted in literature from the United States Holocaust Museum.

11 Letter from Adolf Hoerlin to his son in Peru, September 2, 1932 with greetings from his mother and sister as well. The Peru uprisings were covered in the German press.

12 Joachim Prinz, *Rebellious Rabbi: The German and Early American Years* (Bloomington: Indiana University Press, 2008), p. 85. Prinz, a leading liberal Rabbi in Berlin, observed ". . . I began to understand that what was happening in Berlin was not as important as what was happening in the countryside. The little towns all over the country told the story more eloquently."

13 Jill Stephenson, *Hitler's Home Front (Hambledon &London, 2006)*, p. 137.

14 Gordon C. Craig, *Germany 1866—1945* (England: Oxford University Press,1978), p. 578.

15 Personal communication from Nicholas Mailaender to the author, June 2, 2009. The data was provided by Martin Achrainer, archivist at the Austrian Alpine Club.

16 Maurice Isserman and Stewart Weaver, *Fallen Giants: A History of Himalayan Mountaineering from the Age of Empire to the Age of Extremes* (New Haven: Yale University Press, 2008), p. 31.

17 Lee Wallace Holt, *Mountains, Mountaineering and Modernity: A Cultural History of German and Austrian Mountaineering, 1900-1945.* (Ph.D dissertation, The University of Texas at Austin, May 2008), p. 16.

[18]   MDOeAV (1925): p. 104

[19]   Holt, ibid., p 133. By 1924, Aryan clauses had been promulgated in 50 Austrian sections; another 40 Austrian sections had passed anti-Jewish declarations.

[20]   as quoted by Rainer Amstaedter, *Der Alpinismus: Kultur, Organisation, Politik* (Vienna: WUV-Universitaetsverlag, 1996), p. 303. The 1924 article appeared in the Neue Deutsche Alpenzeitung: ". . . Ihr heftet an die Schwelle eurer Schutzasyle die Frage nach Herkunft und Blut und vergesst statt dessen auf Geist und Fuehlen! Ihr forscht nach Stammbaum und Schaedelform und ueberseht den Herzschlag und den Seelenklang. Was wird das Ziel, das Ende sein?"

[21]   personal communication from Nicholas Mailaender, February 19, 2009.

[22]   Deutsche Alpenverein website, accessed February 2009. The meeting took place in December 1924.

[23]   Nicholas Mailaender, *Im Zeichen des Edelweiss* (Zurich: AS Verlag & Buchkonzept AG, 2006), p. 208.

[24]   Isserman and Weaver, ibid., p. 156

[25]   Mailaender, ibid., p. 208-9. In May of 1933, the Aryan clause applied only to new members of the Alpenverein. If you already belonged to the Alpenverein and were Jewish, membership could continue. By that summer, it was obvious Jews could no longer be part of the Alpenverein.

[26]   Ralf-Peter Maertin, *Nanga Parbat. Wahrheit und Wahn des Alpinus.* (Berlin: Berlin Verlag, 2002), p. 104.

[27]   Isserman and Weaver, ibid., p. 135

[28]   Mailaender, ibid., p. 202.

[29]   personal communcation from Nicholas Mailaender to author, February 5, 2009.

[30]   Hermann Hoerlin postcard to Erwin Schneider, July 9, 1933.

[31]   Victor Regener (1913-2006) left Germany in 1938 and later became a Professor of Physics and Astronomy at the University of New Mexico.

[32]   The research station, opened in 1930 was under the stewardship of W.R. Hess, who won the 1949 Nobel Prize in Physiology/Medicine.

[33]   Bara Sahb is the Indian expression for "leader." Sahib is a term referring to European climbers.

[34]   The Karakorum includes K2, Gasherbrum I or Hidden Peak, Gasherbrum II and Broad Peak.

[35]   July 16, 1933 letter from Dyhrenfurth to Schneider with a copy to Hoerlin. "Wir setzen hier Himmel und Hoelle in Bewegung, um unsere Karakoram-Exedition 1934 auf die Beine zu stellen. Wenn es zum Klappen kommt, wie ich dringend

hoffe, so kann ich doch auft Deine und Pallas' geschaetzte Mitwirkung bestimmt rechnen? Hoffentlich kann auch Uli wieder mitmachen."

[36] Letter from Schneider to Pallas (Hoerlin) July 7, 1933. "Bara Sahb (Dyhrenfurth) hat unter diesen Umstaenden geringe Chancen, ich sehe fuer ihn aeusserst black. Mit seinem Geburtsfehler wird er im dritten Reich kaum mehr einen Blumentopf gewinnen koennen ... "

[37] Letter from Schneider to Hoerlin, September 9, 1933. ". . . die boesen Knaben aus dem dritten Reich." Dyhrenfurth's team included two Americans, two Austrians, and two Swiss. Hettie, Dyhrenfurth's wife, wanted to be sure that Germans on the Expedition had not joined the Nazi party.

[38] Letter from Merkl to Hoerlin, July 12, 1933. "Nun moechte ich sagen, wie sehr ich mich freuen wuerde, wenn Sie sich naechster Jahr unserer Expedition zum Nanga Parbat anschliessen wollten."

[39] Postcard from Merkl to Hoerlin, July 27, 1933. "Ich moechte naechster Dienstag oder Donnerstag vorm. 10:43 nach Stuttgart kommen um mich Ihnen und H.Prof. R verschiedenes zu besprechen"

[40] Letter from director W.R. Hess to Merkl and Welzenbach, September 8, 1933. The letter granted them special permission and entry cards to the high altitude facility.

[41] Letter from Schneider to Hoerlin, September 9, 1933. "Wir kennen B.S. (Bara Sahb) genau, uns kann er nicht mehr viel vormachen, wir wissen auch, dass wir ihn sicher beeinflussen koennen und mit ihm gut auskommen werden. DAS WISSEN WIR ALLES VON MERKL NICHT!"

[42] Letter from Schneider to Hoerlin, September 9 letter. "Merkl ist, trotzdem er sicher ein netter Kerl ist, eitel und eingebildet und ein Dickschaedel."

[43] Letters from Wieland to Hoerlin: July 16 and August 2, 1933.

[44] Letter from Wieland to Hoerlin, September 2, 1933. Wieland and Merkl had climbed Moench.

[45] Letter from Philipp Wieland (father of Uli) to Dinkelacker, thanking him for the Alpenverein's condolence letter. August 3, 1934. ". . . So zog es ihn wieder nach dem Himalaya als er den Ruf des Reichssportfuehrers Herrn von Tschammer-Osten bekam."

[46] Letter from Schneider to Pallas (Hoerlin), August 17, 1933. "Faules Schwein, Suesser . . . Lass Dir das alles durch deinen Krautschaedel gehen und schreibe mir moeglichst bald deine Ansicht, die mir immerhin wichtig erscheint."

[47] Hermann Hoerlin, "Deutsche Bergsteiger im Ausland". *Mitteilungen des Deutschen und Oesterreichischen Alpenvereins* (Winter, 1933). "Es ist ein alter Trieb . . . der Trieb in die Ferne, die Sehnsuch in die weite Welt."

Chapter 5 Notes (Pages 59-74)

[1]   Letter from Merkl to Hoerlin, December 3, 1933. "... ich kann es einfach nicht glauben dass Sie nicht dabei sein sollen und ich hoffe nur, dass Ihre Teilnahm noch moeglich werden wird . . . es waere meine groesste Freude, wenn Sie im Maerz mit uns starten wuerden." (note use of formal "Sie"—although they had met several times)

[2]   Fritz Bechtold, *Deutsche am Nanga Parbat: Der Angriff 1934* (Muenchen: Verlag F. Bruckmann, 1935), p. 16.

[3]   *Mitteilungen des Deutschen und Oesterreichischen Alpenvereins*, June 1, 1934. The sports store was Welt-Sporthaus Schuster in Munich.

[4]   Several people have commented on this, including the famous climber Reinhold Messner: "Schneider war Anarchist. Schneider hat sich sehr negativ ueber Hitler geaeussert . . ."

[5]   Isserman and Weaver, ibid, p. 173. Richard Finsterwalder, the Expedition's cartographer, appealed directly to Hitler's deputy Rudolf Hess to grant permission for Misch to participate. In 1936, Misch fled Germany with his family for China. It is not clear which of his parents or whether both were Jewish. According to Isserman and Weaver, Misch's father was; other sources specify his mother.

[6]   Jean Friedman-Rudovsky, "The Last Days of a Nazi-Era Photographer," TIME, September 23, 2008. While it is debated as to whether or not Ertl officially became a Nazi, there is no question about his prominent role in Nazi filmmaking.

[7]   W. Fiedler, "Der Daemon des Himalaya," *Deutsche Allgemeine Zeitung* [Berlin] March 21, 1935.

[8]   Letter to Hoerlin from Erwin Schneider (written on board the Viktoria) April 1, 1934. "Sie wollen in Gegend K2 einen "leichten" 8000er behuepfen und einen Film drehen, dessen Manuskript ich einmal sah. Ich sag Dir, dabei wurde mir schon ganz schwach."

[9]   India-Ton was owned by Gottfried Treviranus, a member of the Conservative People's party, who barely escaped being arrested—and most probably killed - by the Nazis on June 30, 1934, the Night of the Long Knives. He fled to Holland, leaving the Expedition without that source of funding. Holt, ibid. p. 302.

[10]   *Augsburger Postzeitung*, July 29, 1934. "So etwas ist nur in Deutschland moeglich. Fuer Deutschland werden wir kaempfen und werden alles daran setzen, den ersten Achttausender fuer Deutschland zu erobern. Heil Hitler!"

[11] Merkl postcard from Munich to Hoerlin in Stuttgart. November 21, 1933. "Wir alle bedauern sehr, dass Sie nicht bei uns waren. Hoffentlich wird es aber doch was."

[12] As quoted in Mailaender, ibid, p. 211. It was Reichssportfuehrer Tschammer und Osten who expounded, "Die Eroberung des Gipfels wird zum Ruhme Deutschlands erwartet."

[13] Richard Finsterwalder, "Der Alpenverein und die Deutsche Himalaja Expedition 1934," *Mitteilungen des Deutschen und Oesterreichischen Alpenvereins*, Winter 1933. The Nanga Expedition had received RM 10.000 from the Club.

[14] Mailaender, ibid., p. 211. December 1933 letter from Max Hoesch of the Dueren section of the Verein to Paul Dinkelacker of the Munich section. The letter also sharply objected to the nazification of the Verein.

[15] Holt, ibid, p. 270

[16] Letter from Uli Wieland, March 19, 1934. Wieland noted concerns about the handling of prior news items by the *Mitteilungen*.

[17] in German there is an umlaut over the "a" in Kate. I have not included the usual "e" as an American substitute, as I have in other cases.

[18] Letter from Kate Schmid to Willy Merkl, January 27, 1934. "Dass sie passierte ist Deine Schuld." This was in relationship to handing out an incomplete press release.

[19] Ibid. "Schau, dass Du zu gernuegenden Schlaft kommst."

[20] Letter from Kate Schmid to Willy Merkl late January/early February 1934. "Ach Bub, das ists ja gerade, dass man als gutes Fuehrer vor allem u. bei allen ein guter Psychologe sein muss."

[21] Bechtold, ibid, p. 21.

[22] Bechtold, ibid., p. 26. Base camp was at 3850 meters/13,012 feet. "Hoch droben am Gipfel . . . flammt das erste Licht des jungen Tages. Langsam flutet die blendende Helle ueber die maechtige Steilmauer herab auf den Gletscher. . . . Wir blicken zu dem Berg auf, wie zu etwas ganz Unwirklichem."

[23] Friedlander ibid., p. 33.

[24] John Cornwell, *Hitler's Scientists: Science, War, and the Devil's Pact (New York: Viking Penguin, 2003)*, p. 127

[25] letter to Hoerlin from Schneider written from the Burzil Pass (Nanga Parbat) May 25, 1934. "Du wirst ja sicher immer am Deutschlandsender haengen und im uebrigen versorgen ja die ueblichen Latrinengeruechte das dritte Reich ausgiebig mit Schauernachrichten. Es ist schon zum Kotzen . . ."

[26] Isserman and Weaver, ibid., p. 173. The map is still in use today. The three scientists were Richard Finstermacher, Peter Misch and Walter Raechl.

27 Letter from Wieland (at Nanga basecamp) to Hoerlin, June 7, 1934. "Grosse Expeditionen sind schrecklich. Immer ist es das Gepaeck, was aufhaelt. So Gott will, werden wir drei, noch einmal eine <u>kleine</u> Expedition, aber auch mit grossem Ziel, machen."

28 Letter from Schneider to Hoerlin, May 8, 1934.

29 Letter from Wieland to Hoerlin, June 7, 1934. "Bevor ich diese glorreiche Staette vielleicht auf Nimmer wiedersehen, jedenfalls fuer einige Tage und hoffentlich fuer mindesten vier, hoechstens sechs Wochen in hoehere Regionen verlasse, will ich dir zu deinem Geburtstag noch gratulieren."

30 Letter from Wieland to Hoerlin. June 7, 1934. ". . . dem Fortschritt alles opfern!"

31 Isserman and Weaver, ibid., p. 175

32 Bechtold, ibid., p. 28 "Aber Befehl ist Befehl" and ". . . der grimme Bara-Sahib empfaengt den Hansel unfreundlicher, als er es eigentlich verdient hat."

33 Bechtold, ibid, p. 34

34 It is interesting to note that "Frau Dr." Schmid (and not her husband) was designated. Clearly she was integral to the press position. The release was written by Welzenbach, who was Drexel's closest friend.

35 Mailaender, ibid., p. 212.

36 Isserman and Weaver, ibid., p. 174

37 Mailaender, ibid, p. 212.

38 As quoted in Mailaender, ibid., p. 212. "Merkl handelt zunehmend wie ein Diktator, der keine Kritik zulaesst. Er scheint wirklich zu glauben, dass eine feste und kompromisslose Haltung seine Autoritaet festigen und seinen Minderwertigkeitskomples, den er als Emporkoemmling offensichtlich fuehlt. unterdruecken koennte."

39 as quoted in Eric Roberts, *Welzenbach's Climbs* (Great Britain: West Col Productions,1980), p. 247.

40 Kate Schmid letter to Willy Merkl, July 2, 1934. ". . . dann werden wir wissen, ob es menschenmoeglich war oder nicht auf den Gipfel zu kommen."

41 Isserman and Weaver, ibid., p. 175

42 As quoted in Mailaender, ibid., p. 213. "Man kann nicht einen Verein von zehn bis zwoelf Leuten auf einen Achtausender bringen wollen. Dann kommt eben keiner hinauf. Aber alles Predigen ist hier vergeblich. Willy weiss alles besser."

43 Letter from Walter Raechl (from Nanga base camp) to Paul Dinkelacker, head of the Stuttgart Section of the Alpenverein, July 31, 1934. ". . . Nanga wie eine Insel aus dem Wolkenmeer herausragte . . ."

[44] Account of Aschenbrenner in Bechtold, ibid, p. 44. "Wie ein Luftballon segelte der grosse Packsack vor unseren Augen . . ."

[45] Karl Herrligkoffer, the half brother of Merkl, as quoted in Isserman and Weaver, ibid, p. 178

[46] Indicative of the confusion surrounding death reports is a July 17, 1934 telegram from Hans Hieronimus, the head man at base camp, to Kate Schmid. The dates of Welzenbach's and Wieland's deaths were confused and the spelling of Welzenbach's name incorrect. "Walzenbach und Wieland am neunten und zwoelften Juli am Berg gestorben. Fuenf Traeger ebenso. Merkl in Lager sechs bisher ohne Rettungsmoeglichkeit."

[47] Letter from Raechl to Dinkelacker, July 31, 1943. ". . . der grundlose Schnee bei steilem Aufstieg brachte das Unternehmen schon auf halbem Wege zum Scheitern".

[48] Letter from Kate to Hoerlin, July 15, 1943. "Aber es ist wohl an der Zeit mit allen guten Wuenschen an die Maenner zu denken."

[49] *Muenchner Neueste Nachrichten,* July 18, 1934. "Schwere Sorgen um die deutsche Himalaja-Expedition: Merkl, Wieland und Welzenbach vermisst."

[50] Roberts, ibid, p. 183-5. It was on the north face of the Grand Charmoz in the Alps.

[51] as quoted in Roberts, ibid, p 260.

[52] Letter from Kate Schmid to Willy Merkl, July 2, 1934. ". . . die Arbeit wird gemacht. . . . Du musst nicht glauben, dass ich die Arbeit im Stich lasse. Gewiss nicht."

[53] Kate Schmid communications to Hoerlin, July 2, 4, 8, and 15, 1934.

[54] Telegram to Hoerlin from Gollwitzer, July 17, 1934. "Himalaya Expedition in groesster Gefahr, Koennten Sie sogleich zu Frau Dr Schmid Muenchen Schackstr 3 kommen".

[55] Bechtold, ibid, p. 48 "Unter ihnen ist einer, den ich dreimal, viermal lesen muss, um ihn zu begreifen. Willi Schmid, unser lieber, froher und gescheiter Kamerad, der Leiter unserer Pressestelle in Muenchen, der zu Hause mit seiner Frau die Riesenarbeit leistete, der uns immer wieder anzufeuern wusste—ist tot . . . Schicksal und Tragik hat die ganze Front zerbrochen, hier am Berg und daheim."

[56] Letter from Bechtold to Hoerlin, August 11, 1934 "Zu groesstem Dank aber verpflichtet bin ich Ihnen, dass Sie Frau Dr. Kaet(h)e Schmid in der Zeit tiefsten Leids beistehen . . . Es ist unsagbar, was diese Frau innerhalb so kurzer Zeit alles tragen u. nebenbei leisten musste . . . . Das ist so ungeheuerlich, dass

man wirklich an dem, an das man so lange, wie an etwas Grosses geglaubt hat, irr werden koennte."

57 Telegram from Bechtold to Kate Schmid, September 9, 1934. "Alle Teilnehmer wuenschen Heimkehr unbemerkt." According to the earlier referenced Raechl letter (July 31, 1934), Bechtold undertook leadership functions for the expedition due to Merkl's and Welzenbach's deaths.

58 Letter from Schneider to Pallas, August 19, 1934. "Dass Du bei Frau Schmid warst, haben wir alle mit grosser Freude vernommen. So hast Du wenigsten der armen Frau helfen koennen."

59 Letter from Bechtold to Hoerlin, August 11, 1934. ". . . dass Sie heute in den schweren Tagen der Expedition fuer sie eingetreten sind" und "in der Trauerkundgebung des Rundfunks fuer unsere am Nanga gebliebenen Kameraden gesprochen haben."

60 Roberts, ibid, p. 25. The first ascent of a 8000er was Annupurna (8091 meters) by the French team of Maurice Herzog and Louis Lachernal.

Chapter 6 Notes (Pages 75-88)

1 Letter from Hoerlin to Kate, December 1934. "Dass Du so ganz anders bist, als alle Frauen . . . die mir bisher begegnet sind . . ."

2 Karl Haniel, a friend of the Schmids, was managing director of the Haniel family's (FA Haniel) vast holdings, which included ownership of the MNN and the Gutehoffnungshuette heavy industry company.

3 William Shirer, *Rise and Fall of the Third Reich* (New York: Simon and Schuster, 1960), p. 223.

4 August 1, 1934 affadavit written by Kate Schmid as translated in 2004 by Duscha Schmid Weisskopf, Kate's eldest child. In 2004 Duscha, my half-sister, wrote a family memoir about her father, *Willi Schmid: A Life in Germany*.

5 The origin of the term, Night of the Long Knives, harks back to a vengeance myth in Arthurian legends. The term "*Roehm Putsch*" is usually italicized since it was used by the Nazis to imply Roehm was the perpetrator of a putative coup, a view now dispelled.

6 Roderick Stackelberg, *Hitler's Germany: Origins, Interpretations, Legacies* (London: Routledge (second edition), 2009), p.131.

7 Ian Kershaw, *Hitler 1889—1936: Hubris* (New York: Houghton Mifflin, 1998), p. 517

8   Letter from Lydia Wieland to Frau Schmid and Herr Hoerlin, July 25, 1934. "... er war nicht geschaffen fuer die boese Welt."

9   *Muenchner Neueste Nachrichten,* July 26, 1934. "... Welzenbach ist bestrebt das Ansehen Deutschlands zu foerdern ..."

10   for an example, see *Muenchner Zeitung,* July 23, 1934: "Gefallen fuer das Vaterland" ("Fallen for the Fatherland"). Other paper headlines, such as the *Berliner Morgen-Post Zeitung* (July 26, 1934) and *Frankfurter Zeitung* (July 25, 1934) emphasized the heroic aspect of the expedition. *The London Times* (July 28, 1934) led with a less expressive headline: "Death in the Himalayas."

11   *Reichsbahn Turn und Sport Zeitung,* December 1934. "Was diese Helden taten, war nur fuer Deutschlands Ehre, war nur fuer Deutschlands Ruhm und Herrlichkeit!" in article "Fuer Deutschlands Ehre!"

12   Alan Bullock, *A Study in Tyranny* (New York: Penguin, 1990), ibid., p. 278. The quote was made by Rudolf Hess.

13   Bullock, ibid., p. 278. Himmler was the overseer of Nazi concentration camps and was one of the most feared men in Nazi Germany.

14   Letter from Kate to Hoerlin, August 1, 1934. "Wir sind ein wenig noch mehr verwaist—aber sonst waeren Sie ja auch gar nicht dargewesen, ging es uns anders."

15   Letter from Kate to Hoerlin, August 1, 1934. "Ich sagte ihm, dass er der erste <u>Mensch</u> sei, der zu mir gekommen ist und dass ich 4 Wochen auf diesen Menschen gewartet habe. Hess drueckte mir, auch im Namen der Fuehrers, das offizielle und tiefe Beileid aus und war darueber hinaus so ehrlich ergriffen und wahrgeruettelt, dass es mir einfach gut tat und mir ueberhaupt wieder Boden unter die Fuesse gab ... Als er ging, konnte er kein Wort mehr hervorbringen. Er beugte tief, nur sehr lange, und tief ueber meine Hand."

16   Robert E. Conot, *Justice at Nuremberg* (New York: Basic Books, 1993), p. 44

17   Hess was mesmerized by Hitler in the early 1920's and remained dedicated to him. He played a prominent part in creating the Nuremberg laws, but is perhaps best remembered for his solo flight to Scotland on May 10, 1941 allegedly to negotiate peace with Great Britain. Hess was widely regarded as mentally unstable.

18   Letter from Hess to Frau Kaethe Schmid, September 24, 1934. "Es ist mir mitgeteilt worden, dass Sie besonders im Hinblick auf Ihre Kinder gern schriftlich bestaetigt haben moechten, was ich Ihnen bei meinem Besuch bereits sagte, naemlich dass Ihr Herr Gemahl nicht etwa erschossen woerden ist, weil er im Zusammenhang mit der Roehm-Revolte oder sonst wie schuldig gewesen sei. Tatsaechlich ist er das Opfer eines Ungluecksfalles."

19 Letter from Kate to Hoerlin, August 6, 1934. "Ich freue mich, wenn Sie jetzt nach Aarau kommen. Freuen—das Wort had einen seltsamen und fernen Klang fuer mich bekommen. Und doch: ich freue mich, wenn Sie kommen."

20 Letter from Hoerlin to Kate, late summer 1934. ". . . ich nehme es als das allergroesste Geschenk und Gnade, dass ich zu Dir kommen darf. Seit jenen Tagen im Juli bin ich Gott naeher, als ich es vielleicht je war."

21 Letter from Kate to Hoerlin. fall 1934. ". . . weil es wie ein Sturm ueber mich hingeht . . . es riss mir die Arme auseinander . . . ich breite die Arme weit and kann danach die Herrlichkeit von Tag und Nacht und Morgen umspannen."

22 Letter from Kate to Hoerlin, fall 1934. ". . . und wie ich an Deiner Seite ueber die Felder ging and mich der Wind und Du abwechselnd kuessten und wie gut der Regen auf der heissen Haut war. Seit dem Wunder jenes einen Tages sah ich Wolken wieder wandern, ich sehe wie gruen und blau die Baeume sind, ich kann wieder tief atmen . . . So ist es jetzt, auch jetzt noch moeglich, dass ich Kraft zu verschenken hab und nicht nur das Unvermoegen der Traurigkeit mein Teil ist . . ."

23 Letter from Hoerlin to Kate. fall 1934. "Ein tiefes Glueck begleitet mich, so tief, dass . . . dieses fast laehmende Gefuehl war mir bisher fremd"

24 Letter from Kate to Hoerlin, fall 1934. ""Das Zurueckmuessen ist kein Heimkommen fuer mich; ich gehe hinein wie in eine sehr dunkle, sternenlose Nacht, aber doch in der Gewissheit, dass irgendwo das Licht immer noch und immer wieder leuchtet. Hab Dank."

25 Letter from Kate to Hoerlin, September 8, 1934. ". . . mitten in der Arbeit an diesen stillen stillen Abenden habe ich doch gewartet auf einen Schluessel, der sich nicht mehr dreht."

26 Letter from Kate to Hoerlin, late September, 1934. "Heute Nacht hatte ich einen seltsamen Traum. Der Pitsch rief mich, ich ging seiner Stimme nach, ich ging und ging. Einmal fragte er mich, ob ich muede sei. Ich antwortete: ich gehe ueber die Welt hin um Dich zu finden. Als ich aufwachte fragte ich mich, ob das wahr sei. Es _ist_ wahr. Es sind mir alle Wege zu ihm hin—wie auch sollte ich fortgehen koennen von ihm?"

27 Letter from Kate to Hoerlin, late October, 1934. "Es wurde mir gestern in diesen intensiven Stunden mit Spengler wieder ganz deutlich—gleichzeitig bin ich der Welt von Pitsch verkettet und unloeslich zugehoerig. Ich kann heute noch nicht entscheiden, wer ich bin: eine Frau, die fortfaerth—oder ein Mensch, der neu beginnt."

[28] Letter from Kate to Hoerlin, late September 1934. "Du lieber, Du junger Mensch. Aber schoen ist es, das Leben ist es, wenn Du mir die Haende reichst und mich hier und da hinueberziehst in Deine Welt."

[29] Letter from Kate to Hoerlin, late October 1934. ". . . meine Lippen zwischen den Zuegen Deiner Stirn, den Bogen Deiner Brauen, dem Schwung Deines Mundes . . . und dann beugst Du Dich ueber mich und schaust mich an, ich kann Dir grade noch uebers Haar streichen. Und dann reisst es mir die Seele auseinander und selig, selig oeffnet sie sich. Und dann kann ich nicht mehr als <u>da</u> sein"

[30] Letter from Kate to Hoerlin, early 1935. "Ich dachte ueber . . . Deine Art nach. Und dass Dich der Beruf, die innere Berufung, das wirklich Verhaftetsein noch gar nicht hat. Und dass der, der einmal die Weite der Welt geschaut hat, sie nur schwer vergessen kann, auch gar nicht vergessen soll. Weiter dachte ich, wie gut Du ertragen kannst, was nur ganz wenige Menschen zu ertragen vermoegen: wochen-, ja monatelange Einsamkeit. Dachte daran wie Du durch fremde Laender reistest in dieser ernsten gar nicht oberflaechlichen Unbekummertheit . . . es waere schad, haette sie fuer das keinen Raum mehr in Deinem Leben."

[31] Letter from Hoerlin to Kate, January or February 1935. ". . . wurde ich wohl herausgerissen aus dem Gewohnten. Und ich danke Gott dafuer. Warum bin ich von der Lisel weggegangen; weil es zum gewohnten Gewoehnlichen geworden war, weil mir das ewig gleichmaessige dahinfliessende verhasst ist, weil sie mich letzten Endes als buergerlichen Menschen haben wollte . . ."

[32] Letter from Hoerlin to Kate, December 2, 1934. ". . . manchmal bin ich wie ein gefangener Mensch, durch eine zweifelnde, unruhevolle Liebe gefangen, die mich zu nichts anderem kommen laesst . . ."

[33] Letter from Hoerlin to Kate, November 1934. "Du ziehst mich weg . . . Du willst es nicht, aber ich will es."

[34] Letter from Kate to Hoerlin, December 6, 1934. "Es ist wunderschoen Dir zuzuschauen, weil Du so gut denken kannst. Ich hab es gewusst und schon oft erfahren—aber dann bin ich doch immer wieder erstaunt, <u>wie</u> bezaubernd Du es kannst, das Denkbarsein."

[35] Letter from Kate to Hoerlin, December 1934. "Du hast mich mit den stillsten Dingen berauscht. Lass es immer so bleiben, lass mich durch Dein Verlangen und Begehren in Deine ganz klare tiefe Stille ein, die ein Heiligtum fuer mich ist, ein grosses, weites, in dem meine Liebe ihre Heimat findet."

[36] Letter from Kate to Hoerlin, December 1934. "Warum presst mich das Schicksal dann so unheimlich nah zu Dir? Dass ich keinen <u>Atem</u> habe ohne ihn mit dem

Deinen zu mischen, dass Dein Herz in mir wie meines klopft . . . weil ich mit allem, was mein ist, bezeugen <u>muss,</u> dass ich Dich liebe.

37 Letter from Hoerlin to Kate, fall 1934. "Du ich brenne, lass mich nicht verbrennen . . . ich kann nichts dafuer, dass ich diese Sehnsucht hab . . . stille mein Blut, mir ist, als ob tausend Naechte zu wenig waeren."

38 Letter from Kate to Hoerlin, November 1934. "Es gibt, denke ich, wohl keinen unbedingteren Beweis fuer unsere Verbundenheit, fuer die Wahrheit und Tiefe meines Gefuehls als diese Liebe meiner Kinder zu Dir. Du bist, von all den vielen, die kommen und gehen, der ihnen liebste Mensch. Das ist die schoenste und klarste Bestaetigung, die ich Dir geben kann."

39 Letter from Kate to Hoerlin, November 2, 1934. "O Bub, es gibt Maenner, die warten auf mich und werben um mich—Jahre, jahrelang. Der Pitsch hat dem mit Gelassenheit, mit der herrlichen Sicherheit unserer Liebe zugeschaut. 'Wollte man die Liebe der Menschen trennen von Dir, man wuerde Dir die Luft zum Atmen nehmen. Das wusste er. Er hat nie gelitten um mich. Der Gedanke nur, dass Du, den ich liebe, es tun koennte, laehmt mich."

40 Letter from Hoerlin to Kate, early November 1934. "Ich habe eine junge und tiefe Liebe zu Dir, voll Verlangen und Sehnsucht, Tu ihr nichts zuleide. Es gibt kaum noch etwas anderes auf der Welt fuer mich, als Dich."

41 Letter from Kate to Hoerlin, November 27, 1934: ". . . daraus spuere ich unmittelbar den Willen von Pitsch—denn wie koennte ohne seinen Willen dies so mit mir geschehen? Ich weiss dass es—trotz der Kinder—<u>die</u> Gnade meines Lebens ist, dass Du kamst."

42 Letter from Kate to Hoerlin, December 1934: "Herz und Arme sind mir schwer von dem vielen, was ich fuer Dich habe, was ich Dir bring, da es Dir gehoert und zu Dir will—mein Leben . . ."

43 Letter from Hoerlin to Kate, December 1934. ". . . mein Herz, mein Blut, <u>alles</u> ist Dein . . ."

44 Letter from Kate to Hoerlin, January 1935. "Deine Decke habe ich nun ausgebreitet auf der Ottomane im Buecherzimmer. Es wird niemand anders darauf liegen als ich. Das Fell ist ueber die Massen schoen . . . fuer mich hat es neben der Begeisterung ueber die Schoenheit an sich noch die ganz unmittelbare Verbindung zu Dir hin, deine helle Waerme hat es, Du Geliebter."

Chapter 7 Notes (Pages 89-102)

1   Letter from Kate to Willi Merkl, February 1934. ". . . wir haben getanzt, getanzt—endlos und doch nicht genug! . . . warum tanz ich denn so verrueckt gern?"

2   John Cornwall, *Hitler's Scientists: Science, War and the Devil's Pact* (New York: Penguin Books, 2003), p. 127.

3   Cornwall, ibid., p. 129

4   Eric Voegelin, *Hitler and the Germans*, vol. 31 (University of Missouri Press, 1999), p. 121. The meeting was between Hitler and physicist Max Planck, a Nobel Prize winner and director of Berlin's prestigious Kaiser Wilhelm Institute.

5   Philipp Lenard wrote a four volume textbook titled *Deutsche Physik* in 1936.

6   Letter from Hoerlin to Kate, February 1935. "Ich brauche Ruhe and Stille um gut arbeiten zu koennen."

7   Letter from Hoerlin to Kate, November 1935. "Du schreibst von meinen Faehigkeiten in die Du glaubst. Er werden welche da sein, es waere falsch das bescheiden abstreiten zu wollen—ich muss mich sehr bemuehen, sie richtig zu erkennen und richtig einzusetzen. Dass hab ich besonders im Laufe der beiden letzten Jahre erkannt, wo ich vieles wollte und doch wenig zur eigenen Befriedigung durchfuhrte. Ich darf mich nich zersplittern, nicht zuletzt weil ich kein sehr schneller Arbeiter bin."

8   Letter from Hoerlin to Kate, December 23, 1935. "Es schmerzt mich heute sehr, dass ich Dir und der wartenden Mutter nicht das aeussere Ergebnis der letzten Jahre zum Fest schenken kann. Eben das eine darf ich Dir mit ganz ehrlichem Glauben, ja mit sicherem Wissen sagen, dass ich im vergangenen Jahr ein gut Stueck vorwaerts gekommen bin und dass noch ein sehr anstaendiger Physiker aus mir wird. Ich freue mich darueber . . ."

9   Isserman and Weaver, ibid., p. 156.

10 Andreas Nickel, *Guenter-Hettie-Norman Dyhrenfurth. Zum Dritten Pol* (Zurich: AS Verlag, 2007), p. 80-81. Letter from Dr. Philipp Borchers, head of foreign expeditions for the *Alpenverein* to Karl Wein, Bauer's close climbing companion, February 16, 1930.

11 Peter Mierau, *Die Deutsche Himalaja-Stiftung von 1936 bis 1998* (Muenchen: Bergverlag Rother.1999), p. 64

12 Letter from Bauer to von Tschammer und Osten, December 10, 1934. ". . . Hoerlin und Schneider hatten auch dafuer, dass es sich hier um eine nationale

Angelegenheit handele, kein Verstaendnis, sie bauten ihren Plan 1930, 31 und 32 auf die Teilnahme begueterter auslaendischer Bergsteiger auf—Schneider und Hoerlin gingen 1930 mit dem Judenstaemmling Dyhrenfurth in den Himalaja . . ."

13 Schneider, Erwin, "Die 1. Ersteigung des Huascarans," Sonderabdruck aus "Die Alpen," Jahrgang IX. p. 61. "Weinend treten wir den Rueckzug an und versuchen nun, zur Einsicht gekommen und den Forderungen der heutigen Zeit folgend, rechts unser Heil (Heil Adolf! Deutschland erwache!)"

14 Letter from Bauer to Hans Wieland, March 26, 1936. ". . . ich handle wieder so, als ob ich den Himalaja gepachtet haette . . ."

15 Nickel, ibid., p 153. Letter from Bauer to Tschammer, December 4, 1934. ". . . Es ist eine feste Regel, dass in unuebersichtlichem Wetter die Mannschaft zusammen bleiben muss . . . Wer wie Schneider und Aschenbrenner . . . voraus-und davonlaeuft, der wird nicht als guter Bergkamerad angesehen werden koennen. Es ist sehr gefaehrlich, wenn Leute von so zweifelhafter Haltung jetzt als Helden auftreten . . ."

16 Letter from Bauer to Wien, February 22, 1935. ". . . Hoerlin an dieser Stelle im Verwaltungsausschuss ganz unmoeglich ist. Er scheint ein Mann zu sein der nichts weiter kennt als seine vorgefasste Meinung, seinen persoenlichen Groll und Hass . . ."

17 Letter from Kate to Hoerlin, March 25, 1935. "Das ist fein, wie Ihr zu Schneider und Aschenbrenner steht und nicht um Haaresbreite nachgebt."

18 letter from Wein to Bauer, February 13, 1935. ""Uberigne moechte ich zu dem oben gesagten noch bemerken, dass tatsechlich Herolin sich derzeit unerhoert bloed auffuehrt und eigentlich ihm nichts anderes uebrig bleibt als zu verschwinden."

19 Nickel, ibid., p. 162. "Das Interesse des Reiches, das Ansehen des Deutschen Bergsteigertums verlangen eine genaue Auswahl der Teilnehmer einer etwaigen neuen Expedition."

20 Letter from Hoerlin to Bauer, September 6, 1935. "Der Leiter dieser Expedition muss eine Persoenlichkeit sein, die in jeder Hinsicht das Vertrauen . . . des D.u.Oe.A.V. geniesst." As quoted in Nickels, ibid, p. 164.

21 Letter from Bauer to Wien, August 5, 1935.

22 letter from Hoerlin to Kate, November 1934. "Gestern abend im Skiklub, ich kann nicht mehr so dabei sein, wie es bisher war. Ein Teil sitzt in der SA Uniform da, einer in der schwarzen SS. Viele sind noch ganz stur. Was such ich da?"

23 Letter from Hoerlin to Kate, March 1935.

24 Roberts, ibid, p. 247.

25   Roberts, ibid, p. 247

26   Letter from Kate to Hoerlin, October 12, 1934. "Seltsam, wieviel verschuettet ist zwischen den Maennern. Und sie selber sind so verstoert dadurch, dass sie <u>meine</u> Muedigkeit gar nicht sehen und aus eigener Not heraus immer nur fordern."

27   Letter from Kate to Hoerlin, July 8, 1935.

28   Letter from Kate to Hoerlin. December 1934. ". . . Tschammer das Vorwort zum Buch schreiben moechte und groessten Wert darauf legt, an einer or lieber noch mehreren Stellen genannt zu werden."

29   September 20, 1934 letter from Kate to Hoerlin. "Ach . . . was ist das fuer eine Welt."

30   November 5 and 6th 1934 letters from Kate to Hoerlin. "Die Herren {im Braunen Haus} . . . wollen endgueltig meine Sache selber in die Hand nehmen und beim Reich vertreten. Es ist ein edler Wettstreit unter den Herren ausgebrochen, <u>wer</u> von ihnen fuer mich und meine Sache nach Berlin fahren darf. Findest Du das nicht suess?!! Ich als Schuetzling des Braunen Hauses—Spiel der Tragikomoedie."

31   November 5, 1934 letter from Kate to Hoerlin. "Heute frueh im Braunen Haus habe ich gespuert Deine ruhige Kraft."

32   Letter from Kate to Hoerlin, February, 1935. "Manchmal kann ich es mir selbst nicht erklaeren, eine wie tiefe Ruhe mich ueberkommt in dem Augenblick, wo es wirklich zu kaempfen und sich zu behaupten gilt."

33   letter from Kate to Hoerlin, February 1935 (continued) "Heute Morgen wurde ich wieder ins Braune Haus gebeten. Es sind wueste Treibereien gegen mich im Gang. Ich wusste, dass sie nicht ausbleiben konnten u. war darauf vorbereitet umso mehr als ich jetzt die Gunst der obersten Stellen habe. Dies liess die unteren (u. das sehr schlechte Gewissen der unteren) nicht ruhen . . . (Ich) kaempfte dort nicht fuer mich—denn ich stehe, wo ich hingestellt wurde and stehe fest—aber fuer die drei. Es ist seltsam: aber ich habe nun aufrichtige Freunde dort, wo meine Feinde sitzen sollen. Sie achten mich . . . besonders Wiedemann. Ich sagte im BH: 'Deutschland dennoch zu lieben . . . vielleicht ist es dies, was von mir verlangt wird."

34   letter from Kate to Hoerlin, December 6, 1934. "Er ist entschieden der Beste, an den ich ueberhaupt kommen konnte, aktiver Offizier u. 4 Jahre lang an der Front gewesen, ritterlich und ganz persoenlich an mir und meinem Schicksal interessiert . . ."

35   letter from Kate to Hoerlin, April 30, 1935. "Es ist wohl eine Art Feigheit, dass ich <u>nie</u> Zeitungen lese.

36 Letter from Kate to Hoerlin, March 7, 1935. ". . . um 10 Uhr dann im Reichsjustizministerium, Staatssekretaer Schlegelberger hoechst angenehm, ein Jurist der alten Zeit, genau, klug, konziliant."

37 Letter from Kate to Hoerlin, March 7, 1935. "Weisst Du, dass der Portier mir gestern im Augenblick, als ich das Hotel verlassen wollte, Deinen Eilbrief gab? Da war ich geborgen, ruhig, fast froh bin ich in die Wilhelmstrasse gefahren, beseelt und gestaerkt von Deiner Treue. Du sollst wissen, wie warm und stark und helfend ich Deine Liebe in diesen Tagen wieder und wieder empfunden . . ."

38 Letter from Hoerlin to Kate, March 7, 1934. "In Berlin war ich gut in Form, sagte und tat nichts Falsches, und alles lief, wie ich—oft unbewusst—es gewuenscht hatte. Soviel ist sicher, dass die ganze Sache jetzt endgueltig aus dem Bereich der SS an die Stelle gekommen ist, wo es absolut sauber, vertrauenswuerdig und wohlmeinend geregelt werden wird—dieses gute and sichere Gefuehl . . . wird mich nicht taeuschen."

39 Over 25 letters regarding this case were retrieved and copied from the Berlin Mitte archives.

40 Letter from Schlegelberger to Wiedemann, March 7, 1935. "Eine solche Klage zu vermeiden, liegt aber im Interesse des Reichs."

41 Letter from Kate to Hoerlin, March 23, 1935. "Jetzt bin ich zu dem Entschluss gekommen: ich will mich nicht mehr quaelen lassen, weil ich sonst unbrauchbar und zu allem unfaehig werde. Ich muss die Unsicherheit und Ungewissheit als einen Bestandteil meines Daseins ertragen lernen—denn wenn ich mich weitere 6 Monate (u. vielleicht dann noch laenger) so wie bisher davon quaelen lasse, bin ich am Ende, Hoerlin—und nur Briefe und Bilder koennten noch das bezeugen, was ich war."

42 Letter from Kate to Hoerlin, March 28, 1935. "Nur ich selber weiss, wie nahe ich der Kapitulation bin. Freilich weiss ich auch dies, dass, je staerker der Druck, umso haerter das Metall wird. Vielleicht ist das ein falscher Satz fuer den Wissenschaftler. Fuer mich ist es richtig und gilt."

43 Letter from Hoerlin to Kate, March 1935. "Soweit kann doch nicht einmal die schlimmste Buerokratie gehen. Gibts denn ueberhaupt noch Maenner in diesem _____?"

44 Letter from Kate to Hoerlin, July 30, 1935. "Wiedemann fand ich bemueht u. anstaendig wie immer. Wir hatten die Unterredung mit einem Herrn des Innenministeriums u. zwar im Zimmer des Fuehrers, einem wunderschoenen, stillen und grossartigen Raum, in dem ein paar herrliche alte Italiener haengen und vor dessen Fenster die Linden wehen. Es scheint nun wirklich die Regelung durch das Reich unmittelbar bevorstehend—obgleich ich skeptisch bin . . ."

45   Letter to Frau Kaethe Schmid from der Reichs-und Preussische Minister des
     Innern, September 14, 1935.

46   There were five other "innocent victims" of the Roehm Putsch who received
     compensation at the same time. Kate's was by far the largest.

47   Letter from Kate to Hoerlin, September 20, 1935. ""... da dies nach 15 Monaten
     geschah, loest es kein Gefuehl ruhevoller Geborgenheit aus und die Wirklichkeit
     des Dokuments erscheint mir ganz und gar unwirklich."

48   Letter from Kate to Hoerlin, September 20, 1935. "Es war nach seinem Tod keine
     Zeit quaelender als diese fuer mich. Ich konnte dies nicht kampflos geschehen
     lassen—trotz oder gerade in meiner Situation nicht. Es handelt sich fuer jetzt
     nur noch um 300 Exemplare, die beschlagnahmt werden koennten... So wandte
     ich mich an das Reichsjustizministerium und die Reichskanzlei und bekomme
     heute von Wiedemann den Bescheid, dass er die GeStaPo um Aufklaerung
     ersucht habe... So muss ich also doch noch des Buches wegen nach Berlin."

49   Her prior meetings with Hess had been in her home and with Himmler at the
     Brown House in Munich.

50   Weisskopf, ibid, p 114.

51   Kershaw, ibid., p 396.

Chapter 8 Notes (Pages 103-117)

1   Heiratsurkunde (marriage certificate) of Adolf Tietz and Hedwig Pinner, June
    18, 1883. Both are listed as belonging to the Jewish religion. Adolf Tietz was
    born in Birnbaum and his father was Jacob Tietz, a brother of Michael Tietz
    who founded the Tietz department store dynasty. Documentation from the
    Berlin Mitte archives.

2   Werner Eugene Mosse, *The German-Jewish Economic Elite, 1820—1935,*
    (Oxford University Press, 1989), p. 71.

3   Duscha Weisskopf, *Willi Schmid, A Life in Germany.* 2004.

4   Weisskopf, ibid., p 95.

5   Weisskopf, ibid, p. 116. This seems to have been among the letters burned by
    Kate upon leaving Germany.

6   The 1935 Nuremberg laws and their ramifications will be discussed later.

7   Letter from Kate to Hoerlin, November 1, 1934. "Seit meine Lippen zum
    erstenmal Deine Stirn beruehrten, habe ich nichts verborgen vor Dir. Nicht das
    Zittern der Seligkeit und nicht die Fragen alle, deren Loesung nur allmaehlich

und mit einem sehr hohen Einsatz an Willen, Entscheidung und Klarheit moeglich sein wird."

8   Letter from Kate Tietz to Willi Schmid, June 28, 1919. As quoted in Weisskopf, ibid., p. 95.

9   Letter from Kate Tietz to Willi Schmid, June 28, 1919. As quoted in Weisskopf, ibid., p 95. The bolding is the author's.

10 Friedlander, ibid., p 69.

11 Friedlander, ibid., p 101.

12 Friedlander, ibid., p. 118

13 Friedlander, ibid., p. 122.

14 Letter from Paul Bauer to the Reichs Cultural Ministry, October 16, 1935. "Zu einem Zeitpunkt, da im Dritten Reich ein voelkisches Urgesetz dem Kampf gegen das Judentum ganz klare Formen gibt. ist es nicht anhaengig zu dulden, dass juedische Wirtschaftstraeger im Reich finstere Geschaefte machen . . ."

15 Letter from Kate to Hoerlin, November 9, 1934. ". . . dass ich jetzt manchmal denke, ich muss mich aus Deinem frohen und uebersichtlichen Leben streichen, ich muss fort von Dir—bald—gleich . . ." The men were, respectively, Karl Vossler and Oswald Bumke.

16 Letter from Kate to Hoerlin, December 8, 1934. ". . . dann, dann musst Du doch ermessen, was da geschieht?"

17 Letter from Kate to Hoerlin, December 9, 1934. "Weisst Du, wie das ist, wenn man weiss, dass man kein Kind mehr haben darf in diesem Deutschland? Ich weiss es jetzt."

18 Stackelberg, ibid., p. 173.

19 Marion J. Kaplan, *Between Dignity and Despair* (Oxford University Press, 1999). p. 82.

20 Ian Kershaw, "Hitler 1889-1936: Hubris." W.W. Norton: 1998. p. 564.

21 letter from Hoerlin to Kate, December 1934. "Ich glaube man wird Rasse verschieden definieren koennen und nichts ist richtig, weil es dann den Vertretern an den Exemplaren fehlt. Entweder gibt es tausende von Rassen oder gar keine jetzt bei uns. Dass aus einer Vereinigung in der das Blut draengt, in solchen Faellen nichts gutes entstehen koenne, das koennen nur Menschen behaupten, die gelinder gesagt ein sehr dickes Brett in dem Kopf haben. Du kannst verstehen, dass ich mir diese Dinge einmal zurecht legen muss. Gerade heute, wo auf diesem Gebiet nur Mist geredet werden darf and geglaubt wird, blindlings."

22 Letter from Kate to Hoerlin, December 1934. "Die Sonne schien auf mich hin, ich lag ganz still unter diesem Worte. Ich lag am offenen Fester und sehnte mich hinaus."

23 Letter from Kate to Hoerlin, November 2, 1934. "Die Frage bleibt nur offen nach dem <u>Weg</u>."

24 Letter from Hoerlin to Kate November 1934. "Ich weiss es, dass wir sehr kaempfen muessen, gegen einen sehr maechtigen Feind aber das Recht unserer Liebe ist ein starker Bundesgenosse. In diesem Sinne rede bitte nie mehr von Belastung, es waere nur dann nie, wenn Du glaubtest deshalb beiseite stehen zu muessen. Da muessen wir ganz eins sein, dann zwingen wir es."

25 Richard L. Miller, *Nazi Justiz: Law of the Holocaust* (Westport, CT: Praeger, 1995), p 145. Several mixed marriage applicants were taken into custody by the SS.

26 Kershaw, ibid., p. 563.

27 Letter from Kate to Hoerlin, December 1934. "Ich weiss, dass ich vor diesem Heute nicht an ein Morgen denken kann, noch an die buergerliche Ordnung, den gesetzmaessigen Bestand des Morgen. Als unbegreifliches Glueck liess die Zeit mir, dir zu schenken was mein ist. Ich trinke und segne jede Minute mit Dir, als sie sei die letzte—was wissen wir dann von Morgen? Und Du, wisse dass ich selig, selig bin."

28 Letter from Hoerlin to Kate, July 2, 1935. "In diesen Wochen ist in mir das koerperliche starker denn je; mit allen Sinnen ist ein ungestuemes, nie erlebtes Draengen und Verlangen nach Dir hin . . . Und Du hast (gluecklicherweise) ein heisses Blut."

29 Stackelberg, ibid. p.178.

30 Friedlander, ibid. p.153.

31 Letter from Kate to Hoerlin, October 9, 1935. "Du, es ist Krieg in der Welt. Es gibt Gesetze, die das Leben auf alle Weise verstuemmeln wollen. Der Tod ist nah . . . Du kuesst mich, Du gehst mit mir und es erfuellt mich mit unsagbarem Glueck Deinem Werden zuzuschauen und immer wieder dabei Deine Augen auf mich gerichtet zu fuehlen in herrlichster Liebe."

32 Whether or not Fredi knew he was a "half" brother is unknown. In her March 6, 1935 claim to the Reich for compensation for Willi Schmid's death, she states she has no siblings ("Frau Schmid hat keine Geschwister"). Kate and Fredi were close for years, but Kate did not get along with Fritz's wife and they leaned on Kate heavily for monetary and organizational support.

33 Quoted by Friedlander, ibid., p. 226.

[34] Letter from Kate to Hoerlin, September 11, 1935. ". . . dann ist auch das vorbei? Von Berlin Anrufe, vom Innen-, Justiz—, Finanzministerium, <u>nie</u> etwas Schriftliches, keine Zeile, die Gewaehr oder Sicherheit bietet."

[35] Letter from Kate to Hoerlin, January 10, 1936. "Fredi befindet sich in einer solchen Verzweiflung . . . Ich verstehe das gut. Es ist wohl etwas Grausames, einen Menschen mit unverbundenen Augen Schritt um Schritt dem Abgrund zuzufuehren. Aber wenn einer auf solchem Gang Frau und Kinder dabei hat, so geht es ueber Menschenkraft."

[36] Letter from Kate to Hoerlin, November 27, 1935. "Mit Hausdorffs habe ich es sehr gut, ich finde in ihnen die ueberlegenen, feinfuehligen und mir sehr nahen Menschen, als die ich sie immer gekannt habe. Die Nor hat sie nicht verzerrt, . . . Felix ist so der Mathematik verhaftet, dass er auf keine Weise herauszureissen ist—welch ein Glueck ist das!" Hausdorff was related to Adolf Tietz.

[37] "Hertie" (a combination of the owner's name, *Her*mann *Tie*tz) sounded less Jewish.

[38] After nine years of trying, my half sister Duscha Weisskopf was successful in procuring modest reparations for the forced sale of the Tietz property in Schwerin. The money, received in April 2009, was evenly distributed among my mother's heirs.

[39] Letter from Kate to Hoerlin from Schwerin. July 22, 1935. "O, es ist traurig hier. Ich war noch nie so traurig um Mutti wie jetzt. Ueberall sehe ich sie, an jeder Ecke, in der Kueche, auf ihrem Stuhl. Sie ging und unendliche Liebe mit ihr. Ich sitze hier inmitten des alten Hausrats, aber es ist nun so, dass auch die Dinge ihr liebes sauberes Gesicht fast verloren haben inmitten der unfasslichen Verhetzung und Verzerrung, die mir den Atem stehen laesst u. die Luft vergiftet. Wie ich gestern im Dunkel lag, toente die Uhr meiner Kindheit um Mitternacht. Doch kam keine Ruhe ueber mich wie damals. Friede war nur ueber den Graebern. Du musst wissen, wie schoen sie liegen, gerade ueber dem grossen See. Es ist ganz still dort, nur die Baeume rauschen . . . die Vorsichtheit hier ist namenlos . . . Und ich muss es geschehen lassen, dass sie mir die Strassen, die Baeume, das geliebte Land meiner Kindheit unrettbar fortnimmt."

[40] Letter from Kate to Hoerlin, July 25, 1935. "Das Schlimme der Zeit, das mir in Schwerin die Heimat nahm, kommt nicht hierher."

[41] Letter from Kate to Hoerlin, December 4, 1934. "Bub, was sind das jetzt fuer Tage. sie zerren mir fast das Herz heraus, sie draengen mich—wohin? wohin? Es war doch einmal Heimat, diese feine Stadt . . . die Mauer waechst mir jetzt ins Riesenhafte. Zuerst war ich zu nahe dran—aber je weiter der Zwischenraum wird, umso deutlicher kann ich ihre unmenschliche Hoehe ermessen."

42 Friedlander, ibid., p. 135. The report of March 17, 1935 emanated from the Socialist Party.

43 postcard from Kate to Hoerlin, November 8, 1935. ". . . ein gesetzlicher Feiertag . . . worauf soll ich mich freuen?!?! Die Trommler droehnen dumpf, der Schritt ihrer Kolonnen erschuettert die Strassen, die Fackeln lagen im voelligen Dunkel."

44 letter from Kate to Hoerlin, June 4, 1935. "Weisst Du denn, wie tief und sehr Du mir Heimat bist? Dass ich um dieser lieben Heimat . . . das Herz dort ruhen und jubeln lasse, wohin es gehoert . . . Und Du weisst, was Du mir bist, Du Mensch, Du Mann, vielgeliebte Heimat Du."

Chapter 9 Notes (Pages 119-132)

1 Friedlander, ibid., p 198. The quote is from a SS educational bulletin, April 22, 1936.

2 Letter from Kate to Hoerlin, September 6, 1936. "Mich laesst es erzittern . . . in diesem sonnenlosen Jahr, ich habe eine Furcht in mir . . ."

3 letter from Kate to Hoerlin, January 10, 1936. "Es ist ein zitterndes Auf und Ab, all ueberall, in mir und um mich herum. Hoerlin, geh fort, geh fort. Du musst leben, wo es still ist . . . erfuellt von der Sicherheit das Gegebenen und Moeglichen. Das ist die Luft, die Du zum Atmen brauchst und mir verschlossen ist."

4 Letter from Hoerlin to Kate, January 12, 1936. "Einmal wirst Du zu dem festen Pol findern, nach dem Du Dich sehnst. Das ist mein sicherer Glaube . . . Es kommt wieder eine Zeit, in der wir Hand in Hand ueber die Huegel gehen, die Schoenheit der Welt sehend und ihre Grausamkeit vergessend."

5 Letter from Hoerlin to Kate, January 12, 1936. "Wenn ein Mensch zu Dir kommst, der mehr ist und Dir mehr ist, als ich bin und sein kann, dann will ich ohne Klage meines Weges gehen."

6 Letter from Kate to Hoerlin, January 27, 1936. "Du bist es, der mich erfuellt, ich atme bei Dir, noch hat sich meine Hand nicht aus der Deinen geloest, noch versucht mein Schritt im Gleichtakt mit dem Deinen zu gehen."

7 Letter from Kate to Hoerlin, April 29, 1935. "Die Geburt der Idee ist ein Ziel, das gewiss alle Kraefteanspannung lohnt—und es ist, das fuehle ich in einer grossen Gewissheit—kein Planen ins Blaue, keine Utopie, kein Phantasieren . . . es ist absolut Dein Plan, Deinem Wesen und drum wohl auch Deinen Faehigkeiten

entsprechend. Das glaube ich and Du sollst mich ganz nah fuehlen, wenn sich hier Dein Wille einen Weg schaffen kann."

[8] A flagship of the German fleet, launched in 1937, was named after Gustloff. In 1945, its sinking by a Russian submarine in the Baltic Sea has been called the greatest ship disaster of all time. Approximately 9000 lives were lost; it carried civilian refugees and wounded soldiers escaping from the advancing Russian army on the eastern front.

[9] Hitler Historical Museum website. Hitler speech in Schwerin: February 12, 1936.

[10] Hitler speech in Schwerin, ibid.

[11] Friedlander, ibid., p. 62.

[12] letter from Kate to Hoerlin, January 14, 1936. "Lieber, ich fuerchte mich vor dieser Reise, in die Einsamkeit und Hoffnungslosigkeit . . . ich habe nicht viel schlafen koennen"

[13] Stackelberg, ibid. p.178.

[14] Jane Kaplan, ed., *Nazi Germany* (Oxford University Press, 2008), p.138.

[15] Miller, ibid., p 100. The term "Jewish-tainted property" was applied to personal property of Jews confiscated and/or forfeited by the Nazis.

[16] Friedlander, ibid., p. 198-9.

[17] Robert Gellately, *The Gestapo and German Society: Enforcing Racial Policy, 1933-45* (New York: Oxford University Press, 1990), p. 71. The SD initially focused on suspected anti-government organizations or groups but soon included investigating the lives of individual citizens. The quote, from 1934, is by Reinhard Heydrich, director of the SD.

[18] Karl A. Schleunes, ed. *Legislating the Holocaust: The Bernhard Loesener Memoirs and Other Documents* (Westview Press, 2001), p. 130.

[19] My mother never shared the first name of von Alvensleben with my siblings and me. The most likely paternal candidate is Albrecht von Alvensleben (1848-1915), who lived at a family estate in Tessenow, a small town approximately 40 kilometers from Schwerin.

[20] Ludolf-Hermann von Alvensleben, known as 'Bubi", was assigned as Commander of the Schwerin region in 1937 and later became Chief of German Police. During WW II on the Eastern front, Bubi was held responsible for the execution of thousands of Poles.

[21] Karl Schleunes, *The Twisted Road to Auschwitz: Nazi Policy toward German Jews 1933-39* (University of Illinois Press, 1990), p. 130.

22 Letter from Kate to Hoerlin, January 29, 1936. "Mutti, wenn Du heimkommst, das ist gerade so wie die Musik von Mozart—man weiss nicht, <u>warum</u> es so schoen ist!"

23 "Ich bin hier, ist dass nicht genug?" Thomas Mann was probably Germany's foremost author. His most famous work was <u>Magic Mountain</u> (1925) and he won the Nobel Prize for Literature in 1929. Married to a Jew, he denounced National Socialism in 1930 and fled to Switzerland when Hitler came to power.

24 letter from Kate to Hoerlin, May 21, 1935. "Sonntag Abend war ein feiner und in seiner Zusammensetzung wohl fast nur in Muenchen moeglicher Kreis beisammen: Professoren, Hochadel, Aerzte und hohe Reichswehroffiziere. Alle geistig sehr interessiert . . ."

25 Letter from Kate to Hoerlin, March 31, 1935. ". . . zum Tee kommen Vosslers und Frau Hutchinson und Spengler und Bumke—also lauter gewichtige Maenner! Siehst Du mich eigentlich verwundert in ihrer Gesellschaft? . . . es handelt sich ja nicht ums Literarische, nicht ums "Geistige", sondern um sehr natuerliche und menschlich nahe Beziehungen und Verbundenheiten."

26 Furtwaengler was conductor of the Berlin Philharmonic and the Leipzig Gewandhaus Orchestra; in 1936 he was offered the conductorship of the New York Philharmonic, a position that did not materialize because of political maneuverings of the Third Reich.

27 Geheimrat was an honorary title, translated as privy counselor. Historically, the term described a secret or private advisor to a head of state.

28 letter from Hoerlin to Kate, March 31, 1936. "Ich bin froh dass ich am Abend zu Dir gesprochen habe . . . ich weiss, es war qualvoll fuer Dich mehr wie fuer mich. Ich aber hatte ein grosse Angst gehabt . . ."

29 Bumke speech to a meeting of psychiatrists in Munich, 1931 as quoted in George J. Annas and Michael Grodin. The *Nazi Doctors and the Nuremberg Code* (Oxford University Press: 1995), pgs. 90-1.

30 Letter from Hoerlin to Kate, July 2, 1935. "Dazu kommt, dass mir der kleine Willy irgendwie nicht sehr sympathisch ist."

31 U.S. Holocaust Memorial Museum website.

32 Susan Bachrach, *The Nazi Olympics Berlin 1936* (New York: Little Brown, 2000), p. 76. Rudi Ball, a hockey player, was Jewish.

33 Fredrick T. Birchall, *New York Times,* February 6, 1936.

34 TIME magazine, February 17, 1936.

35 Bachrach, ibid., 76.

36   According to my sister, Duscha Weisskopf, Bogner once substituted fish for
     flowers, presenting Kate with a bouquet of freshly caught trout, proclaiming, "I
     picked these for you."

37   After WW II, the Olympic salute was discontinued. It was too easily confused
     with a Nazi salute.

38   Nickel, ibid., p. 179. ". . . fuer eine Reihe bemerkenswerter Besteigungen und
     wissenschaftlicher Expeditionen im Himalaja."

39   Nickel, ibid., p. 180. Letter from M. Messerli, General Secretary of the Swiss
     Olympic Committee to the Dyhrenfurths.

40   When working as an assistant to Hans Ertl for a film on the Winter Olympics,
     a uniformed Nazi questioned whether the 17 year old, in spite of his Aryan
     looks, was Jewish. Norman later on became a first-rate climber, leading the first
     all-American ascent of Everest in 1963.

41   As quoted in Nickel, ibid., p. 242. "So etwas kann vorkommen, mein junger
     Freund!"

42   Mailaender, ibid., p. 239 and Nickel, ibid., p. 198.

43   David Cassidy, *Uncertainty: The Life and Science of Werner Heisenberg* (New
     York: W. H. Freeman,1992), pgs. 354-5.

44   Letter from August 1936, ibid. "Euere Freude an allem Schoenen und Guten,
     Euer Schauen, Dein Zeigen and Lehren, und noch viel mehr, wie werde ich das
     alles vergessen koennen."

45   Letter from Hoerlin to Kate, August 1936. "Schoen ist es zu wissen, wie
     hervorraegend gut man mit Euch wandern und bergsteigen kann. Es waren
     sicher die schoensten Ferien, die ich je erlebt habe . . . die zwei Wochen waren
     so voll Schoenheit und voll gluecklichster Liebe, dass sie mir heute noch fast
     wie ein maerchenhafter Traum erscheinen."

46   Friedlander, ibid. pgs. 179-180.

47   Friedlander, ibid. pgs. 224-5.

48   Miller, ibid., pgs. 109-11.

49   Akten der Partei-Kanzlei der NSDAP, Rekonstruktion eines verlorengegangenen
     Bestandes, Regesten, Bd. 1, bearbeitet von Hermut Heiber unter Mitwirkung
     von Gerhard Weiher und Hildegard von Kotze, Muenchen u.a. 1983.

50   Letter from Kate to Hoerlin, October 19, 1936. "Ich kann fast nicht schreiben,
     so sehr setzt sich das innere Zittern in einem Zittern der Hand fort."

51   Letter from Kate to Hoerlin, November 5, 1936. "Nun schreibe ich an Dich
     mit der Maschine, weil es dabei nichts macht, dass meine Haende zittern. Der
     Inhalt des Berliner Bescheids ist in jeder Beziehung und absolut erfreulich,
     ganz erstaunlich wohlwollend, man laesst mir in bezug auf das Wohin

voellig freie Wahl, d.h. man raeumt mir Sonderrechte und eine unbedingte Ausnahmestellung in jeder Beziehung ein . . ."

52 Letter from Hoerlin to Kate, September 15, 1936. "Ich weiss, dass das dunkle Tor ins Licht fuehrt."

53 Letter from Kate to Hoerlin, November 5, 1936. "Liebster, ich muss mir jetzt alle Kraft fuer den Abschied und fuer den Anfang aufsparen, fuer die Kinder, fuer Dich und fuer mich."

Chapter 10 Notes (Pages 133-145)

1 Letter from Kate to Hoerlin, November 15, 1936. "Das Duttli habe ich heut nicht im Einzelenen, aber doch im Grossen einweisen muessen, ich habe diesen grossen fragenden sorgenden Augen gesagt, dass wesentliche Veraenderungen in unseren Leben notwendig geworden sind und nahe bevorstehen. Der Kind hat ja lang etwas gespuert und ich fand sie unglaublich verstaendig und suess."

2 Letter from Kate to Hoerlin, November 29, 1936, in which Kate quotes from her letter to her Swiss friend, Marguerite Oehler. ". . . wo man doch kein guter Auskommen hat und nicht belaestigt wird."

3 Yehuda Bauer, *The History of the American Jewish Joint Distribution Committee* (Philadelphia: The Jewish Publication Society of America, 1974), pgs. 59-60.

4 Bruce F. Pauly. *From Prejudice to Persecution: A History of Austrian Anti-Semitism* (Chapel Hill: University of North Carolina Press, 1998), p. 10.

5 Letter from Kate to Hoerlin, December 22, 1936. "Von der Schweiz . . . kommen erschuetternd unverstaendige Briefe. "Dass Du nach Schweiz gehst, sehen wir nicht mit reiner Freude."

6 Letter from Kate to Hoerlin, November 29, 1936. "Den Brief von M. Oehler ist mir sehr schmerzlich. Kann man dann mit mir befreundet sein und mich so wenig kennen. Oder ists gar nicht so sehr die Margrit als die Schweiz, das andere Land, in diese fremde Welt, die sich in meine seelisch Not ueberhaupt nicht hineindenken kann und es fuer unnoetig haelt weg zu gehen . . .", Jedenfalls kann mein Entschuluss, nicht in die Schweiz zu gehen, nicht mehr bekraeftigt werden als durch diesen Brief."

7 Bruce F. Pauly. ibid., p. 32.

8 Pauly, ibid., pgs. 121-7.

9 Shofar Archive of the Nizkor Project, *Nazi Conspiracy and Aggression*, volume 2, chapter XIV, pgs. 944-45.

10 The hall was part of the headquarters for Olympic officials, built at a cost of $1,200,000 (TIME magazine, February 17, 1936), a considerable expense for the times.

11 Nicholas Mailaender email to the author, August 10, 2009.

12 Mailaender, ibid. p. 236.

13 *Anschluss* had a more benign association that we now attribute to it. It means connection or integration.

14 Mailaender, ibid. p 239.

15 letter from Kate to Hoerlin, November 5, 1936. "Ich bitte Dich sehr, keinesfalls jetzt den Posten im Alpenverein aufzugeben—vielleicht werden wir schon sehr blad erfahren, dass diese Deine Arbeit ihren Lohn bringt in bezug auf unser Leben."

16 Thomas Ferguson and Hans-Joachim Voth, "Betting on Hitler—The Value of Political Connections in Nazi Germany," *Quarterly Journal of Economics* (MIT Press, v. 123(1), 2008), p. 114.

17 John Loftus and Mark Aarons, *The Secret War against the Jews: How Western Espionage Betrayed the Jewish People* (St. Martin's Griffin, 1997), p. 57.

18 Oron J. Hale, *The Captive Press in the Third Reich*. (Princeton University Press, 1964), p. 212.

19 By 1936, Reusch had distanced himself from Hitler, which subsequently became a sourse of tension between him and Karl Reusch who continued to support Hitler. When it became known in 1938 that Haniel's wife was "not pure Aryan," Haniel was no longer part of Hitler's circle.

20 Alan E. Steinweis, *Art, Ideology and Economics in Nazi Germany* (University of North Carolina Press, 1996), p. 111. The President of the Reich Music Chamber was Hans Hinkel.

21 Steinweis, ibid., p.115. In 1938, Jews were excluded from attending concerts and other cultural events. Outside concert hall signs read, "No entry to Jews."

22 letter from Kate to Hoerlin, December 15, 1935. "Und Reusch rief eben von Nuernberg an. Er bittet mich um den Mittwochabend—und wir haben ja immer unser Weihnachten gehabt, der herrliche alte Mann und ich."

23 David Blackbourne and Richard J. Evans, editors. *The German Bourgeois: Essays on the Social History of the German Middle Class from the Late Eighteenth to the Early Twentieth Century* (London: Routledge, 1993), p.71.

24 recalled in a letter from Elfriede Gamow to the author, February 15, 2009.

25 Peter Hayes, "Profits and Persecution: German Big Business and the Holocaust," Center for Advanced Holocaust Studies (Washington, D.C.: U.S. Holocaust Memorial Museum, 1998), p. 5.

[26] Peter Hayes, "I.G. Farben Revisited: Industry and Ideology Ten Years Later," in Lesch, Hayes, p. 6.

[27] Hayes, ibid., p. 12.

[28] Hayes, ibid., pgs. 7-9.

[29] Loftus and Aarons, ibid. p. 58.

[30] Loftus and Aarons, ibid., p. 59.

[31] Peter Loehnert and Manfred Gill, "The Relationship of I.G. Farben's Agfa *Filmfabrik* Wolfen to its Jewish Scientists and to Scientists married to Jews, 1933—1939" in *The German Chemical Industry in the Twentieth Century*, John E. Lesch, editor (The Netherlands: Kluwer Academic Publishers, 2000), p. 125.

[32] Letter from Hoerlin to Kate, July 8, 1936. "Wir sind jetzt ein gutes Stuck Weges zusamen gegangen. Ich glaube wir sind weiter gekommen und nicht im Kreise gegangen; was kann ich schoeneres wuenschen, als dass dieser Weg fuer uns beide keine Ende nimmt."

[33] Letter from Kate to Hoerlin, September 23, 1936. "Ich will mir den Blick ganz freihalten fuer unser Ziel und durch gar nichts anderes ablenken lassen."

[34] Letter from Hoerlin to Kate, October 17, 1936. "Liebste, Du konntest mir nichts schoeneres schreiben als diesen Satz—'Ich stehe nur ganz und gar unter dem Gesetz der Liebe zu Euch Vieren.' Ich bin unsaeglich gluecklich darueber."

[35] Letter from Kate to Hoerlin, December 11, 1936. "Das hat mich nachdenklich gemacht und es beschaeftigt mich sehr—gewiss nicht nur um der romantischen und ritterlichten Note willen, sondern auch wegen das Gesetzes, der Realitaet, die unbeugsam hinter diesen Geschehen steht."

[36] Letter from Hoerlin to Kate, January 1935. "Gestern der Abend mit Furtwaengler sehr schoen, voll Kontakt. Er ist so klug dass man es kaum fuer moeglich haelt, dass er trotzdem ein solch guter Musiker ist." Furtwaengler had been home-schooled by his father, an eminent professor of archeology and his mother, a gifted painter.

[37] Sam H. Shirakawa, *The Devil's Music Master* (Oxford University Press, 1992), p. 157. According to Furtwaengler's 2nd wife, whom he married in 1943, the conductor never intended to marry any of his mistresses in spite of their bearing his children. According to Furtwaengler's 2nd wife, whom he married in 1943, the conductor never intended to marry any of his mistresses in spite of their bearing his children.

[38] Letter from Kate to Hoerlin, February 1935. "F schickte mir sein Auto…ich hatte Muehe beim Gespraech zu blieben, zumal es sich um die allerpersoenlichsten Dinge zwischen diesen beiden Menschen drehte . . . da er die Frau zu lange

allein liess, ist nun vieles schwierig geworden . . . <u>Darum</u> reisst er ab. Ich stand betroffen ob diese ploetzlichen Naehe . . . und war froh, als das Gespraech sich kunst-politischen Dingen zuwandte . . ."

³⁹ Shirakawa, ibid., p. 183.

⁴⁰ Letter from Kate to Hoerlin, January 21, 1937. "Soll ich sagen, dass ich mich freue? Wie schwach ist dies Wort fuer meine Erloesung, Du lieber Mann."

⁴¹ Letter from Kate to Hoerlin, December 1, 1936. "Es geht nun alles Schlag auf Schlag—fast zu rasch! Heute schon kam die amtliche Bescheinigungen der Reichtskanzlei, um die ich Wiedemann bat. Es ging wie gedacht: als ich dieser Dokument unten bei der Wohnungsfuersorge verwies, wurde ich sofort aus meinem bis Oktober 1938 laufenden Mietvertrag entlassen und meine Kuendigung zum 1 Maerz angekommen. So waere auch das erledigt."

⁴² Julia Menz, a former student of Wanda Landowska, performed throughout Europe.

⁴³ In addition to the musicians and "the Garmischers", guests included the Vosslers, Bumke, Elsaesser (an architect), the Schoeninghs (of the prominent publishing house), the Roths, Honigmanns, Frau Hutchinson and Marguerite Oehler.

⁴⁴ Letter from Kate to Hoerlin, November 18, 1936. "Einmal wird die Zeit kommen, wo es so still sein wird, dass wir den Wind hoeren und den Wolken und Sternen nachschauen koennen und wo ich gar nichts Neues, nur sehr viel lieber Altes fuer Dich weiss."

Chapter 11 Notes (Pages 147-160)

¹ Letter from Kate to Hoerlin, November 6, 1936. "Ich gehe ja nicht fort—ich komme zu Dir."

² Letter from Kate to Hoerlin, January 8, 1937. "Das Getrenntsein von Dir scheint mir jetzt oft, immer oefter, nicht mehr tragbar. Aber es moegen wohl die Umstaende um uns herum schuld sein an diesem Versagen. Ich sehe Dich immer vor mir . . ."

³ Letter from Kate to Hoerlin, March 12, 1937. ". . . jetzt wird sie (die Waesche) nach Luft und Wind und Sonne duften, wie Ihr mir jahrelang gewuenscht hat. Du wirst ja den Kopf schuetterln, was fuer wichtige Dinge ich Dir da erzaehle, aber sie machen mich so gluecklich . . . die Berge sind zum Greifen nah, die Luft warm und weich—hier ist kein Stadt, sind keine Maueren . . ."

4   letter from Kate to Hoerlin, June 7, 1937. "Es war gut, dass ich nach Dessau kam und sah, dass man dort nicht sehr lange atmen kann. Wiedemann kennt es und ist der gleichen Meinung—es sei das Allermindeste und Scheusslichste in Deutschland."

5   Isserman, ibid., p. 201.

6   Mailaender, ibid., p. 241.

7   Mailaender, ibid., p. 241.

8   Letter from Schneider to Hoerlin, June 27, 1937. "Glaeubig Gemueter koennten es als ausgleichende Gerechtigkeit auffassen . . ."

9   Letter from Schneider to Hoerlin, June 27, 1937. "Ich kann es mir wirklich nicht vorstellen . . . die Leute das Lager an eine Stelle gelegt haben, die den Lawinenstuerzen in hoechstem Masse ausgesetzt war. Jedenfalls ist damit der Rekord gebrochen, die Bergsteiger zu 100% ausradiert, das hat es doch noch nie gegeben."

10   Loehnert and Gill in Lesch, ibid., p. 126.

11   Letter from Kate to Hoerlin, June 7, 1937. "Ich komm eben von der Reichskanzlei. Wiedemann machte sich sofort frei, als ich anrief . . . dann sass ich bei ihm . . . und als ich ihm die Bilder von Freisaal zeigt und meines dabei . . . fragte er, ob ers behalten duerfte, es sei so schoen und lieb, und tats in seine Brieftasche und freute sich sehr. Und dann fragte er nach Dir. Da habe ich ihm nun deinen Namen gesagt und dass ich Dich lieb haette und lieb behalten wuerde, von der I.G. habe ich ihm gesagt und dass man in Dessau nicht leben koenne. Und nachem er mir lang und genau zugehoert hat, will er Dich diesen Samstag zwischen 11 und 12h sprechen. Ich soll dann mitkommen und er will mit uns ueberlegen . . . Ich schriebe Dir dies mit ruhigen Saetzen, aber mein Herz zittert vor Freude ueber diesen Mann und dass Du nun zu ihm kommen wirst und vielleicht ein Weg sich findet."

12   Martha Schad, *Hitler's Spy Princess: the Extraordinary Life of Stephanie von Hohenlohe* (England: Sutton Publishing, 2004), p. 43.

13   Schad, ibid., p. 52.

14   Schad, ibid., p. 54.

15   Letter from Kate to Hoerlin, September 15, 1935. "Da ich grosse Sorge um ihm hatte, rief ich Bumke neulich und als dieser eine Weile beobachtet hatte, sagte er mir, dass <u>alles</u> ganz in Ordnung sei, solange ich . . . unmittelbare Verbindung mit ihm haette, das sei wichtiger als alles andere."

16   Letter from Kate to Hoerlin, August 10, 1937. "Thompsi ist prima am Berg, besser als das Dutteli."

17   Letter from Kate to Hoerlin, March 12, 1937. "Es ist jeden Tag verschieden und immer ueberraschend, . . . Die Zeit bemueht sich so anders hier wie in der Stadt, nach Wetterverhaeltnissen, der Ablauf der Tages haengt von allem anderen mehr ab als von Stundenzeiger."

18   Letter from Kate to Hoerlin, August 10, 1937. "O Du, Du mit den 3 paar Ski auf deinen Schultern, was faengst Du mit uns an??!"

19   Letter from Kate to Hoerlin, August 10, 1937. "Wir waren so gluecklich, waren allein droben, rings um uns die schoene schoene Welt—und wir legen im Sommerwind, der Thymien duftete und die Hohe trug uns oft zu Dir."

20   Letter from Kate to Hoerlin, August 18, 1937. "Von den Kindern Herzensgruesse und ihre grenzenlose Freude auf Dich. Sie jauchzen . . ."

21   Letter from Kate to Hoerlin, June 29, 1937. "Drei Jahre sind es, dass Du nach dem 30. June unser Haus betretst—so nahe liegen Tod und Geburt nebeneinander. Und nun nach drei Jahren werde ich Deiner Liebe folgen, wohin sie mich ruft."

22   Letter from Hoerlin to Kate, August 1937. "Gestern sass ich Stunden ueber einem Brief, der nicht in die Feder wollte, weil ich nich sah wo der Weg geht, aber weiss, dass er geht."

23   Loehnert and Gill, ibid., p. 9.

24   Loehnert and Gill (see prior citations), in reviewing all of Gajewski's extensive work files (36 meters high), could find no hint of him as an active Nazi.

25   Letter from Hoerlin to Kate, October 20, 1937. "Er hat viel gefragt, offensichtlich bestrebt zu helfen, nicht nur ueber die Firme sondern auch persoenlich-menschlich. Er war herzlicher und naher als das erstemal. Am liebsten wurden sie mich hier behalten, weil sie mich brauchen (einerseits freut mich das naturlich sehr, den Anerkennung wegen). Im ubrigen aber ist es schwierig jetzt etwas geeignetes, meinen Faehigkeiten entsprechendes zu finden. Er sagte mir aber zu, dass er sich weiterhin umsehen will."

26   Letter from Kate to Wiedemann, October 24, 1937. ". . . was Sie darin schreiben, brauche ich Ihnen gewiss nicht zu sagen, dass wissen Sie and machen Sie tausendmal besser als ich . . ."

27   Letter from Kate to Hoerlin, August 13, 1937.

28   Letter from Kate to Wiedemann, October 17, 1937. ". . . an jedem Tag steht das Tor von Freisaal Ihnen weit offen . . . und ich gruesse Sie mit Dankbarkeit vollen Vertrauens."

29   Schad, p 66.

30   Kershaw, ibid., p. 536. The original modest house had been expanded at considerable cost into a grandiose residence.

31   Ignatius Phayre, "Hitler's Moutain Home," *House and Garden*, November 1938.

32   Schad, ibid., p 67.

33   Letter from Hoerlin to Kate, November 7, 1937. "Fuer Dich ist es schwer, reisen-schwer die naehsten Monate wie untatig zu sitzen. Ich bitte Dich innig, behalt mich lieb und glaub an mich."

34   Loehnert and Gill, ibid., p. 6.

35   Letter from Kate to Hoerlin, November 7, 1937. ". . . all unsere Freude findet ihre Heimat in Dir . . . so still, so sehr gesegnet sind die Tage mir, dass ich gut weiss dies kann nicht so bleiben, aber es ist mir geschenkt um Kraft zu schoepfen fuer die Zeit, wann ich sie brauche."

36   Reminiscense (June 27, 1951) written by Kate Hoerlin after attending the Casals Festival in Prades, France.

37   Letter from Kate to Hoerlin, December 7, 1937. ". . . Ueberirdisch schoen. Furtwaengler sass neben mir—auch er empfand es so, als 'verklaerten Klang.' Ich war viele Stunden mit Casals zusammen—er besitz die wunderbare Zartheit und tiefe Zaertlichheit, die aus einer grenzenlosen Guete kommt."

38   As quoted in a letter from Kate to Hoerlin, January 7, 1938. "Er sieht sehr leidend aus," was said by poet Regina Ullman, a protégé of Rainer Maria Rilke, who moved to Austria from Germany in 1936.

39   Letter from Hoerlin to Wiedemann, January 9, 1938. ". . . Auf eine schnelle Loesung habe ich nicht gehofft . . . aber der geringe Fortschritte der Angelengenheit seit Oktober macht mir jetzt allerdings ziemliche Sorge . . . In Frage kommt fast nur eine Taetigkeit bei der Schwesterfirm der Filmfabrik in USA, der Agfa Ansco in Binghamton. Doch raet Herr Dr. Gajewski ab, weil er glaubt, dass ich mich in diesem kulturarmen Lande nicht wohlfuehlen wuerde. Auf Grund der gestrigen Unterredung mit Ihnen will ich nun Binghampton ernstlicher ins Auge fassen und sofort die notwendigen Schritte unternehmen."

40   Letter from Kate to Hoerlin, January 31, 1938. "Es ist etwas geschehen gestern Abend, ich kann es nicht mit Werten sagen, aber ich weiss, dass es ausschlaggebend fuer unsere Zukunft ist. Was war das fuer ein Abend, voll von Dir, von uns und unserm Leben. Ich lege deine Haende auf meine Augen—grenzenlos ist, was sich in mir nach Dir sehnt. Und mein Wollen ist da. Du warst so schoen gestern in der Kraft Deiner Glaubens."

41   Letter from Kate to Hoerlin, February 4, 1938. "Und dann, nennte ich Deinen Namen . . . und er sagte dass er sich vor Wochen schon nach Dir erkundigt und eine sehr gute, sehr erfreuliche Auskunft bekommen haette aus Stuttgart und

von der IG Farben. Und er wusste <u>genau</u> ueber Dich—so ist Reusch!!! Und er sagte sein Ja zu uns mit tiefer und unbedingter Freude."

42   Letter from Hoerlin to Wiedemann, February 24, 1938.

Chapter 12 Notes (Pages 161-175)

1   *The Holocaust Chronicle* (Publications International Ltd: 2000), p. 127.

2   Ingo Mueller, *Furchtbare Juristen* (Muenchen: Kindler Verlag, 1987), p. 49. Erwin Bumke was the Reichsgerichtspraesident and a trusted friend of Hitler's; in spite of this, the brothers remained close.

3   Letter from Kate to Hoerlin, October 18, 1937. "Seit . . . lebe ich der Zukunft (und der nicht gar fernen, glaube ich) mit einer grossen Bereitschaft und Stille des Herzens entgegen."

4   Letter from Kate to Hoerlin, March 7, 1938. "Ich weiss nichts, fast nichts von Indien, von 'fremden Laendern und Menchschen.' Da musst Du mir alles sagen, Du lieber Mann. Ich hoere Dir zu, bald bin ich da—o Du, wie alt und neu ist dieser Zusammenkommen."

5   These included the pianist Rudolf Serkin, members of the Budapest String Quartet and the harpsichordist Yella Pessl.

6   Letter from Kate Schmid to Wiedemann, March 5, 1938. Request from Hermann Hoerlin referred to in Wiedemann response to him of March 11, 1938.

7   Wolfgang Uwe Eckart, *Man, Medicine and the State: the Human Body as Object of Government.* (Germany: Fritz Stein Verlag, 2006), p. 218.

8   Letter from Hoerlin to Dr. K. Blome at the Ministry of the Interior, March 20, 1938.

9   Letter from Dr. K. Blome to Hoerlin, March 24, 1938. "Es muss, gemeinsam von Ihnen und Frau Schmidt (sic), ein Antrag bei der zustaendigen hoehere Verwaltungsbehoerde des Ortes, an dem der Mischling, in Ihrem Falle also Frau Schmidt, seinen Wohnsitz hat."

10   Letter from Kate Schmid to German Consul/Salzburg, March 31, 1938. ". . . Frau Kate Schmid ist nicht arischer Abstammung . . ."

11   Deutschen Konsulat Salzburg, Salzburg, April 1, 1938, "Gesehen und auf Grund des Schreibens der Reichskanzlei vom 11.3.38 Hauptmann a.D.Wiedemann Wi/Si. befeuerwortet."

12   letter from Hoerlin to Blome, April 2, 1938 and from Hoerlin to Wiedemann, April 3, 1938.

13   Letter from Blome to Hoerlin, April 8, 1938. "Hierdurch teile ich Ihnen mit, dass ich am heutigen Tage Ihren Antrag auf Ehegenehmigung zustaendigkeitshalber an den Herrn Reichs—und Preussischen Minister des Innern weitergeleitet habe. Heil Hitler!"

14   Letter from Wiedemann to Kate Schmid and letter from Wiedemann to Herman Hoerlin, both dated March 11, 1938. "Ich habe mit dem zustaendigen Referenten, Herrn Dr. Blome gesprochen, der in Ihrem Fall fuer einen Dispens eintreten wird. Diese Antwort kann als definitiver Enscheid noch nicht angesehen werden, ist jedoch guenstiger als ich selbst es erwartet habe."

15   Karl A. Schleunes, ed. *Legislating the Holocaust: The Bernhard Loesener Memoirs and Other Documents* (Westview Press, 2001), p. 63. Blome was subsequently tried for medical experimentation in the 1947 Nuremberg doctor trials.

16   Schleunes, ibid., pgs. 63-4.

17   Letter from Hoerlin to Wiedemann, March 20, 1938. ". . . ob es notwendig ist auf die Abstammungsunterlagen von Frau Kate Schmid, die im Sippenamt am Shiffsbauerdamm liegen, zu verweisen, das weiss ich nicht."

18   Letter from Hoerlin to Kate, October 7, 1937. "Mir ist es recht, dass Du den Weg ueber den Schiffbauerdamm nicht mehr weiterverfolgst, nicht nur recht sondern auch lieb."

19   Email from Dr. Matthaus Juergen to the author, July 20, 2006. Dr. Juergen is Director of the Applied Research Scholars, Center for Advanced Holocaust Studies, U.S. Holocaust Memorial Museum.

20   I have found no documents or explanatory correspondence regarding this although Kate and Hoerlin mention in respective letters exchanged in October 1937 that Kate would not pursue further the "Erledigung" (settlement) from the "Schifffsbauerdamm."

21   Akten der Partei-Kanzlei der NSDAP, Rekonstruktion eines verlorengegangenen Bestandes, Regesten, Bd. 1, bearbeitet von Hermut Heiber unter Mitwirkung von Gerhard Weiher und Hildegard von Kotze, Muenchen u.a. 1983.

22   Loehnert and Gill, ibid., p. 130.

23   Letter from Wiedemann to Frau Lily (sic) von Schnitzler, January 10, 1938. "Ich selbst sehe die einzige Moeglichkeit einer Loesung darin, dass Herr Dr. Hoerlin rasch im Ausland unterkommt. Wenn Sie fuer Dr. Hoerlin und damit auch fuer Frau Dr. Schmid sich in diesem Sinne irgendwie einsetzen koennten, waere ich Ihnen, sehr geehrte gnaedige Frau, sehr verbunden."

24   Letter from Wiedemann to Gajewski, April 4, 1938. ". . . bei einem zufaelligen Besuch von Frau Dr. Schmid erfahre hat, in welch liebenswuerdiger Weis Sie sich des Falls Dr. Hoerlin angenommen haben."

25 Letter from Wiedemann to Konsul Raymond H. Geist, general counsel of the
    U.S.A. to Berlin, March 23, 1938. ". . . Frau Kaete Schmid beabsichtigt eine
    kurze Reise nach USA. Koennten Sie ihr nicht das Visum ausstellen? Dafuer,
    dass gegen Frau Schmid keine Bedenken verliegen, weder von unserer Seite
    noch—so weit ich das beurteilen kann, von Seiten der Vereinigten Staaten,
    uebernehme ich die Buergschaft."

26 Loehnert and Gill, ibid.8.

27 Hayes in Lesch, ibid., p. 130.

28 Hayes in Lesch, ibid., p. 9

29 Loehnert and Gill in Lesch, ibid., p. 129.

30 Letter from Kate to Hoerlin, April 26, 1938. ". . . und am allerwunderbarsten
    in diesem neuen Land scheint mir die immer immer wachsende Liebe . . . Mit
    welchen tiefen Glueck mich dieses Land beschenkt, in dem ich Deine Frau bin
    und fuer Dich leben wurde . . . Ich glaube, wir duerfen Vertrauen haben, dass
    unser Leben gesegnet ist. Wir gehen ja nun auf unserm Weg."

31 Letter from Hoerlin to Kate, May 26, 1938. "Ich fuehle mich heute schon
    heimischer in Binghamton als ich es je in Dessau tat. Wir fuenf werden es gut
    und schoen haben hier . . ."

32 Letter from Kate (at Hotel Wellington in New York City) to Hoerlin (in
    Binghamton) April 28, 1938. "Der Herrgott meint es sehr gut, wann er uns in
    die kleine Stadt und in unser stilles gutes Leben dort fuehrt."

33 Letter from Kate to Hoerlin, April 28, 1938. ". . . ich lerne, lerne, lerne."

34 Mosse, ibid., p. 210.

35 Ron Chernow, *The Warburgs: The 20ᵗʰ Century Odyssey of a Remarkable Jewish
    Family* (New York: Random House, 1993), p. 441.

36 Letter from Max Warburg to Nina Loeb Warburg, March 26, 1938.

37 Letter from Max Warburg to Kate, March 26, 1938. Email (March 13, 2006) to
    the author from Jana Leichsenring, who on my behalf, reviewed the Warburg
    archives in Hamburg on March 4, 2006 and wrote: "Paul Reusch's Empfehlung
    fuehrte dazu, dass sich Max Warburg regelrecht verpflichtet fuehlte, sich Kaethe
    Schmid zur Verfuegung zu stellen—was er ihr am 27. Maerz 1938 mitteilte. Er
    liess sie wissen, dass sie ihm "ungeniert" wissen lassen koenne, an wen sie in
    Amerika empfohlen zu werden wuensche."

38 Letter from Kate to Hoerlin, April 26, 1938. ". . . die japanischen Quitten, die
    deutschen Apfelbaume—und wir gingen langsam hindurch." The 500 acre
    Westchester estate, "Woodlands," owned by Nina's brother-in-law Felix, was
    treated as a family compound. Nina and Paul had a house on the property.

39 Paul had left W.W. Warburg to marry Nina Loeb, the daughter of a founding partner of Kuhn & Loeb Co., considered the last of the "gentleman investment banking" firms. Nina and Paul married in 1895 and had two children, James Paul Warburg and Dr. Bettina Warburg. The character, "Daddy" Oliver Warbucks in *Little Orphan Annie* cartoon and in the Broadway musical *Annie*, was supposedly based on the life and times of Paul Warburg.

40 Letter from Kate to Hoerlin, April 26, 1938. "... und dass ich seit seinen Tod der ersten Mensch bin, mit dem sie in Ruhe und fast in Freude dort sein kann."

41 Letter from Kate to Hoerlin, May 14, 1938. "Und dann war ich den Abend zum Essen in dem schoenen, ehrwuerdigen Haus und hatte die erste Begegnung mit diesem ausserordentlichen Menschen. Ich ging dann Mittwoch nochmals zu ihm, wir sprachen alles aus genaueste durch. Es ist alles sehr kompliziert, er wird mich wieder nach Hamburg rufen, wenn es an der Zeit ist."

42 Notation from Max Warbug to Herrn Dr. Hirsch und Herrn Behrmann, May 13, 1938. Kate spoke of assets between 30,000 and 50,000 RM.

43 Chernow, ibid., pp 148-9.

44 Chernow, ibid., p. 460.

45 Chernow, ibid., p. 472

46 Letter from Kate to Hoerlin, May 14, 1938. "Gestern Abend habe ich ihnen bis 11 Uhr erzaehlen muessen, sie haben atemlos zugehoert, liebe nachdenkliche Fragen gestellt, bereit fuer das Neue, das wir ihnen bereiten.

47 Letter from Maria Hoerlin to Hermann Hoerlin, June 4, 1938.

48 Letter from Maria Hoerlin to Kate Schmid, May 28, 1938. "Ich freue mich von Herzen wieder eine geliebte Tochter zu haben."

49 Letter from the German Reich Interior Ministry to the Austrian Reichsstatthalter in Vienna, May 21, 1938 and validated on June 20, 1938. "Dem jued. Mischling 1. Grades Kaete Schmid geb. Tietz aus Muenchen, z.Zt. in Salzburg wohnhaft, erteile ich im Einvernehmen mit dem Stellvertreter des Fuehrers die auf Grund des Paragraphen 3 der Ersten Verordnung zur Ausfuehrung des Gesetzes zum Schutze des deutschen Blutes und der deutschen Ehre vom 14.11.1935 (RGB1.IS. 1334) beantragte Genehmingung zur Eheschliessung mit dem deutschbluetigen deutschen Staatsangehoerigne Dr. Ing. Hermann Hoerlin aus Dessau, z.Zt. in Binghampton N.Y. USA, wohnhaft. Ich ersuche ergebenst, die Antragstellerin so wie das zustaendige Matrikenamt hiervon umgehend zu benachrichtigen."

50 as discussed in Friedlander, ibid. 151.

51 Sammelaktenheft zum Familienbuch (Blatt Nr. 341, Jahr 1938). "Wir die Verlobten versichern, dass wir deutschen bzw. artverwanten Blutes sind." "Ich, die Verlobte, bin Mischling ersten Grades."

52 Email from Jana Leichsenring to the author, June 21, 2005. "Dann auch jedem Beamten des Dritten Reiches waere auf den ersten Blick auf die Heiratsurkunde aufgefallen, dass da was nicht 'in Ordnung' ist. Und diese Heiratsurkunde waere fuer denjenigen, der sie ausstellte, gefaehrlich geworden. Es sei denn, er haette legitimierten koennen . . ."

53 Notation from Elli Schmid Ringler in letter from Kate to Hoerlin, March 13, 1938.

Chapter 13 Notes (Pages 179-194)

1 Following a request by Swiss authorities to restrict Jewish immigration to Switzerland, the Third Reich required all Jewish passports to be stamped with the letter "J" as of October 7, 1938.

2 The Klepper kayak became popular in Germany in the 1930's. It could be carried in a backpack, assembled in 10 minutes and according to advertising, promised ". . . memorable, affordable vacations."

3 The Intent of Citizenship was stated officially on January 30, 1939, according to their Petition for Naturalization to the Supreme Court of Broome County in Binghamton submitted on August 17, 1943.

4 Stackelberg, ibid., p.181

5 These estimates vary according to source. Friedlander reports 267 synagogues destroyed. (Friedlander, ibid., p.276).

6 Kristallnacht was instigated by the assassination of a German diplomat by a 17 year old Jewish youth in Paris.

7 Deborah E. Lipstadt, *Beyond Belief: The American Press and the Coming of the Holocaust* (The Free Press/Simon & Schuster, 1986), p. 38

8 Lipstadt, ibid., p. 38

9 Quentin Reynolds, *Colliers*, February 1939.

10 Friedlander, ibid., pgs. 270-271. Letter from State Secretary and chief of the Reich Chancellery Hans Lammers to Minister of Interior Wilhelm Frick, November 4, 1938.

11 Friedlander, ibid., pgs. 284-285.

12 Stackelberg, ibid., p. 184.

13 Prior to the introduction of the Arlberg method, skiing was largely viewed as a somewhat laborious way of traveling or touring in the snow. One long pole was originally used to steer and slow the skier; around WW I, the short two-pole method came into use but recreational skiing was still rare.

14 Gerard Fairlie, *Flight without Wings: The Biography of Hannes Schneider.* (A.S. Barnes, 1957), pgs. 207-208.

15 Hannes' flight from the Third Reich was a result of a deal between Harvey Gibson, founder of the North Conway ski resort, who was Chairman of New York's Metropolitan Trust and Hjalmar Schacht, President of the *Reichsbank.* See Fairlie, ibid., pgs. 206-10.

16 *New York Post,* October 21, 1938.

17 Musical circles debated whether Feuermann or Casals was the greatest living cellist. Feuermann's untimely death at age 39 in May 1942 stilled the question.

18 Lipstadt, ibid., pgs. 79-99

19 *Binghamton Press,* November 19, 1938.

20 Duscha was at the Cambridge School near Boston and Thomi at the George School, a Quaker school near Philadelphia.

21 The Trapps changed their stage name from the Trapp Family Choir to the Trapp Family Singers when they introduced more popular songs into their repertoire. Their original focus was on more sophisticated, classical music: Renaissance and Baroque repertoire, Bach cantatas, etc. See Joan Gearin, "The Real Story of the von Trapp Family" in *Prologue* (Winter issue 2005, vol. 37, no. 4: National Archives).

22 Thomas Gale, "GAF" (General Aniline Film Corporation), *International Directory of Company Histories* (1988). By January 1944, the *Agfa* name was dropped and the company was known as Ansco.

23 TIME magaine June 3, 1940. A rebuttal letter to these accusations was printed in TIME on July 15 with the president of General Aniline denouncing the claims.

24 Letter from Hoerlin to Trude Pratt, January 22, 1941.

25 Letter from Kate to Hoerlin, April 28, 1938. ". . . Schwarz hatte auch so schreckliche Angst, dass etwas vom 30. Juni bekannt werden koennte . . ." The meeting between Schwarz and Kate took place in New York City.

26 Letter from the R.M. Gaffney, Vice President of the First National Bank, to Herman Hoerlin, January 15, 1942.

27 Letter from Foreign Property Control Department of Federal Reserve Bank to Herman Hoerlin, February 24, 1942.

28   Letter from SS Brigadier Leader Fritz Breithaupt to Frau Kaete Hoerlin-Schmid, August 18, 1941. The monthly stipend of 600 RM for the three Schmid children (roughly $150 per month/$2000 per year at the time) was not insignificant.

29   Chernow, ibid., pgs. 312-13.

30   The Kara Corporation was established by Bettina and her uncle Max Warburg. See Chernow, ibid., p. 439.

31   Joseph Lash was a member of the radical left and became an advisor to Eleanor Roosevelt. He headed the Democratic National Committee's youth contingent and became the official biographer of Eleanor. His books on the Roosevelts, especially *Eleanor and Franklin* (1971), were groundbreaking.

32   Trude married Joseph Lash in 1944, thereby becoming Trude Lash. From 1945-1953, she was Secretary to the United Nations Commission on Human Rights and thereafter founded and served as director of Citizens for Children and Youth of New York.

33   My mother told me that she advised Trude *against* divorcing Eliot, a stance that I suspect Joe became well aware of. When Trude discovered she was pregnant with Joe's child, the debate became moot. Joe and my mother did become friendly, although never particularly close.

34   Letter from Hermann Hoerlin to Trude Pratt, January 22, 1942 and letter from Herman Hoerlin to Bettina Warburg, January 22, 1942

35   Letter from Trude Pratt to Hermann Hoerlin, January 25, 1942.

36   Otto Brodnitz emigrated to the U.S. from Germany in 1927.

37   Letter from Hermann Hoerlin to Otto W. Brodnitz, German Agencies, U.S. Treasury Department. March 5, 1942.

38   Goebbels, Hitler's Propaganda Minister, was the chief architect of *Kristallnacht*. The October 24, 1938 quote from his diary is cited in Schad, ibid., pgs. 104-105.

39   A subsidiary of I.G. Farben's in Peru (La Quimica-Bayer) had small film division and told the expedition they would be able to process black and white film (although not color), but ending up sending all the film to the I.G. Farben *Agfa* subsidiary in the United States, *Agfa*/Ansco. This occurred before *Agfa*/Ansco was seized by the U.S. Government in February 1942.

40   Most of the letters were from expedition member Dr. Walther Brecht, with several from the expedition leader, Professor Hans Kinzl, as well.

41   Letter from Walter Brecht to Herman Hoerlin, October 12, 1939. "Doch noch hoffen wir auf ein rasches, vielleicht auch ueberraschendes Ende dieses wahnsinnigen Spiels. Vielleicht gibt es Zeit ... um einige Herren bei uns so oder

so—d.h. mit Gewalt—zur Vernunft zu bringen, auch ohne diese unnuetzen Opfer."

[42] Letter from Otto W. Brodnitz to Dr. Bettina Warburg, March 1, 1942. The **bolding** is mine.

[43] Letter from William Honkala, Investigator, U.S. Treasury Dept. to E.J. Ford, Special Assistant Attorney General, Department of Justice. June 22, 1943

[44] As documented in the Honkala/Ford letter above

[45] As documented in letters from Tom C. Clark, Assistant Attorney General, Department of Justice, to Herman Hoerlin. May 21, 1943 and June 16, 1943.

[46] Honkala letter, ibid.

[47] As documented in letters between Herman Hoerlin and U.S. Department of Justice Attorney General Norman Bursler, February 15 and March 3, 1943.

[48] Letter from Herman Hoerlin to Norman Bursler, U.S. Department of Justice Attorney General, April 6, 1943.

[49] Cellulose acetate and nitrate films contained these chemicals.

[50] As documented in a letter from Herman Hoerlin to Brigadier General Frederick Osborn, August 20, 1942. Hoerlin had met Osborn, who was Chief of the Morale Branch of the War Department, at an event he attended at the Cambridge School, where Duscha was enrolled.

[51] The appeal from Mr. A.E. Marshall, President of *Agfa*/Ansco and Vice-President of General Aniline and Film Corporation was sent to the Secretary of the Navy by way of the Office of the Alien Property Custodian, Leo T. Crowley.

[52] Letter from Leo T. Crowley, Alien Property Custodian, to Mrs. Roosevelt, September 30, 1942.

[53] Letter from Trude Pratt to Hermann Hoerlin, October 5, 1942.

[54] Even after my parents became U.S. citizens in 1944, the cameras had to be removed from the house. Duscha, by then 20, still had alien status. Although she was away at college, the U.S. Attorney (letter to Hoerlin from Irving Higbee, September 8, 1944) did not want her to have access to them during vacations at home.

[55] All German consulates were ordered closed by Roosevelt on June 16, 1941.

[56] After the war, the photographs were compiled into one of the most beautiful mountaineering photograph albums, *Cordillera Blanca: Peru* by Hans Kinzl und Erwin Schneider (Innsbruck: Universitaets-Verlag Wagner, 1950). The photos have also been of recent use in documenting global warming.

[57] Bettina Warburg was born in Hamburg, during a seven year stay of her parents. In 1902 her father left the M.M. Warburg office there to become a partner in his wife's family firm of Kuhn, Loeb and Co, investment bankers in New York.

Chapter 14 Notes (Pages 195-211)

[1] Letter from Captain G.F. Switzer, U.S. Army, June 4, 1945. The letter was posted on June 7, 1945.

[2] "Luftangriffe auf die Stadt Stuttgart," *Stuttgart in Luftkrieg* (Germany: Klett Verlag, 1967) There were 53 missions over the city; the largest offensive was in March 1944 with 863 Royal Air Force bombers. The last offensive was in April 1945.

[3] Letter from Maria Hoerlin to Hoerlin family, September 23, 1945. ". . . ich kann ruhig sagen, dass auch ich es fuer eine besondere Gnade ansehe, dass ich bewahrt geblieben bin . . . Die Nachtruhe, dren wir uns nun keine Alarme mehr schrecken, tut einem gut; lange haette man es nicht mehr ausgehalten bei der Luftkriegslage in den letzten Monaten des Krieges."

[4] Earl F. Ziemke, *The U.S. Army in the Occupation of Germany 1944-46* (U.S. Army, Center for Military History, 1975), p. 408. In a misguided policy, the military did not want to give Germans any advantage over the average conditions in surrounding European nations. CARE packages were not allowed until June 1946.

[5] "Schau wie schlampig sie marschieren." "Ja, deswegen haben wir den Krieg gewonnen."

[6] Chernow, ibid., p. 562.

[7] Chernow, ibid., p. 541.

[8] Toby Thacker, *The End of the Third Reich: Defeat, Denazification and Nuremberg, January 1944-November 1946* (England: NPI Media Group, 2006), p. 43.

[9] Jonathan Petropoules and John K. Roth, *Gray Zones: Ambiguity and Compromise in the Holocaust and its Aftermath* (Berghahn Books, 2006), p. 327.

[10] Frederic Sondern, "Captain Fritz: Hitler's old Superior Officer runs into trouble selling Nazism to West," *LIFE* magazine, June 26, 1939, p. 26.

[11] The report was submitted by Sir William Wiseman. See Schad, ibid., pgs.132-138.

[12] *TIME* magazine: October 8, 1945.

[13] Quoted in Robert Conot, *Justice at Nuremberg* (Basic Books, 1993), p. 511.

[14] William Stevenson, *A Man Called Intrepid* (Lyons Press, 2000), pgs. 205-207.

[15] *Lewiston Evening News Journal*, November 17, 1948. The original charge, adjudicated by Court President Ludwig Salisco, was as a "major offender."

[16] In early 1947, the Allies held 90,000 Nazis in detention according to Herbert Hoover's press release of the President's Economic Mission to Germany and Austria, report #1, February 28, 1947, p. 2.

[17] Wiedemann wrote a memoir entitled "Der Mann, der Feldherr werden wollte" (The Man who wanted to become Commander) in 1964; he died at the age of 78 in 1970.

[18] Hanns Hippius, H.J. Moeller, N. Mueller and G.Neundoerfer-Koh, *The University Department of Psychiatry in Munich: from Kraepelin and his Predecessors to Molecular Psychiatry* (Springer Verlag, 2007), p. 126. The change in name was also motivated by broader issues around labeling; as Bumke astutely commented, ". . . the word psychiatric is almost never applied correctly."

[19] Hanns Hippius et al, ibid., pgs. 111-130.

[20] Loehnert and Gill in Lesch, ibid., p.139. Dr. Gerhard Ollendorff had petitioned Hitler to be declared as a German despite his Jewish descent. The request was denied.

[21] In 1953, Gajewski was awarded one of Germany's highest honors: the Great Cross of Merit.

[22] S. Jonathan Wiesen, *West Germany and the Challenge of the Nazi Past* (University of North Carolina Press, 2001), p. 83. Reusch had relinquished leadership of one of Germany's largest industries, refusing to cooperate with Hitler's agenda. After the war, the Allies put Reusch's son in charge of dismantling the empire his father had built.

[23] Edward R. Murrow, CBS radio broadcast, April 16, 1945.

[24] These estimates are from the U.S. Holocaust Museum.

[25] In 1946 Hermann and Liese Bohm joined their son in Chicago; he had immigrated there before war broke out.

[26] J.J. O'Conner and E.F. Robertson, *MacTutor History of Mathematics Archives* (Scotland: University of St. Andrews, 2004).

[27] The numbers of deaths are disputed (ranging from 500,000 to three million). See R.J. Rummel's book, *Death by Government* (Transaction Publishers, 1997). Rummel describes the Polish resettlement as "the greatest forcible dislocation of persons in European history" and the 1,585,000 deaths (his figure) of ethnic Germans as genocide.

[28] Letters to Max Lerner, *PM Daily*; Arthur Hays Sulzberger, *New York Times*; and Senators Robert F. Wagner and James M. Mead from Herman Hoerlin, January 10, 1946.

[29] The group consisted of 10 professional physicists and 14 technicians and focused on improvements of color film technology, optics, x-ray films and

radioactive monitoring. The *Agfa* portion of the name had been dropped in 1944.

30 Hoerlin's talk in November 1949 to the Isotope Committee of Wilson Memorial Hospital focused on "atomic cocktails" for hyperthyroid patients.

31 Exterminator had started in 99 races, of which he won 50. He was the subject of a popular children's book, "Old Bones: the Wonder Horse."

32 In the obituary for Exterminator in the *Binghamton Press* (September 27, 1945), the care of stable manager, Mike Terry, is credited for Exterminator's long life of 30 years.

33 The Bund was a pro-Nazi organization formed in the United States in the 1930's. At a 1939 rally at Madison Square Garden attended by 20,000 followers, the head of the Bund kept on referring to President Franklin D. Roosevelt as Frank D. Rosenfeld.

34 Unpublished memoir of 1951 Casals Festival by Kate Hoerlin, Fall 1951.

35 Postcard from Alexander Schneider and Pablo Casals to Kate Hoerlin, July 4, 1950.

36 Unpublished memoir of 1951 Casals Festival, Kate Hoerlin, ibid.

37 Letter from Erwin Schneider to Hoerlin, March 10, 1940. "Jedenfalls habe ich bei beiden Operationen Morphium und Pillen abgelehnt und konnte den Schmerz ertragen, der gerade an der Grenze war."

38 Robert Kostka, "Erwin Schneider 1906-1987 Leben und Arbeit," p.14.

39 Isserman and Weaver, ibid., p. 300. The expedition was not supported by the German Alpine Club because of Merkl's brother's lack of experience but was endorsed by the Austrian Alpine Club and the Munich branch of the German Alpine Club.

40 Isserman and Weaver, ibid., pgs. 299—303. German newspapers reported erroneously that Buhl had raised the German flag.

Chapter 15 Notes (Pages 213-230)

1 U.S. Department of Justice Application for Certificate of Identification (Aliens of Enemy Nationalities); U.S. Department of Treasury Application to Unblock Accounts (5b of the Trading with the Enemy Act); U.S. Department of Treasury January 24, 1942 Report of all Property Types belonging to Nationals; U.S. Department of Justice Application for a Certificate of Arrival and Preliminary Form for Petition for Naturalization (August 17, 1943).

2   David S. Wyman, *"The Abandonment of the Jews: America and the Holocaust 1941-1945"* (New York: Pantheon Books, 1985), p. 9.

3   Rose's father, Paul Ewald, was a well-known x-ray physicist; my father completed his undergraduate and graduate studies at Stuttgart.

4   Letter from Kate to Hoerlin, May 12, 1953.

5   Letter from Hoerlin (in Binghamton) to Schwabian section of the *Alpenverein*, September 1, 1949. "... mit einem leisen Heimweh ..."

6   Since the 1950's, residents have been able to buy and build their homes, in contrast to renting them from the government. Accordingly, the town's architecture has improved.

7   Originally called the Los Alamos Laboratory, "Scientific" was added to its title in 1947. At the time, LASL had approximately 1000 employees, down from its wartime high of 1400 civilian employees and 1600 military technicians. Since then it once again changed its acronym to LANL (Los Alamos National Laboratory) and employs around 10,000 people.

8   Harold Agnew and Raemen E. Schreiber, *Obituary for Norris Bradbury, director of Los Alamos from 1945-1970*; 1995.

9   Letter from Kate to Mother Hoerlin, June 3, 1953. "Aber vorlaeufig saust Dein Sohn ja immer noch in der Weltgeschichte herum. Er ist einfach zu sehr mit allem Neuen und Wissenswerten beschaeftigt, konzentriert sich ganz darauf ..."

10   United States Atomic Energy Commission, Official Transcript of Interview with Herman Hoerlin, AEC # CH-2221-SF, January 11, 1954.

11   United States Atomic Energy Commission interview, ibid.

12   My parents and I first went to Aspen in 1954, a time when only one street was paved and before it had been "discovered."

13   The Los Alamos Scientific Laboratory, the Department of Defense, and the University of California Lawrence Radiation Laboratory (Livermore) were the respective leads in 331 high altitude tests from 1953—1963.

14   Herman Hoerlin, "United States High-Altitude Test Experiences: A Review Emphasizing the Impact on the Environment," *Los Alamos Scientific Laboratory Monograph 6405*, October 1976.

15   Rolf Mueller, "A Brief History of Stratospheric Ozone Research," *Meteorological Zeitschrift*, v. 18, No. 1, February 2009.

16   "Operation Teapot" lasted from February until the end of May 1955. The blast I witnessed was 3.2 kilotons.

17   Victor Randlett, Scott Kirsch and Lisa Marshall, "Nuclear Nevada." *The AAG (Association of American Geographers) Newsletter*, January 2009, p. 8.

18   "Casals at the U.N.", editorial of *The New York Times*, October 24, 1958.

19 *Los Alamos Scientific Laboratory News*, December 13, 1962. Vol. 4, No. 28.

20 Underground testing continued in Nevada.

21 "H-Bomb Destroyed in Air after Rocket Radio Fails," *New York Times*, June 4, 1962.

22 John Zinn, Los Alamos Scientific Laboratory, to author, e-mail communication, March 30, 2010. During one test, the rocket exploded on the launch pad, resulting in very serious contamination of Johnston Island.

23 On July 9, 1962, Starfish created an EMP (electromagnetic pulse) that sent power line surges through the Hawaiian island of Oahu 800 miles away, knocking out street lights, blowing fuses and circuit breakers and triggering burglar alarms. A man-made radiation belt disabled and destroyed several satellites. See Palmer Dyal, "Particle and Field Measurements of the Starfish diamagnetic cavity," *Journal of Geophysical Research*, 2006.

24 *Field Evaluation of Optical Instrumentation for Detection of Nuclear Explosions in Space*, Transcript of Statement and Response to Questions by Dr. Herman Hoerlin, Los Alamos Scientific Laboratory, before the Joint Committee on Atomic Energy, Congress of the United States, March 8, 1963.

25 As quoted in the *Los Alamos Scientific Laboratory Report 1962*.

26 Letter from Guy E. Barasch to the author, January 27, 2003.

27 Letter from Kate to Hoerlin, June 20, 1962. Letters to him were sent to a Post Office Box at the University of California, San Francisco.

28 Mariner and Piehlen, *The Atomic Bomb and American Society* (University of Tennessee Press, 2009), p. 275.

29 Hoerlin, *LASL Monograph*, October 1976, ibid., p. 12. The test was moved from the Bikini to the Johnston Atoll.

30 Letter from Guy E. Barasch to author, January 27, 2003.

31 Jeremy Bernstein, *The Life it Brings: One Physicist's Beginnings* (New York: Houghton Mifflin, 1987), p. 131.

32 *I.F. Stone's Bi-Weekly*, March 18, 1963, p. 2.

33 Transcript of Hoerlin testimony to the Joint Committee, ibid. The remark was made by Representative Jack Westland (Republican from state of Washington).

Chapter 16 Notes (Pages 231-241)

[1] Hans Bethe with Donald Kerr and Robert Jeffries, "Herman W. Hoerlin," *The Road from Los Alamos* (The American Institute of Physics, 1991), p. 234.

[2] Peggy, the first-born of my brother and his wife Jean died tragically in 1960 at the age of eight from meningitis. She had been my parents' first grandchild.

[3] Early signs of Steve and Kristine's vocations were born out: Steve has become a landscape gardener and Kristine a doctor.

[4] Popocateptl erupted in 1947 and 1994 and is often off limited for climbing. According to Hoerlin's Mexican guide, their two day ascent was well below average time.

[5] The Stettner's Ledges climb up the east face of Long's (14,225 feet) required technical know-how and endurance.

[6] Smythe had been with my father on the 1930 International Expedition. On the 1949 Himalayan expedition, Smythe contracted a fatal case of malaria in Delhi. My father's last letter to him and his wife on June 28, 1949, was written the day before Smythe's death at age 48 . . . on his birthday.

[7] Schneider had gone back to the Himalayas and Andes several times, no longer to make hair-raising climbs but as a cartographer whose exquisite maps survive to this day. Schneider died in 1987.

[8] Hannes died in 1955, having established the well-known Eastern Slope Ski School in New Hampshire. In 1947, he returned to St. Anton where he was greeted "like a king" (letter from Schneider to Hoerlin, October 9, 1947). His two children chose to return there permanently.

[9] Letter from my father to me, December 28, 1981.

[10] Thomi was head of the rare book library at the University of Utah, where he had moved with his family after years in the publishing business in New York.

[11] Victor Regener, son of Erich, was also a physicist who left Germany in 1938. In 1946, he joined the Physics Department of the University of New Mexico and served as its chair for a number of years.

[12] Donald Kerr was head of Los Alamos National Laboratory from 1979-1985. Currently he is Deputy Director of the National Reconnaissance Office.

[13] Remarks were made by Hoerlin's son-in-law, Charles Randall, and grandson, Thomas Hoerlin Schmid. Renate Zinn, a friend from Los Alamos who happened to be born in Schwabisch Hall, also spoke. The violist was Walter Trampler, a world-class performer who was a family friend.

14 Letter from Kate to Hoerlin, May 24, 1953. "Die Moral von der Geschichte: ich erleb alles nur mit Dir, durch Dich, nichts aber ohne Dich."

15 Letter from Kate to Hoerlin, January 19, 1937. "Ich weiss keinen Menschen auf der Welt, der mir dieses Geleit so geben kann wie Du."

BIBLIOGRAPHY

BOOKS and ARTICLES

Amstaedter, Rainer. *Der Alpinismus: Kultur, Organisation, Politik.* Vienna: WUV-Universitaetsverlag, 1996.

Annas, George J and Grodin, Michael. The *Nazi Doctors and the Nuremberg Code.* Oxford: Oxford University Press, 1995.

Bachrach, Susan. *The Nazi Olympics Berlin 1936.* New York: Little Brown, 2000.

Bauer, Yehuda. *The History of the American Jewish Joint Distribution Committee.* Philadelphia: The Jewish Publication Society of America, 1974.

Bechtold, Fritz. *Deutsche am Nanga Parbat: Der Angriff 1934.* Muenchen: Verlag F. Bruckmann, 1935.

Bethe, Hans with Donald Kerr and Robert Jeffries, "Herman W. Hoerlin," *The Road from Los Alamos.* College Park, MD: The American Institute of Physics, 1991.

Bernstein, Jeremy. *The Life it Brings; One Physicist's Beginnings.* New York: Houghton Mifflin Company, 1987.

Blackbourne, David and Evans, Richard J. editors. *The German Bourgeois: Essays on the Social History of the German Middle Class from the Late Eighteenth to the Early Twentieth Century.* London: Routledge, 1993.

Borchers, Philipp et al, "Die Forschungsreise des D, u Oe.A.V. in die Cordillera Blanca (Peru)," *Zeitschrift des Deutschen und Oesterreichischen Alpenverein, 1933.*

Borchers, Philipp. *Die Weisse Kordillere.* Berlin: Verlag Scherl, 1935.

Botting, Douglas. *Humboldt and the Cosmos.* New York: Harper&Row, 1973.

Bullock, Alan. *A Study in Tyranny.* New York: Penguin, 1990.

Cassidy, David. *Uncertainty: The Life and Science of Werner Heisenberg.* New York: W. H. Freeman, 1992.

Chernow, Ron. *The Warburgs: The 20th Century Odyssey of a Remarkable Jewish Family.* New York: Random House, 1993.

Conot, Robert E. *Justice at Nuremberg.* New York: Basic Books, 1993.

Cornwell, John. *Hitler's Scientists: Science, War, and the Devil's Pact.* New York: Viking Penguin, 2003.

Craig, Gordon C.,*Germany 1866 – 1945.* Oxford: Oxford University Press,1978.

Dyhrenfurth, Guenter Oskar. *Himalaya-Fahrt: Unsere Expedition 1930.* Zurich: Orell Fuessli Verlag, 1942.

Dyhrenfurth, Guenter Oskar. *Himalaya: Unsere Expedition 1930 .* Berlin: Verlag Scherl, 1931.

Dyhrenfurth, Hettie. *Memsahb im Himalaya.* Leipzig: Deutsche Buchwerkstaetten G.M.B.H., 1931.

Eckart, Wolfgang Uwe. *Man, Medicine and the State: the Human Body as Object of Government.* Germany: Fritz Stein Verlag, 2006.

Fairlie, Gerard. *Flight without Wings: The Biography of Hannes Schneider.* New York: A.S. Barnes, 1957.

Ferguson, Thomas and Voth, Hans-Joachim ."Betting on Hitler – The Value of Political Connections in Nazi Germany," *Quarterly Journal of Economics.* MIT Press, v. 123(1), 2008.

Finsterwalder, Richard. "Der Alpenverein und die Deutsche Himalaja Expedition
1934," *Mitteilungen des Deutschen und Oesterreichischen Alpenvereins,* Winter 1933.

Friedlander, Saul. *Nazi Germany and the Jews, volume I: The Years of Persecution, 1933-39.* New York: HarperCollins, 1997.

Fritzsche, Peter. *Life and Death in the Third Reich.* Cambridge: Harvard University Press, 2008.

Gale, Thomas. "GAF" (General Aniline Film Corporation). *International Directory of Company Histories,* 1988.

Gearin, Joan. "The Real Story of the von Trapp Family." *Prologue,* Winter issue 2005. Washington, D.C.: National Archives.

Gellately, Robert. *The Gestapo and German Society: Enforcing Racial Policy, 1933-45.* New York: Oxford University Press, 1990.

Gritschneder, Otto. *"Der Fuehrer hat Sie zum Tode verurteilt": Hitlers Roehm-Putsch-Morde vor Gericht.* Muenchen: Verlag C.H. Beck, 1993.

Hale, Oron J. *The Captive Press in the Third Reich.* Princeton: Princeton University Press, 1964.

Hayes, Peter "I.G. Farben Revisited: Industry and Ideology Ten Years Later," in John E. Lesch, editor, *The German Chemical Industry in the Twentieth Century.* The Netherlands: Kluwer Academic Publishers, 2000.

Hayes, Peter. "Profits and Persecution: German Big Business and the Holocaust," *Center for Advanced Holocaust Studies*. Washington, D.C.: U.S. Holocaust Memorial Museum, 1998.

Herrligkoffer, Karl. *Willy Merkl – Ein Weg zum Nanga Parbat*. Muenchen: Bergverlag Rudolf Rother, 1936.

Hippius, Hanns; Moeller H.J; Mueller, N; Neundoerfer-Koh, G., *The University Department of Psychiatry in Munich: from Kraepelin and his Predecessors to Molecular Psychiatry*. Germany: Springer Verlag, 2007.

Hoerlin, Hermann. "Deutsche Bergsteiger im Ausland," *Mitteilungen des Deutschen und Oesterreichischen Alpenvereins*. Winter, 1933.

Hoerlin, Herman. "United States High-Altitude Test Experiences: A Review Emphasizing the Impact on the Environment," *Los Alamos Scientific Laboratory Monograph 6405*, October 1976.

Hoerlin, Hermann. "Winterfahrten im Mont-Blanc-Gebiet" Sonderabdruck aus *Die Alpen*, Jahrg. IX, Heft 1, 1933.

Holt, Lee Wallace. *Mountains, Mountaineering and Modernity: A Cultural History of German and Austrian Mountaineering, 1900-1945*. Ph.D dissertation, The University of Texas at Austin: May 2008.

Humboldt, Alexander von. *"Ueber einen Versuch den Gipfel des Chimborazo zu ersteigen"* Halle: Otto Hendel, 1894.

Isserman, Maurice and Weaver, Stewart. *Fallen Giants: A History of Himalayan Mountaineering from the Age of Empire to the Age of Extremes*. New Haven: Yale University Press, 2008.

Kaplan, Jane ed.. *Nazi Germany*. Oxford: Oxford University Press, 2008.

Kaplan, Marion J. *Between Dignity and Despair*. Oxford: Oxford University Press, 1999.

Kershaw, Ian. *Hitler 1889-1936:Hubris*. New York: W.W. Norton,1998.

Kevles, Daniel J. *The Physicists*. New York: Knopf, 1971,

Kinzl, Hans und Schneider, Erwin. *Cordillera Blanca Peru*. Innsbruck: Universitatsverlag Wagner, 1950.

Lesch, John E. editor, *The German Chemical Industry in the Twentieth Century*. The Netherlands: Kluwer Academic Publishers, 2000.

Lipstadt, Deborah E. *Beyond Belief: The American Press and the Coming of the Holocaust*. New York: The Free Press/Simon & Schuster, 1986.

Loehnert, Peter and Manfred Gill, Manfred. "The Relationship of I.G. Farben's Agfa *Filmfabrik* Wolfen to its Jewish Scientists and to Scientists married to Jews, 1933—1939" in John E. Lesch, editor, *The German Chemical Industry in the Twentieth Century*. The Netherlands: Kluwer Academic Publishers, 2000.

Loftus, John and Aarons, Mark, *The Secret War against the Jews: How Western Espionage Betrayed the Jewish People*. New York: St. Martin's Griffin, 1997

Mailaender, Nicholas. *Im Zeichen des Edelweiss*. Zurich: AS Verlag & Buchkonzept AG, 2006.

Maertin, Ralf-Peter. *Nanga Parbat. Wahrheit und Wahn des Alpinus*. Berlin: Berlin Verlag, 2002.

Mariner and Piehlen, *The Atomic Bomb and American Society*. Nashville: University of Tennessee Press, 2009.

Messner, Reinhold. *The Big Walls*. Oxford: Oxford University Press, 1978.

Mierau, Peter. *Die Deutsche Himalaja-Stiftung von 1936 bis 1998.* Muenchen: Bergverlag Rother, 1999.

Miller, Richard L. *Nazi Justiz: Law of the Holocaust.* Westport, CT: Praeger, 1995.

Morreau, Annette. *Emanuel Feuermann.* New Haven; Yale University Press, 2002.

Mosse, Werner Eugene. *The German-Jewish Economic Elite, 1820—1935.* Oxford: Oxford University Press, 1989.

Mueller, Ingo. *Furchtbare Juristen.* Muenchen: Kindler Verlag, 1987.

Mueller, Rolf. "A Brief History of Stratospheric Ozone Research," *Meteorological Zeitschrift,* v. 18, No. 1, February 2009.

Neale, Jonathan. *Tigers in the Snow: how one fateful Climb made the Sherpas Mountaineering Legends.* New York: St. Martin's Press, 2002.

Nickel, Andreas. *Guenter-Hettie-Norman Dyhrenfurth. Zum Dritten Pol.* Zurich: AS Verlag, 2007.

O'Conner, J.J. and Robertson, E.F. *MacTutor History of Mathematics Archive.* Scotland: University of St. Andrews, 2004.

Pauly. Bruce F. *From Prejudice to Persecution: A History of Austrian Anti-Semitism.* Chapel Hill: University of North Carolina Press, 1998.

Petropoules, Jonathan and Roth, John K. *Gray Zones: Ambiguity and Compromise in the Holocaust and its Aftermath.* Oxford: Berghahn Books, 2006.

Prinz, Joachim. *Rebellious Rabbi: The German and Early American Years.* Bloomington: Indiana University Press, 2008.

Randlett, Victor; Kirsch, Scott; Marshall, Lisa. "Nuclear Nevada." *The AAG (Association of American Geographers) Newsletter,* January 2009.

Rhodes, Richard. *The Making of the Atomic Bomb.* New York: Simon & Schuster, 1986.

Richie, Alexandra, *Faust's Metropolis: A History of Berlin.* New York: Carrol & Graff, 1988.

Ricker, John. *Yuraq Janka: Guide to the Peruvian Andes.* New York: American Alpine Club, 1977.

Roberts, Eric. *Welzenbach's Climbs.* Great Britain: West Col Productions, 1980.

Rossi, Bruno. *Cosmic Rays.* New York: McGraw Hill, 1964.

Rummel, R.J. *Death by Government.* Piscataway, N.J.: Transaction Publishers, 1997.

Rutherford, Earnest. "Discussion on Ultra-Penetrating Rays," *Proceedings of the Royal Society of London A 132. 1931.*

Sacher, Abram Leon. *A History of the Jews.* New York: Alfred A. Knopf, 1967.

Schad, Martha. *Hitler's Spy Princess: the Extraordinary Life of Stephanie von Hohenlohe.* England: Sutton Publishing, 2004.

Schleunes, Karl A. ed. *Legislating the Holocaust: The Bernhard Loesener Memoirs and Other Documents.* Westview Press, 2001.

Schleunes, Karl A. *The Twisted Road to Auschwitz: Nazi Policy toward German Jews 1933-39.* Chicago: University of Illinois Press, 1990.

Schmid, Willi. *Unvollendente Symphonie.* Muenchen: R. Oldenbourg, 1935.

Schulle, Diana. *Das Reichssippenamt: Ein Institution nationalsozialistischer Rassenpolitik.* Berlin: Logos Verlag, 2001.

Shirakawa, Sam H. *The Devil's Music Master.* Oxford: Oxford University Press, 1992.

Shirer, William L. *The Rise and Fall of the Third Reich: A History of Nazi Germany.* New York: Simon and Schuster, 1960.

Shrecker, Ellen. *Many are the Crimes – McCarthy in America.* New York: Little, Brown and Company, 1998.

Smythe, Frank S. *Climbs and Ski Runs.* London: A&C Black Limited, 1929.

Smythe, Frank S. *The Kanchenjunga Adventure.* London: Victor Gollancz Ltd,, 1930.

Stackleberg, Roderic. *Hitler's Germany: Origins, Interpretations, Legacies.* New York: Routledge, 1999.

Steinweis, Alan E. *Art, Ideology and Economics in Nazi Germany.* Chapel Hill: University of North Carolina Press, 1996.

Stephenson, Jill. *Hitler's Home Front.* London: Hambledon & London, 2006.

Stevenson, William. *A Man Called Intrepid.* Guilford, CT.: Lyons Press, 2000,

Thacker, Toby. *The End of the Third Reich: Defeat, Denazification and Nuremberg, January 1944-November 1946.* England: NPI Media Group, 2006.

Voegelin, Eric. *Hitler and the Germans*, vol. 31. Kansas City: University of Missouri Press, 1999.

Weisskopf, Duscha. *Willi Schmid: A Life in Germany.* Family Memoir, 2004.

Weyer, Helfried and Dyhrenfurth, Norman G. *Nanga Parbat.* Karlsruhe: Badenia Verlag, 1980.

Wiesen, Jonathan S. *West Germany and the Challenge of the Nazi Past.* Chapel Hill: University of North Carolina Press, 2001.

Wyman, David S. *"The Abandonment of the Jews: America and the Holocaust 1941-1945."* New York: Pantheon Books, 1985.

Zebhauser, Helmut. *Alpinismus im Hitlerstaat.* Munich: Bergverlag Rother, 1998.

Ziemke, Earl F. *The U.S. Army in the Occupation of Germany 1944-46.* U.S. Army: Center for Military History, 1975

ANNUAL REPORTS

Akademischer Alpen-Verein Berlin XXIII. und XXIV. Jahresbericht 1926-1927

Akademischer Alpen-Verein Berlin XXVI. und XXVII. Jahresbericht 1928/29 und 1929/30

Akademischer Alpen-Verein Berlin XXVIII. und XXIX. Jahresbericht 1930/31 und 1931/32

Akademischer Alpen-Verein Berlin 1903-1928

"100 Jahre Sektion Schwaben des Deutschen Alpenverein 1869/1969"

Jahresbericht 1924/25 des Akademischen Skiklub Stuttgart

Jahresbericht 1925/26 des Akademischen Skiklub Stuttgart

Jahresbericht 1926/27 des Akademischen Skiklub Stuttgart

Rundbriefe des Sonderbundes February 1971

Oesterreichische Alpenzeitung/ Oesterreichischen AlpenKlub. September/ Oktober 1974

ARCHIVAL SOURCES

Bielefeld Stadtarchiv
Bundesarchiv Berlin
Berlin-Mitte Stadtesamt Archiv
Dioezesanarchiv Berlin
Erzbischoeflische Archiv Muenchen/Freising
Los Alamos Historical Society Archives
Schwaebisch Hall Stadtarchiv
United States Holocaust Archives
United States National Archives
Warburg Institute Archive
Mecklenburg-Vorpommern Archiv

NEWSPAPERS and PERIODICALS

Augsburger Postzeitung
Berliner Morgen-Post Zeitung
Binghamton Press
Colliers magazine
Deutsche Allgemeine Zeitung
Frankfurter Zeitung
House and Garden magazine
I.F. Stone's Bi-Weekly
LASL (Los Alamos Scientific Laboratory) News
Lewiston Evening News Journal
LIFE
The London Times
Mitteilungen des Deutschen und Oesterreichischen Alpenverein
Muenchner Neueste Nachrichten

Muenchner Zeitung
New York Post
New York Times
Reichsbahn Turn und Sport Zeitung
Stuttgart Tagblatt
TIME

PHOTOGRAPHS

Photographs are all from the collection of Herman and Kate Hoerlin with the following exceptions:

Photos # 125, 126, 129 and 142 from the collection of the German Alpine Club

Photo # 141: photo credit Preston-Steinheimer, 1939

Images # 138 and # 139 from the Bielefeld Stadtarchiv.

Images # 100 and # 148 are emblems in the public domain

Photo restoration work was done by Elfie Harris.

INDEX

CPSIA information can be obtained at www.ICGtesting.com
Printed in the USA
LVOW111116190212

269367LV00004B/12/P